Node.js for Full-Stack Developers

Build Scalable, High-Performance
Applications with Server-Side JavaScript

Dennis Rambert

Copyright Page

Table of Contents

Preface

The world of web development is evolving at an unprecedented pace. As applications become more complex and user expectations for speed and scalability rise, developers are expected to build high-performance, real-time, and scalable web applications. **Node.js** has emerged as a powerful technology that enables developers to achieve this with **JavaScript on both the frontend and backend**.

This book, **Node.js for Full-Stack Developers: Build Scalable, High-Performance Applications with Server-Side JavaScript**, is designed to be your **comprehensive guide** to mastering Node.js for full-stack development. Whether you are a frontend developer looking to dive into backend programming, a backend developer exploring JavaScript for server-side development, or a full-stack developer seeking to optimize your skills, this book will equip you with **everything you need to build robust and scalable applications using Node.js.**

What Makes This Book Different?

Unlike many other books that focus solely on the fundamentals or advanced concepts of Node.js, this book takes a **full-stack approach**. It bridges the gap between **frontend and backend development** by demonstrating how Node.js integrates seamlessly with modern frontend frameworks like **React, Vue, and Angular**.

This book is **practical and hands-on**, ensuring that every chapter includes:

- **Real-world use cases** to illustrate concepts
- **Hands-on examples and projects** to reinforce learning
- **Best practices** for writing clean, maintainable, and efficient code
- **Performance optimization and security techniques** for production-ready applications

By the end of this book, you won't just understand **how** Node.js works—you'll be able to build **real, production-ready applications with it.**

Who This Book Is For

This book is ideal for:

◆ **Frontend Developers** – If you're comfortable with JavaScript and want to expand into backend development, this book will help you transition smoothly.

◆ **Full-Stack Developers** – If you already have experience with both frontend and backend development, this book will help you optimize and scale your Node.js applications.

◆ **Backend Developers** – If you're coming from another backend language like PHP, Python, or Ruby, this book will introduce you to the efficiency and power of Node.js.

◆ **Entrepreneurs & Startups** – If you want to build scalable applications with a modern tech stack, this book will give you the knowledge to do so efficiently.

◆ **Computer Science Students & Hobbyists** – If you're looking to enhance your web development skills, this book will provide a structured and practical learning experience.

What You'll Learn

This book is structured to take you from **the basics to advanced concepts** in a step-by-step manner:

Part 1: Getting Started with Node.js

- Understanding Node.js and its role in full-stack development
- Setting up your development environment
- Learning core Node.js concepts like the Event Loop, Streams, and Modules
- Mastering modern JavaScript (ES6+) for backend development

Part 2: Backend Development with Node.js

- Creating web servers and APIs using Express.js
- Connecting Node.js with databases like MongoDB and PostgreSQL
- Implementing authentication and authorization with JWT and OAuth
- Building RESTful APIs for frontend integration

Part 3: Full-Stack Integration with Node.js

- Connecting Node.js with frontend frameworks like React, Vue, and Angular
- Implementing real-time features with WebSockets and Socket.io
- Handling file uploads, processing, and cloud storage
- Building scalable microservices architecture

Part 4: Deployment, Performance Optimization & Security

- Deploying Node.js applications on cloud platforms like AWS, Vercel, and Heroku
- Optimizing performance with caching, load balancing, and clustering
- Writing unit and integration tests for Node.js applications
- Implementing security best practices to protect applications from vulnerabilities

By the time you finish this book, you'll be confident in **designing, developing, and deploying full-stack applications** using Node.js, following industry best practices.

Prerequisites

To get the most out of this book, you should have:

- Basic familiarity with JavaScript (including ES6+ features)
- Some experience with frontend development (React, Vue, or Angular is helpful but not required)
- A fundamental understanding of web technologies like HTML, CSS, and APIs

Don't worry if you're new to backend development! This book explains **everything from scratch** and gradually builds up to advanced concepts.

How to Use This Book

This book is structured to be **progressive**—each chapter builds on concepts from the previous ones. However, if you already have some experience with Node.js, feel free to **jump to the sections that interest you most.**

Each chapter includes:
Concepts & Theory – A detailed explanation of the topic with real-world

examples

Code Walkthroughs – Hands-on coding exercises and projects

Best Practices – Tips for writing clean, maintainable, and efficient code

Challenges & Exercises – Additional exercises to reinforce learning

Why Node.js Matters in Today's Web Development Landscape

Over the years, Node.js has become a **go-to technology** for building fast, scalable, and real-time applications. **Big tech companies like Netflix, PayPal, LinkedIn, Uber, and eBay** use Node.js to handle millions of users and massive workloads efficiently.

By mastering Node.js, you're gaining a **highly valuable skill** that opens up opportunities in **backend development, API design, microservices architecture, and cloud computing**.

This book is **not just about learning Node.js—it's about mastering full-stack development with JavaScript**. Whether you're a beginner or an experienced developer, you'll find valuable insights and techniques to **build better, faster, and more scalable applications**.

So, let's dive in and start our journey into **Node.js for Full-Stack Development!**

Chapter 1: Introduction to Node.js

The Role of Node.js in Full-Stack Development

Node.js plays a significant role in modern web development by enabling developers to use JavaScript on both the frontend and backend. This creates a unified development environment where the same language, libraries, and data structures can be used throughout an application. This approach simplifies the development process, reduces context switching between different programming languages, and improves efficiency.

Before the introduction of Node.js, web applications typically required different languages for different parts of the stack. JavaScript was primarily used in the browser for client-side interactions, while backend logic and server-side tasks were handled using languages such as PHP, Python, Ruby, or Java. This separation required developers to manage multiple language ecosystems, leading to increased complexity in both development and maintenance.

Node.js removes this barrier by allowing JavaScript to run on the server. It is built on **Chrome's V8 JavaScript engine**, which compiles JavaScript directly to machine code for fast execution. Unlike traditional server-side technologies, which often handle requests synchronously, Node.js is **asynchronous and non-blocking**, meaning it can handle multiple requests at the same time without waiting for one to finish before processing the next. This makes it particularly well-suited for applications that require high performance, such as real-time messaging, live streaming, and APIs handling a large number of concurrent users.

Another advantage of Node.js in full-stack development is its **event-driven architecture**. Instead of following a step-by-step execution model, Node.js reacts to events as they occur. This is useful for real-time applications, where actions such as user interactions, notifications, or data updates need to be processed immediately. By using this approach, applications can remain responsive and efficient, even under heavy load.

In addition to its technical advantages, Node.js benefits from a **large ecosystem of open-source libraries** through **npm (Node Package Manager)**. Developers have access to a vast collection of pre-built modules and tools that simplify common development tasks such as authentication, database integration, file handling, and API development. This accelerates the development process and reduces the need to build functionality from scratch.

Node.js is also highly compatible with **modern frontend frameworks** like React, Vue, and Angular. Since all these technologies use JavaScript, developers can share code between the frontend and backend, making it easier to maintain and scale applications. For example, validation logic can be written once and used on both the client and server, ensuring consistency and reducing redundancy.

Scalability is another reason why Node.js is widely used in full-stack development. It is designed to handle a large number of simultaneous connections with minimal resource consumption. Many traditional backend technologies rely on multi-threading, which requires allocating additional system resources for each new connection. In contrast, Node.js operates on a **single-threaded, event-driven model**, allowing it to efficiently process thousands of concurrent requests with minimal overhead. This makes it a preferred choice for applications that experience high traffic or require real-time updates.

Node.js is used by companies of all sizes, from startups to large enterprises, to build scalable and high-performance applications. Companies like Netflix, LinkedIn, PayPal, and Uber have adopted Node.js to improve application speed, reduce server costs, and enhance the overall user experience.

For developers, Node.js provides a flexible and efficient way to build full-stack applications. It allows for a more streamlined development workflow, better code reusability, and improved application performance. By using Nodc.js, full-stack developers can work with a single programming language across the entire application stack, reducing complexity and increasing productivity.

Why JavaScript for the Backend?

JavaScript has traditionally been associated with frontend development, handling interactions within the browser. However, with the introduction of **Node.js**, JavaScript is now used to build server-side applications, making it a key language for full-stack development. This shift has raised an important question: **Why use JavaScript for backend development instead of more traditional server-side languages like PHP, Python, or Java?**

There are several reasons why JavaScript is well-suited for backend development, including its efficiency, scalability, ease of use, and ecosystem support.

One of the main advantages of using JavaScript for backend development is that it allows developers to use the **same language** for both frontend and backend. This eliminates the need to switch between different programming languages, which simplifies development and reduces cognitive load.

In a typical web application, the frontend is responsible for the user interface and interactions, while the backend handles data storage, authentication, and business logic. Traditionally, developers would use JavaScript for the frontend and a different language, such as Python or PHP, for backend operations. This required maintaining expertise in multiple languages, dealing with language-specific debugging tools, and managing different development workflows.

With **JavaScript running on both the client and server**, developers can write and maintain **shared code** between the frontend and backend. For example, form validation logic that ensures a user enters a valid email address can be written once and used on both the client (in the browser) and the server. This reduces redundancy and ensures consistency across the application.

Performance and Scalability

JavaScript, when used with Node.js, offers **asynchronous, non-blocking execution**, making it highly efficient for handling multiple requests at the same time.

Traditional backend languages often follow a **blocking execution model**, meaning that each request is handled sequentially. This can create performance bottlenecks, especially when multiple users are accessing the application simultaneously.

Node.js operates differently. It uses an **event-driven, non-blocking architecture**, allowing it to handle multiple requests concurrently without waiting for each one to finish. This is particularly useful for applications that require:

Real-time functionality, such as chat applications and live notifications.

High concurrency, where multiple users access the system at the same time.

Streaming services, where large amounts of data are transmitted continuously.

This ability to efficiently process multiple requests at once makes JavaScript a strong choice for building scalable backend systems.

Asynchronous Programming Model

Asynchronous programming allows applications to execute multiple tasks **without waiting for each task to complete** before moving on to the next. This is particularly useful in backend development, where operations like database queries, API calls, and file system access can take time.

JavaScript supports **asynchronous programming** using features like:

Callbacks – Functions that execute after an asynchronous operation completes.

Promises – Objects that represent a future value that will be available once an operation is finished.

Async/Await – A modern syntax that makes working with asynchronous code easier to read and write.

By using these techniques, JavaScript can perform tasks efficiently without blocking the execution of other parts of the application.

Large Ecosystem and Community Support

JavaScript has a **vast ecosystem** supported by a large community of developers. One of the most important aspects of this ecosystem is **npm (Node Package Manager)**, which provides access to **over a million open-source packages** that can be easily integrated into applications.

These packages help developers build backend functionality more efficiently by providing pre-built solutions for common tasks such as:

Database management (e.g., Mongoose for MongoDB, Sequelize for PostgreSQL).

User authentication (e.g., Passport.js, Firebase Auth).

Real-time communication (e.g., Socket.io for WebSockets).

Server frameworks (e.g., Express.js, Fastify, NestJS).

This vast collection of tools allows developers to focus on building application logic rather than writing repetitive code from scratch.

Additionally, JavaScript has one of the **largest and most active developer communities**. This means that resources, tutorials, forums, and online support are readily available, making problem-solving easier.

Seamless Integration with Modern Web Technologies

JavaScript is designed to work well with modern frontend technologies such as **React, Vue, and Angular**. Since all these frameworks are built on JavaScript, they can easily communicate with a backend written in Node.js.

For example, a React application can send **API requests** to a Node.js backend using **fetch()** or **Axios**, and the backend can respond with JSON data. Because both systems use JavaScript and the JSON format, communication is straightforward and efficient.

This seamless integration allows full-stack developers to build applications faster while ensuring that different parts of the application work well together.

Microservices and Serverless Compatibility

Modern backend architectures are shifting away from monolithic applications toward **microservices** and **serverless computing**. JavaScript, particularly with Node.js, is well-suited for these architectures.

Microservices are small, independent services that work together to form an application. Node.js makes it easy to build and deploy microservices because of its lightweight and efficient processing model.

Serverless computing allows developers to run backend functions without managing servers. Cloud platforms such as **AWS Lambda, Google Cloud Functions, and Azure Functions** support Node.js, enabling developers to write scalable backend code that only runs when needed, reducing operational costs.

The compatibility of JavaScript with these modern backend solutions makes it an excellent choice for developers looking to build scalable and cost-effective applications.

Adoption by Leading Companies

JavaScript is used for backend development by some of the largest companies in the technology industry. Businesses that require high performance and scalability have adopted JavaScript and Node.js for their backend infrastructure.

For example:

Netflix improved load times by migrating its backend services to Node.js.

PayPal experienced a significant decrease in response times after switching to a Node.js-based backend.

LinkedIn improved its mobile app's performance by transitioning from Ruby on Rails to Node.js.

These real-world examples demonstrate that JavaScript is not only a practical choice for backend development but also a **proven** one that powers large-scale applications.

JavaScript has become a major player in backend development due to its ability to handle **asynchronous operations, scalability, and seamless integration with modern web technologies**. The introduction of **Node.js** has enabled JavaScript to function efficiently on the server, reducing the need for multiple programming languages in full-stack applications.

By using JavaScript for both frontend and backend development, developers benefit from **code reusability, shared knowledge, and a unified development workflow**. Additionally, the **large ecosystem, strong community support, and compatibility with microservices and cloud**

computing make JavaScript a flexible and future-proof choice for backend development.

With these advantages, it is clear why JavaScript is widely adopted for building modern, high-performance web applications.

Key Features of Node.js

Node.js is widely used for backend development due to its efficiency, scalability, and ability to handle real-time applications. Unlike traditional backend environments, Node.js offers a unique set of features that make it well-suited for modern web applications. These features contribute to its popularity among developers and its adoption by large-scale enterprises.

Asynchronous and Non-Blocking Architecture

One of the most important characteristics of Node.js is its **asynchronous, non-blocking execution model**. This means that Node.js can handle multiple tasks at the same time without waiting for one to finish before starting another.

Traditional backend systems often follow a **blocking (synchronous) execution model**, where each request must be processed sequentially. If a database query takes time to execute, the server has to wait before handling the next request. This can lead to slower performance, especially when multiple users are interacting with an application simultaneously.

In contrast, Node.js uses an **event-driven, non-blocking approach**, allowing it to handle thousands of requests concurrently. When a request involves a time-consuming operation, such as reading from a database or accessing an API, Node.js continues executing other tasks while waiting for the response. This improves efficiency and performance, making Node.js an excellent choice for applications that require high scalability.

Example of non-blocking behavior in Node.js:

```
const fs = require("fs");

// Asynchronous file read
fs.readFile("example.txt", "utf8", (err, data) => {
  if (err) throw err;
```

```
  console.log("File content:", data);
});

console.log("This message prints before the file is
read.");
```

In this example, the file read operation does not block execution. Instead, Node.js moves on to the next task while waiting for the file to be read.

Single-Threaded, Event-Driven Model

Unlike traditional multi-threaded server environments, Node.js operates on a **single-threaded event loop**. A **thread** is a sequence of instructions that a server follows to process a request. Many backend environments use multiple threads to handle requests concurrently, but this requires significant system resources.

Node.js, however, efficiently manages multiple client connections using a **single thread** by relying on an **event loop**. This event loop listens for incoming requests and delegates tasks to system resources, allowing Node.js to handle many connections at once with minimal overhead.

This makes Node.js particularly efficient for applications that require **real-time updates**, such as messaging platforms, live dashboards, and online gaming servers.

Fast Execution with the V8 JavaScript Engine

Node.js is built on **Google's V8 JavaScript engine**, which is the same engine that powers the Chrome browser. This engine **compiles JavaScript directly into machine code**, making execution significantly faster compared to traditional interpreted languages.

Since V8 continuously improves with optimizations from Google, Node.js benefits from these enhancements, making it one of the fastest JavaScript execution environments available. This performance advantage allows developers to build applications that are both responsive and efficient.

Built-In Package Manager (npm)

Node.js comes with **npm (Node Package Manager)**, which provides access to a vast collection of reusable JavaScript libraries and modules. This package manager simplifies development by allowing developers to install and integrate third-party packages instead of writing everything from scratch.

For example, if a developer needs authentication functionality, they can use a package like **Passport.js** instead of building an authentication system manually.

Common npm packages include:

Express.js – A framework for building web applications and APIs.

Mongoose – A library for interacting with MongoDB databases.

Socket.io – A tool for enabling real-time communication.

Installing a package using npm is straightforward:

```
npm install express
```

This installs the Express.js framework, which can then be used to build web applications efficiently.

Support for RESTful APIs and Microservices

Node.js is frequently used to build **RESTful APIs**, which allow applications to communicate with servers using HTTP requests. These APIs provide a structured way for frontend applications to retrieve or modify data from a backend server.

Because of its non-blocking nature, Node.js is also well-suited for **microservices architecture**, where applications are divided into smaller, independent services that communicate with each other. This approach improves scalability and makes applications easier to maintain.

For example, an e-commerce application might have separate microservices for:

User authentication

Product inventory

Payment processing

Order management

Each of these services runs independently but communicates through APIs, allowing the application to scale more effectively.

Real-Time Capabilities with WebSockets

Node.js is an excellent choice for applications that require **real-time functionality**, such as live chat applications, online multiplayer games, and live notifications.

This is made possible through **WebSockets**, a protocol that enables bidirectional communication between clients and servers. Unlike traditional HTTP requests, which require a new connection for each interaction, WebSockets keep a persistent connection open, reducing latency and improving performance.

The **Socket.io** library simplifies the implementation of WebSockets in Node.js, allowing developers to build real-time features with minimal effort.

Example of a simple WebSocket server using **Socket.io**:

```
const io = require("socket.io")(3000);

io.on("connection", (socket) => {
  console.log("User connected");

  socket.on("message", (data) => {
    console.log("Message received:", data);
    io.emit("message", data); // Broadcast message
to all connected users
  });
});
```

With this setup, messages sent by one user can be instantly received by others, enabling real-time interactions.

Cross-Platform Compatibility

Node.js is designed to run on multiple operating systems, including **Windows, macOS, and Linux**. This makes it highly portable, allowing developers to build applications that can be deployed on different environments without modification.

In addition to running on traditional servers, Node.js can be used in **cloud environments and serverless computing platforms**, making it a flexible choice for modern development.

For example, cloud providers like **AWS Lambda, Google Cloud Functions, and Azure Functions** support Node.js, allowing developers to run backend logic without managing dedicated servers.

Scalability and Load Balancing

Scalability is a critical factor in backend development, especially for applications with a large number of users. Node.js is designed to scale efficiently by leveraging its event-driven model and lightweight execution.

For even greater scalability, Node.js can be configured to use **clustering**, which allows multiple instances of an application to run simultaneously across different processor cores. This ensures that requests are distributed efficiently, improving overall performance.

The **cluster module** in Node.js makes it easy to enable multi-process scaling:

```
const cluster = require("cluster");
const http = require("http");
const os = require("os");

if (cluster.isMaster) {
  for (let i = 0; i < os.cpus().length; i++) {
    cluster.fork();
  }
} else {
  http.createServer((req, res) => {
    res.writeHead(200);
    res.end("Hello, world!");
  }).listen(3000);
}
```

This example creates multiple worker processes, ensuring that requests are handled efficiently across multiple CPU cores.

Node.js provides several advantages for backend development, making it an efficient, scalable, and flexible choice for modern web applications. Its **asynchronous, non-blocking architecture**, combined with the **V8 JavaScript engine**, ensures high performance. Features like **event-driven execution, real-time capabilities, built-in package management, and cross-platform support** further enhance its usability.

With its growing adoption in cloud environments, microservices, and scalable systems, Node.js continues to be a leading technology for building high-performance applications. Understanding these features allows developers to make informed decisions when designing and developing backend systems.

Event Loop and Non-Blocking I/O in Node.js

Node.js is designed to handle multiple operations efficiently without blocking execution. This capability is made possible through its **event loop** and **non-blocking I/O model**. Understanding how these work is essential for writing high-performance applications in Node.js.

The Event Loop: How Node.js Handles Multiple Tasks Efficiently

The **event loop** is a core feature of Node.js that allows it to manage multiple tasks without creating multiple threads. Instead of handling each request in a separate thread, as some traditional backend technologies do, Node.js operates on a **single-threaded, event-driven architecture**.

This approach ensures that Node.js can process many requests **concurrently** without waiting for one task to complete before starting another. The event loop continuously monitors events and executes tasks when they are ready, preventing the system from becoming unresponsive.

How the Event Loop Works

To understand the event loop, consider how a restaurant operates. Imagine a waiter taking multiple orders from customers. Instead of waiting at the kitchen for one dish to be prepared before taking the next order, the waiter moves on to serve the next customer while the chef prepares the food in the background. The waiter only returns to deliver the food when it is ready.

Similarly, Node.js listens for incoming requests and delegates tasks such as database queries, file operations, or API calls to the system. While waiting for these operations to complete, Node.js continues processing other tasks. Once a task is ready, the event loop picks it up and executes the callback function associated with it.

Phases of the Event Loop

The event loop operates in a cycle consisting of different phases. Each phase processes a specific type of task. The key phases of the event loop include:

Timers Phase

Executes scheduled functions like `setTimeout()` and `setInterval()`.

Pending Callbacks Phase

Handles completed I/O operations such as network requests and database responses.

Idle, Prepare Phase

Internal processes used by Node.js (not commonly used in application development).

Poll Phase

Retrieves new I/O events and executes callbacks for completed operations.

If there are no pending operations, Node.js waits for new events.

Check Phase

Executes immediate functions like `setImmediate()`.

Close Callbacks Phase

Handles cleanup operations such as closing database connections or file handles.

Example: Understanding the Event Loop in Code

The following example demonstrates how the event loop processes different types of tasks:

```
console.log("Start");

setTimeout(() => {
  console.log("Timeout callback executed");
}, 0);

setImmediate(() => {
  console.log("Immediate callback executed");
});

process.nextTick(() => {
  console.log("Next tick executed");
});

console.log("End");
```

Expected Output:

`Start`

`End`

`Next tick executed`

`Immediate callback executed`

`Timeout callback executed`

Explanation:

Synchronous code (`console.log("Start")` and `console.log("End")`) runs immediately.

`process.nextTick()` runs before other queued operations.

`setImmediate()` executes in the "Check" phase.

`setTimeout()` executes in the "Timers" phase.

This demonstrates how the event loop prioritizes different types of operations.

Non-Blocking I/O: How Node.js Avoids Delays

Traditional server-side languages like PHP and Python often use **blocking I/O operations**, meaning that when an input/output task (such as reading a file or fetching data from a database) is performed, the execution is paused until the operation is complete. This can slow down applications that need to handle multiple requests at the same time.

In contrast, **Node.js uses non-blocking I/O operations**, which means it does not wait for tasks to complete before continuing execution. Instead, it delegates the task to the system and moves on to the next operation. When the task is completed, Node.js retrieves the result and processes it asynchronously.

Example: Blocking vs. Non-Blocking I/O

Blocking (Synchronous) I/O Example:

```
const fs = require("fs");

console.log("Start");
const data = fs.readFileSync("example.txt",
"utf8"); // Blocks execution
console.log(data);
console.log("End");
```

Output:

```
Start
```

```
(File contents)
```

```
End
```

Explanation:

The program **waits** for `fs.readFileSync()` to complete before executing the next line.

If the file is large, this can cause delays, making the application unresponsive.

Non-Blocking (Asynchronous) I/O Example:

```
const fs = require("fs");

console.log("Start");
fs.readFile("example.txt", "utf8", (err, data) => {
  if (err) throw err;
  console.log(data);
});
```

```
console.log("End");
```

Output:

```
Start

End

(File contents)
```

Explanation:

`fs.readFile()` starts the file read operation but does **not block** execution.

The program moves on to execute `console.log("End")` immediately.

Once the file read is complete, the callback function is executed, printing the file contents.

This approach allows applications to handle multiple operations efficiently without being delayed by slow tasks.

Benefits of the Event Loop and Non-Blocking I/O

Improved Performance – Node.js can handle thousands of concurrent requests efficiently without slowing down.

Faster Response Times – Applications remain responsive since tasks are processed asynchronously.

Scalability – The event-driven model allows applications to scale effectively without requiring additional threads.

Efficient Resource Utilization – Single-threaded execution reduces memory and CPU overhead compared to multi-threaded environments.

These advantages make Node.js a preferred choice for applications that require real-time interactions, such as **chat applications, live notifications, and streaming services**.

When to Use Blocking vs. Non-Blocking Code

Although non-blocking code is generally preferred, there are cases where blocking operations may be suitable:

Blocking Code is useful for **small tasks** where performance is not a concern (e.g., reading a configuration file during application startup).

Non-Blocking Code should be used for **time-consuming tasks** (e.g., fetching data from a database, handling network requests).

Choosing the right approach depends on the application's requirements and the impact on performance.

The event loop and non-blocking I/O model are fundamental to how Node.js manages concurrent operations efficiently. The **event loop** allows Node.js to process multiple requests without creating multiple threads, while **non-blocking I/O** ensures that operations do not delay execution.

Understanding these concepts is essential for building high-performance applications in Node.js. By leveraging the event loop and non-blocking execution, developers can create scalable, responsive, and efficient applications that handle multiple tasks without performance bottlenecks.

Chapter 2: Setting Up Your Development Environment

Before you start building applications with Node.js, it's essential to set up a well-organized development environment. A good setup makes coding more efficient, reduces errors, and ensures that your code is maintainable. In this chapter, we'll go through the steps to install **Node.js and npm**, set up a **modern development workflow** using **VS Code, ESLint, and Prettier**, understand **npm and yarn**, and finally, **run your first Node.js script**.

Installing Node.js and npm

When setting up a **Node.js** development environment, installing **Node.js** and **npm (Node Package Manager)** is the first and most crucial step. These two tools provide everything needed to run JavaScript on the backend, manage project dependencies, and build scalable applications. Whether you are a beginner or an experienced developer, understanding how to install and manage these tools properly will ensure a smooth development experience.

Before getting into installation, it is important to understand what **Node.js** is and why it is essential for JavaScript-based development.

Node.js is a **runtime environment** that allows JavaScript code to be executed outside of a browser. Unlike traditional JavaScript, which runs only within web browsers like Chrome or Firefox, Node.js enables JavaScript to run on servers, desktop applications, and even IoT devices.

At its core, Node.js is powered by **Google's V8 JavaScript engine**, the same engine that runs JavaScript in Chrome. However, Node.js extends JavaScript's capabilities by adding modules that allow it to interact with files, databases, networks, and other system resources that browser-based JavaScript cannot access.

For example, with Node.js, you can:

Create web servers that handle multiple client requests

Read and write files on a computer

Communicate with databases

Build APIs that power modern web applications

One of the reasons developers prefer Node.js is its **asynchronous, event-driven architecture**, which allows it to handle multiple requests simultaneously without blocking execution. This makes it particularly useful for building applications that require high performance, such as real-time chat apps, streaming platforms, and data-intensive APIs.

With a basic understanding of why Node.js is useful, the next step is to install it properly on your system.

Downloading and Installing Node.js

The first step in setting up Node.js is downloading and installing it from the official **Node.js website**. The installation process varies depending on the operating system you are using.

Choosing the Right Version of Node.js

When you visit the official Node.js website, you will see two versions available for download:

LTS (Long-Term Support) – This version is recommended for most users because it is stable, well-tested, and receives security updates for an extended period.

Current – This version includes the latest features and improvements but may not be as stable. It is mainly intended for developers who want to experiment with the newest updates.

If you are unsure which one to choose, always go with the **LTS version**, as it is more reliable for production applications.

Installing Node.js on Windows

For Windows users, the process of installing Node.js is straightforward.

Go to the Node.js website (nodejs.org) and download the **Windows Installer** for the LTS version.

Run the downloaded file and follow the installation steps:

Accept the license agreement.

Choose an installation location (the default is usually fine).

Select components (the default selection is recommended).

Complete the installation.

Verify the installation by opening a Command Prompt (`cmd.exe`) or PowerShell and running:

```
node -v
```

This should display the installed Node.js version, confirming that the installation was successful.

```
v18.16.0
```

Next, check if **npm** (which is installed automatically with Node.js) is available:

```
npm -v
```

If the installation was successful, it should return a version number:

```
9.5.1
```

At this point, Node.js and npm are ready for use on your Windows machine.

Installing Node.js on macOS

On macOS, you have multiple ways to install Node.js. The most common methods include:

Using the Official Installer

Visit the Node.js website (nodejs.org) and download the macOS installer for the LTS version.

Run the installer and follow the setup instructions.

Verify the installation by opening the Terminal and running:

```
node -v
```

If installed correctly, this command will output the Node.js version.

Confirm that npm is installed:

```
npm -v
```

This should return the installed npm version.

Using Homebrew (Recommended for macOS Users)

Homebrew is a package manager for macOS that simplifies software installation. Many developers prefer using it to install Node.js.

Open the Terminal and ensure **Homebrew** is installed by running:

```
brew -v
```

If Homebrew is not installed, install it using:

```
/bin/bash -c "$(curl -fsSL
https://raw.githubusercontent.com/Homebrew/install/
HEAD/install.sh)"
```

Install Node.js using Homebrew:

```
brew install node
```

Verify the installation:

```
node -v
npm -v
```

Using Homebrew ensures that you can easily update Node.js later by running:

```
brew upgrade node
```

Installing Node.js on Linux

Linux users can install Node.js using their system's package manager. The installation steps depend on the Linux distribution.

Ubuntu/Debian-based Systems

Open a Terminal window and update the package lists:

```
sudo apt update && sudo apt upgrade
```

Install Node.js and npm:

```
sudo apt install nodejs npm
```

Verify the installation:

```
node -v
```

```
npm -v
```

For the latest version of Node.js, you can use **nvm (Node Version Manager)** instead, which allows you to switch between different versions easily.

CentOS, Fedora, and RHEL

Enable the Node.js repository:

```
sudo dnf module enable nodejs:18
```
Install Node.js:

```
sudo dnf install nodejs
```
Verify the installation:

```
node -v
npm -v
```

Using a package manager ensures that Node.js can be easily updated when new versions are released.

Updating Node.js and npm

Over time, newer versions of Node.js and npm are released with bug fixes, security updates, and performance improvements. Keeping them updated ensures that you are using the latest features.

To update Node.js, visit the official website and download the latest LTS version or use the appropriate package manager for your system.

To update npm separately, run the following command:

```
npm install -g npm
```
This installs the latest npm version globally.

Testing Your Installation with a Simple Script

Now that Node.js is installed, it's a good idea to test it by running a simple script.

Open a code editor or terminal and create a new file named `app.js`.

Add the following code:

```
console.log("Node.js is working!");
```

Save the file and run it using the terminal:

```
node app.js
```

If everything is set up correctly, you should see the following output:

```
Node.js is working!
```

This confirms that Node.js is installed and functioning correctly on your system.

Installing Node.js and npm is the foundation for JavaScript backend development. Whether you are using **Windows, macOS, or Linux**, the installation process is straightforward and ensures you have access to the powerful tools provided by Node.js. Once installed, verifying the setup and keeping your environment updated will help you maintain a smooth development experience.

With Node.js properly installed, you are now ready to explore its features and start building applications that take full advantage of its efficiency and scalability.

Setting Up a Modern Development Workflow

A well-structured development workflow is essential for writing clean, maintainable, and error-free code. A modern development setup ensures that your environment is optimized for efficiency, reducing common issues that arise from inconsistent formatting or undetected errors.

To achieve this, you need a **powerful code editor**, tools that enforce **consistent coding standards**, and an **automatic formatting system**. This section focuses on setting up **Visual Studio Code (VS Code)**, configuring **ESLint** to catch potential coding mistakes, and integrating **Prettier** to keep your code consistently formatted.

Choosing the Right Code Editor: Visual Studio Code (VS Code)

A code editor is where you will spend most of your time writing and debugging code, so it is important to choose one that enhances productivity.

Visual Studio Code (VS Code) is widely regarded as one of the best code editors for JavaScript and Node.js development. It is lightweight, highly customizable, and comes with built-in support for debugging, version control, and intelligent code suggestions.

To set up VS Code, follow these steps:

Download and Install VS Code
Go to the official VS Code website and download the installer for your operating system (Windows, macOS, or Linux). Once the download is complete, install it by following the on-screen instructions.

Open VS Code and Set Up a Project Folder
After installation, launch VS Code and create a new project folder where you will store your Node.js projects. You can do this by opening VS Code, selecting **File > Open Folder**, and choosing or creating a new directory.

Install Recommended Extensions
VS Code allows you to enhance its functionality using extensions. To improve your development experience, open the Extensions Marketplace by clicking the Extensions icon on the left sidebar or pressing `Ctrl + Shift + X` (Windows/Linux) or `Cmd + Shift + X` (macOS).

Search for and install the following extensions:

ESLint – Helps identify and fix coding issues.

Prettier - Code formatter – Automatically formats code to maintain consistency.

Node.js Extension Pack – Provides additional Node.js tools and debugging support.

Once installed, these extensions will integrate seamlessly with your workflow.

Setting Up ESLint for Code Quality

ESLint is a tool that analyzes your JavaScript code and enforces best practices by identifying errors and potential problems. It helps maintain a consistent coding style and ensures that code is free of common bugs.

Installing ESLint

To use ESLint in your project, you first need to install it as a dependency. Open VS Code and launch the integrated terminal by pressing **Ctrl + ** `(Windows/Linux) or **Cmd +` (macOS).

Navigate to your project folder and initialize a new Node.js project:

```
npm init -y
```

This creates a `package.json` file, which keeps track of your project's dependencies. Next, install ESLint as a development dependency:

```
npm install eslint --save-dev
```

Once installed, run the following command to configure ESLint:

```
npx eslint --init
```

This command prompts you with a series of configuration options. Answer the questions based on your preferred setup:

How would you like to use ESLint? – Choose: `To check syntax and find problems`

What type of modules does your project use? – Choose `CommonJS` if using Node.js

Which framework does your project use? – Select `None` (unless you are using React, Vue, or another framework)

Does your project use TypeScript? – Choose `No` unless working with TypeScript

Where does your code run? – Select `Node`

What format do you want your config file to be in? – Choose `JSON`

This process generates an `.eslintrc.json` file in your project folder, which contains ESLint's configuration settings.

Customizing ESLint Rules

By default, ESLint follows JavaScript best practices, but you can customize it by modifying `.eslintrc.json`.

For example, if you want to allow `console.log` statements (which ESLint flags by default), you can modify your rules like this:

```
{
  "env": {
    "node": true,
    "es6": true
  },
  "extends": ["eslint:recommended"],
  "rules": {
    "no-console": "off",
    "indent": ["error", 2],
    "quotes": ["error", "double"]
  }
}
```

In this configuration:

`"no-console": "off"` allows `console.log` statements.

`"indent": ["error", 2]` enforces a 2-space indentation.

`"quotes": ["error", "double"]` ensures double quotes are used consistently.

Now, whenever you write JavaScript code that violates these rules, ESLint will flag it with an error or warning in VS Code.

To check for ESLint errors manually, run:

```
npx eslint yourfile.js
```

This helps maintain code quality by catching potential issues before execution.

Setting Up Prettier for Code Formatting

Prettier is an automatic code formatter that ensures consistency in code structure, indentation, and spacing. Unlike ESLint, which mainly checks for coding errors, Prettier focuses on formatting your code according to predefined rules.

To install Prettier, use the following command:

```
npm install --save-dev --save-exact prettier
```

Next, create a **Prettier configuration file** in your project root directory by running:

```
echo {} > .prettierrc.json
```

This file can be customized to enforce specific formatting rules. For example:

```
{
  "singleQuote": true,
  "trailingComma": "es5",
  "tabWidth": 2,
  "semi": false
}
```

In this configuration:

`"singleQuote"`: `true` enforces single quotes instead of double quotes.

`"trailingComma"`: `"es5"` adds trailing commas where valid in ES5 syntax.

`"tabWidth"`: `2` ensures indentation is two spaces per tab.

`"semi"`: `false` removes semicolons from the end of statements.

To apply Prettier formatting manually, run:

```
npx prettier --write .
```

However, the best way to use Prettier is by integrating it with VS Code. Open **VS Code Settings** (`Ctrl + ,` or `Cmd + ,` on macOS) and search for **Format on Save**. Enable this option so that Prettier automatically formats your code every time you save a file.

To ensure that Prettier and ESLint work together without conflicts, install the following additional dependencies:

```
npm install eslint-config-prettier eslint-plugin-prettier --save-dev
```

Then, update `.eslintrc.json` to include Prettier's recommended settings:

```
{
  "extends": ["eslint:recommended",
"plugin:prettier/recommended"],
  "plugins": ["prettier"],
  "rules": {
```

```
      "prettier/prettier": "error"
  }
}
```

With this setup, ESLint will now flag any formatting issues that do not match Prettier's rules, ensuring both tools work in harmony.

By setting up **VS Code**, **ESLint**, and **Prettier**, you create a development workflow that enforces clean, consistent, and error-free code.

VS Code provides an optimized coding environment.

ESLint helps catch potential bugs and enforces coding standards.

Prettier ensures that formatting remains uniform across your project.

This setup not only improves code quality but also enhances productivity by reducing manual formatting and debugging efforts. With these tools in place, you are now ready to write cleaner and more maintainable Node.js applications.

Introduction to npm and Yarn

Every modern JavaScript developer relies on package managers to handle dependencies, automate tasks, and streamline development. When working with **Node.js**, two major package managers stand out: **npm (Node Package Manager)** and **Yarn**. These tools allow developers to install, update, and manage external libraries and frameworks, making development more efficient.

What is npm?

npm (Node Package Manager) is the default package manager that comes with Node.js. It allows developers to install and manage third-party JavaScript libraries and tools. These libraries, known as **packages**, are stored in an online registry at npmjs.com, where millions of reusable code modules are available for developers to integrate into their projects.

Whenever you install Node.js, npm is installed automatically. To verify that it is available on your system, open a terminal or command prompt and run:

37

```
npm -v
```
If npm is installed correctly, this command will return the version number of npm installed on your system.

Why npm is Essential

Without npm, developers would have to manually write and organize code for every feature in an application. Instead of reinventing the wheel, npm provides access to a vast ecosystem of open-source modules, allowing developers to integrate existing solutions rather than building everything from scratch.

For example, if you need to handle HTTP requests in your Node.js application, you don't have to write the entire networking logic yourself. You can install a well-tested library like `axios` using npm:

```
npm install axios
```
With this single command, npm fetches the package from the online registry and makes it available for use in your project.

Using npm to Manage Dependencies

Before installing any packages, a Node.js project must be initialized with a `package.json` file. This file keeps track of project dependencies, scripts, and configuration settings.

To initialize a new project, navigate to your project folder in the terminal and run:

```
npm init -y
```
This command generates a `package.json` file with default settings. The file looks like this:

```
{
  "name": "my-project",
  "version": "1.0.0",
  "description": "",
  "main": "index.js",
  "scripts": {
    "test": "echo \"Error: no test specified\" &&
exit 1"
  },
  "author": "",
```

38

```
  "license": "ISC"
}
```

This file serves as the blueprint for your project, keeping track of installed packages and settings.

Installing Packages with npm

npm allows you to install packages either **locally** (for a specific project) or **globally** (accessible across all projects on your system).

To install a package locally, use:

```
npm install express
```

This installs `express`, a popular web framework, and adds it to the `node_modules` directory. The dependency is also recorded in `package.json` under the `dependencies` section:

```
"dependencies": {
  "express": "^4.18.2"
}
```

To install a package globally, use:

```
npm install -g nodemon
```

This installs `nodemon`, a tool that automatically restarts a Node.js application when file changes are detected, making development easier. Global packages are useful for command-line tools that you want to use across multiple projects.

Uninstalling Packages with npm

If a package is no longer needed, it can be removed using:

```
npm uninstall express
```

This deletes the package and removes its reference from `package.json`. If you uninstall a globally installed package, add the `-g` flag:

```
npm uninstall -g nodemon
```

Updating Packages with npm

To update a package to the latest version, run:

```
npm update axios
```
If you want to update all dependencies in your project, use:

```
npm update
```
For major updates, where breaking changes might occur, check the available versions first:

```
npm outdated
```
This command lists packages that have newer versions available.

To update to a specific version, use:

```
npm install express@5.0.0
```
This installs Express version 5.0.0 instead of the latest version.

Running Scripts with npm

npm allows developers to define **custom scripts** in `package.json`. These scripts automate tasks like running tests, starting servers, or executing build commands.

For example, if you frequently start a Node.js server using:

```
node server.js
```

You can define a script in `package.json`:

```
"scripts": {
  "start": "node server.js"
}
```
Now, you can start the server with:

```
npm start
```

This reduces repetitive commands and improves workflow efficiency.

What is Yarn?

Yarn is an alternative package manager developed by Facebook. It was created to address some of the performance and security issues in npm. While npm has improved significantly over the years, Yarn remains a popular choice due to its speed and deterministic package installation.

To check if Yarn is installed on your system, run:

```
yarn -v
```
If it is not installed, install it using npm:

```
npm install -g yarn
```
Now, Yarn can be used as an alternative to npm for managing dependencies.

Using Yarn to Manage Dependencies

Similar to npm, Yarn requires a project to be initialized. To create a `package.json` file using Yarn, navigate to your project folder and run:

```
yarn init -y
```
This generates a `package.json` file, just like npm.

Installing Packages with Yarn

To install a package using Yarn, use:

```
yarn add axios
```
This installs `axios` and updates `package.json`. Unlike npm, Yarn also creates a `yarn.lock` file, which ensures that the same package versions are used across different environments.

To install a package globally:

```
yarn global add nodemon
```
To uninstall a package:

```
yarn remove axios
```
To update all packages:

```
yarn upgrade
```
These commands perform the same functions as npm but often execute faster.

Comparing npm and Yarn

Although npm and Yarn serve the same purpose, they have differences in performance, security, and workflow.

Speed: Yarn is generally faster due to parallel package downloads.

Deterministic Installs: Yarn ensures that all installations produce the same results across different environments with `yarn.lock`.

Security: Yarn uses checksums to verify package integrity, reducing the risk of compromised dependencies.

Simplicity: npm has improved over time and now includes features like `package-lock.json` for deterministic installs.

Both tools are widely used, and the choice often depends on project requirements and developer preferences.

npm and Yarn are essential tools for managing JavaScript dependencies efficiently. npm is the default package manager for Node.js and provides a robust ecosystem of libraries. Yarn offers performance improvements and security enhancements, making it a strong alternative.

By understanding how to install, update, and remove packages using these tools, you can streamline development, reduce redundancy, and maintain a well-organized project structure. With a solid grasp of npm and Yarn, you are now ready to manage dependencies effectively in your Node.js applications.

Running Your First Node.js Script

Getting started with **Node.js** is an exciting step toward building powerful server-side applications using JavaScript. Whether you're working on a backend service, automating a task, or creating a full-stack application, writing and running your first Node.js script lays the foundation for everything that follows.

Before writing your first script, it's important to have a well-organized environment. If you haven't installed **Node.js** yet, make sure it is installed on your system by opening a terminal or command prompt and running:

```
node -v
```
If Node.js is installed correctly, this command will display its version number.

Next, create a dedicated folder for your Node.js project. Open your terminal and navigate to a directory where you want to store your project. Then, create a new folder and move into it:

```
mkdir my-node-project
cd my-node-project
```

Inside this folder, initialize a new Node.js project by running:

```
npm init -y
```

This command creates a `package.json` file, which acts as the metadata file for your project. Although not strictly necessary for running a basic script, this file becomes useful as you start managing dependencies and adding scripts in the future.

Writing Your First Node.js Script

Now that your environment is ready, it's time to write and execute your first Node.js script.

Create a new JavaScript file in your project folder. You can name it `app.js`.

Open `app.js` in a code editor (such as VS Code) and enter the following JavaScript code:

```
console.log("Hello, Node.js!");
```

This script contains a single line of JavaScript that prints a message to the console when executed.

Save the file and return to your terminal.

To execute the script, use the `node` command followed by the filename:

```
node app.js
```

If everything is set up correctly, you should see the following output in your terminal:

```
Hello, Node.js!
```

Congratulations! You have successfully written and executed your first Node.js script.

Understanding How Node.js Executes Scripts

Unlike JavaScript in a web browser, where scripts are executed within an HTML page, Node.js runs JavaScript directly in the system's terminal. This is possible because Node.js provides a **runtime environment** that allows JavaScript to interact with the file system, databases, and networks.

When you execute `node app.js`, Node.js does the following:

Loads the script into memory

Compiles the JavaScript using the V8 engine (the same engine used in Chrome)

Executes the script line by line

Prints output to the terminal (if there are `console.log` statements)

Since Node.js executes JavaScript outside of the browser, you are not limited by browser security restrictions, making it an ideal choice for server-side programming.

Expanding Your First Script with Variables and Functions

A simple `"Hello, Node.js!"` script is a great start, but let's go a step further by adding variables and functions. Modify your `app.js` file as follows:

```
// Define a variable
const message = "Welcome to Node.js!";

// Define a function
function greetUser(name) {
    return `Hello, ${name}!`;
}

// Call the function and display the output
console.log(message);
console.log(greetUser("Alice"));
```

Save the file and run it using:

```
node app.js
```
The expected output will be:

```
Welcome to Node.js!
Hello, Alice!
```

This script introduces variables, functions, and string interpolation using template literals. It demonstrates how Node.js executes JavaScript just like a browser would, but without requiring an HTML file.

Working with the File System in Node.js

One of the key advantages of Node.js is its ability to interact with the file system. Unlike browser-based JavaScript, which is restricted from accessing files for security reasons, Node.js allows you to **read and write files** directly from your operating system.

To demonstrate this, let's modify our script to **create and read a file**.

Writing to a File

Replace the contents of app.js with the following code:

```
const fs = require("fs");

// Write to a file
fs.writeFileSync("message.txt", "This is a message
from Node.js!");

console.log("File has been created successfully.");
```

In this script:

The fs module (which stands for **file system**) is imported using require().

The writeFileSync method is used to create a file named message.txt and write content into it.

A success message is logged to confirm that the file has been created.

Run the script again:

```
node app.js
```
After execution, check your project folder—you should see a new file named message.txt. Open it, and you'll find the text "This is a message from Node.js!" inside.

Reading from a File

Now, modify app.js to read the contents of message.txt and display them in the terminal:

```
const fs = require("fs");

// Read from a file
```

```
const data = fs.readFileSync("message.txt",
"utf8");

console.log("File Content:", data);
```

This script reads the file content synchronously and prints it. Run it using:

```
node app.js
```

You should see the following output:

```
File Content: This is a message from Node.js!
```

This is a simple demonstration of how Node.js interacts with the file system, allowing you to read and write files effortlessly.

Handling User Input in Node.js

Node.js can also process user input directly from the terminal. This is useful for interactive applications, command-line tools, or gathering input before executing a task.

Modify `app.js` to accept user input:

```
const readline = require("readline");

const rl = readline.createInterface({
    input: process.stdin,
    output: process.stdout
});

rl.question("What is your name? ", (name) => {
    console.log(`Hello, ${name}! Welcome to
Node.js.`);
    rl.close();
});
```

This script:

Uses the `readline` module to accept user input from the terminal.

Prompts the user with a question (`"What is your name?"`).

Prints a greeting message based on the user's response.

Run the script:

```
node app.js
```
When prompted, enter your name:

```
What is your name? John
Hello, John! Welcome to Node.js.
```

This demonstrates how Node.js can interact dynamically with users, making it a powerful tool for building interactive command-line applications.

Running your first Node.js script is a foundational step in understanding how Node.js executes JavaScript outside the browser. You have learned how to:

Write and execute a basic Node.js script.

Work with variables, functions, and string manipulation.

Read and write files using the built-in **fs module**.

Accept and process user input from the terminal.

With these concepts in place, you are now ready to explore more advanced Node.js features, such as creating web servers, handling APIs, and managing databases. From here, the possibilities are endless.

Chapter 3: Core Concepts of Node.js

Node.js is built on a few fundamental principles that make it unique compared to other backend technologies. Understanding these **core concepts** will not only help you write better Node.js applications but also enable you to take full advantage of its efficiency, scalability, and flexibility.

In this chapter, we'll explore the **module system**, work with the **file system**, understand how **buffers and streams** handle data efficiently, and break down **asynchronous programming** techniques using **callbacks, promises, and async/await**.

Understanding Modules

Modules are one of the most fundamental building blocks of Node.js applications. They allow developers to break down a program into smaller, reusable pieces of code that can be managed and maintained independently. Instead of writing an entire application in one large, unreadable file, modules help organize code into separate files, making development more efficient and scalable.

Node.js provides two primary ways to work with modules: **CommonJS (CJS)** and **ES Modules (ESM)**. Each approach has its own syntax and characteristics, and understanding how they work will help you make informed decisions when structuring your Node.js applications.

When building applications, you often need to split functionality across multiple files to keep the codebase organized. For example, a web application might have separate files for handling authentication, database interactions, and API routes. Without modules, all these features would be written in a single file, making it difficult to manage and debug.

Modules solve this problem by enabling you to:

Encapsulate functionality in separate files.

Reuse code across different parts of an application.

Avoid naming conflicts by keeping variables and functions local to a module.

48

Improve maintainability by organizing code into logical sections.

In Node.js, every JavaScript file is treated as a module, and you can import and export functions, objects, or variables between them.

CommonJS Modules (require/exports)

CommonJS (CJS) is the **default module system** used in Node.js. It has been around since the early days of Node.js and is widely supported. If you are working in a Node.js environment without explicitly enabling ES Modules, you are using CommonJS by default.

How CommonJS Works

CommonJS uses two primary keywords:

`require()` – Used to import modules.

`module.exports` – Used to export functions, objects, or variables.

Creating and Exporting a Module

Let's create a simple module that provides a greeting function.

Create a file named `greet.js` and define the function:

```
function greet(name) {
    return `Hello, ${name}!`;
}

module.exports = greet;
```

Here, `module.exports` is used to make the `greet` function available for use in other files. Without this, the function would remain private to `greet.js` and would not be accessible elsewhere.

Import and Use the Module

Now, create another file named `app.js` and use `require()` to import the `greet.js` module:

```
const greet = require("./greet");

console.log(greet("Alice"));
```

When you run the script using:

```
node app.js
```

The output will be:

```
Hello, Alice!
```

This demonstrates how CommonJS allows you to export and import functions across files in a Node.js project.

Exporting Multiple Values in CommonJS

You can also export multiple functions or variables from a module. Modify `greet.js` to export multiple values:

```
function greet(name) {
    return `Hello, ${name}!`;
}

function farewell(name) {
    return `Goodbye, ${name}!`;
}

module.exports = {
    greet,
    farewell
};
```

Now, update `app.js` to import both functions:

```
const { greet, farewell } = require("./greet");

console.log(greet("Alice"));
console.log(farewell("Alice"));
```

Running `node app.js` will produce:

```
Hello, Alice!
Goodbye, Alice!
```

This approach allows you to keep related functions grouped within a single module, improving organization.

ES Modules (import/export)

ES Modules (ESM) is the **modern JavaScript module system**, introduced as part of the ECMAScript standard. It is commonly used in frontend development and is now fully supported in Node.js as well. Unlike CommonJS, which loads modules synchronously, ES Modules **use asynchronous loading**, making them more efficient in some cases.

How to Enable ES Modules in Node.js

By default, Node.js assumes you are using CommonJS. To enable ES Modules, you must **explicitly set your project to use ESM**.

Open `package.json` and add:

```
{
  "type": "module"
}
```

This tells Node.js to treat `.js` files as ES Modules.

Use **export** and **import** instead of `module.exports` and `require()`.

Creating and Exporting an ES Module

Modify `greet.js` to use ES Module syntax:

```
export function greet(name) {
    return `Hello, ${name}!`;
}

export function farewell(name) {
    return `Goodbye, ${name}!`;
}
```

Instead of using `module.exports`, ES Modules use the `export` keyword to define what should be made available to other files.

Importing an ES Module

Now, modify `app.js` to use ES Module syntax:

```
import { greet, farewell } from "./greet.js";

console.log(greet("Alice"));
console.log(farewell("Alice"));
```

When you run:

```
node app.js
```

The output will be:

```
Hello, Alice!
Goodbye, Alice!
```

Unlike CommonJS, which requires `.js` file extensions to be omitted, ES Modules **require the `.js` extension** when importing files.

Key Differences Between CommonJS and ES Modules

1. Syntax

CommonJS uses `require()` and `module.exports`, while ES Modules use `import` and `export`.

2. Synchronous vs. Asynchronous Loading

CommonJS loads modules **synchronously**, meaning it waits for the entire module to be processed before continuing execution. ES Modules, on the other hand, **load asynchronously**, improving performance in some cases.

3. Default Behavior in Node.js

Node.js **defaults to CommonJS** unless explicitly configured to use ES Modules by adding `"type": "module"` in `package.json`.

4. Usage in Frontend vs. Backend

CommonJS is primarily used in **Node.js**, while ES Modules are the standard in **modern frontend JavaScript development** (React, Vue, etc.).

When to Use CommonJS vs. ES Modules

If you are working on a **Node.js-only project**, CommonJS is a safe and widely used option. It has been around for years, and most Node.js libraries still use it.

If you are working on a **full-stack project** that involves both frontend and backend JavaScript, ES Modules provide a consistent syntax across the entire codebase, making it a better choice.

For new projects, ES Modules are becoming the preferred standard due to their modern syntax and better compatibility with browser-based JavaScript.

Modules are essential for writing scalable Node.js applications. Whether you use **CommonJS** or **ES Modules**, understanding how to structure and reuse code effectively will make development more organized and efficient.

CommonJS (`require()` and `module.exports`) is the traditional module system used by Node.js.

ES Modules (`import` and `export`) is the modern JavaScript module system that is now fully supported in Node.js.

CommonJS is synchronous, while **ES Modules support asynchronous loading**.

Node.js defaults to CommonJS, but you can enable ES Modules by adding `"type": "module"` in `package.json`.

Both module systems are powerful, and the choice depends on your project's needs. Understanding both ensures that you can work on any Node.js project, regardless of which module system is used.

Working with the File System (`fs` Module)

One of the biggest advantages of using **Node.js** for backend development is its ability to interact directly with the file system. Whether you need to create, read, update, or delete files and directories, Node.js provides a built-in module called **`fs` (File System)** that allows you to perform these operations efficiently.

Unlike JavaScript in the browser, which is restricted from directly accessing files for security reasons, **Node.js has full access to the file system**. This is particularly useful for applications that deal with file storage, logging, configuration management, or reading and writing large amounts of data.

The **`fs` module** is a **core module** in Node.js, meaning it is built into the platform and does not require any additional installation. To use it in your application, you need to import it using **`require()`**:

```
const fs = require("fs");
```

53

With the `fs` module, you can:

Read the contents of a file

Write data to a file

Append data to an existing file

Rename or delete files

Create, read, and remove directories

The **fs module** supports **both synchronous and asynchronous methods** for most operations.

Synchronous methods block execution until the operation is completed.

Asynchronous methods do not block execution and use **callbacks, promises, or async/await** to handle results.

For most real-world applications, it is recommended to use **asynchronous methods** to keep the application responsive and scalable. However, synchronous methods can be useful for scripts where execution order matters.

Reading a File in Node.js

One of the most common tasks when working with the file system is reading a file's contents. Let's assume we have a file named `example.txt` with the following content:

`Node.js makes working with files easy and efficient.`

Reading a File Synchronously

A **synchronous** method reads the file completely before allowing further execution.

```
const fs = require("fs");

const data = fs.readFileSync("example.txt",
"utf8");
console.log(data);
```
When this script runs, it will print the file's content to the console:

`Node.js makes working with files easy and efficient.`

Since this method blocks execution, it is not ideal for applications that handle multiple tasks simultaneously.

Reading a File Asynchronously

To prevent blocking, you should use the **asynchronous version** of `fs.readFile()`, which takes a callback function:

```
const fs = require("fs");

fs.readFile("example.txt", "utf8", (err, data) => {
    if (err) {
        console.error("Error reading file:", err);
        return;
    }
    console.log(data);
});
```

In this version, Node.js reads the file in the background and executes the callback function once the operation is complete. This allows the application to continue running other tasks while waiting for the file to be read.

If an error occurs, such as if the file does not exist, it is handled inside the callback function.

Writing to a File

Creating and writing files is another essential file system operation. The `fs.writeFile()` method allows you to write data to a file.

Writing a File Synchronously

A synchronous write operation creates a new file or **overwrites an existing file** if it already exists.

```
const fs = require("fs");

fs.writeFileSync("output.txt", "This is a new file created with Node.js.");
console.log("File written successfully.");
```

After running this script, a new file named `output.txt` will be created in your project directory with the following content:

```
This is a new file created with Node.js.
```

Writing a File Asynchronously

Using the asynchronous version ensures that other tasks continue running while the file is being written.

```
const fs = require("fs");

fs.writeFile("output.txt", "This file was created
asynchronously.", (err) => {
    if (err) {
        console.error("Error writing to file:",
err);
        return;
    }
    console.log("File written successfully.");
});
```

This method is more suitable for web applications or services where blocking execution could degrade performance.

Appending Data to a File

If you need to **add** content to an existing file rather than overwriting it, use `fs.appendFile()`.

```
fs.appendFile("output.txt", "\nThis is an
additional line.", (err) => {
    if (err) {
        console.error("Error appending data:",
err);
        return;
    }
    console.log("Data appended successfully.");
});
```

Running this script will add a new line to `output.txt` instead of replacing the existing content.

Renaming a File

To rename a file, use `fs.rename()`.

```
fs.rename("output.txt", "renamed.txt", (err) => {
    if (err) {
```

```
        console.error("Error renaming file:", err);
        return;
    }
    console.log("File renamed successfully.");
});
```

This will rename `output.txt` to `renamed.txt`. If a file with the new name already exists, it will be **overwritten** without warning.

Deleting a File

If you need to remove a file, use `fs.unlink()`.

```
fs.unlink("renamed.txt", (err) => {
    if (err) {
        console.error("Error deleting file:", err);
        return;
    }
    console.log("File deleted successfully.");
});
```

This permanently deletes the file, so be cautious when using this operation.

Working with Directories

Node.js also allows you to manage directories using the `fs` module.

Creating a Directory

To create a directory, use `fs.mkdir()`:

```
fs.mkdir("newFolder", (err) => {
    if (err) {
        console.error("Error creating directory:",
err);
        return;
    }
    console.log("Directory created successfully.");
});
```

Reading a Directory's Contents

To list all files and folders inside a directory, use `fs.readdir()`:

```
fs.readdir(".", (err, files) => {
```

```
    if (err) {
        console.error("Error reading directory:",
err);
        return;
    }
    console.log("Files in directory:", files);
});
```

Deleting a Directory

To remove an empty directory, use `fs.rmdir()`:

```
fs.rmdir("newFolder", (err) => {
    if (err) {
        console.error("Error deleting directory:",
err);
        return;
    }
    console.log("Directory deleted successfully.");
});
```

If the directory is **not empty**, this method will throw an error. You must delete all files inside before removing the directory.

Best Practices for Working with the File System

Use Asynchronous Methods for Performance
Always prefer asynchronous methods (`fs.readFile()`, `fs.writeFile()`) over synchronous methods (`fs.readFileSync()`, `fs.writeFileSync()`) in real-world applications to avoid blocking the event loop.

Handle Errors Properly
Always check for errors in the callback function to handle unexpected issues like missing files or permission errors.

Use Path Module for Cross-Platform Compatibility
When working with file paths, use the **path module** to avoid issues between Windows and Linux file systems.

```
const path = require("path");
const filePath = path.join(__dirname,
"example.txt");
console.log("File Path:", filePath);
```

Ensure File Security

Avoid exposing sensitive files in a publicly accessible directory. Use proper **permissions** and **environment variables** to store confidential data.

The **fs module** is a powerful tool for managing files and directories in Node.js. It allows you to read, write, modify, and delete files efficiently. By understanding both **synchronous and asynchronous** methods, you can build applications that handle files effectively without blocking execution.

With this knowledge, you are now equipped to manage file operations in Node.js confidently, whether for **logging, configuration management, or user file uploads**.

Understanding Buffers and Streams

Handling data efficiently is a fundamental part of backend development, especially when dealing with **large files, real-time processing, and network communication**. Unlike traditional programming environments where data is handled all at once, **Node.js processes data in small, manageable chunks**. This approach reduces memory usage and improves performance, making it particularly useful for **file operations, streaming video or audio, reading large datasets, and handling network requests**.

At the core of this system are **Buffers** and **Streams**. These two concepts allow Node.js to **handle data efficiently without loading everything into memory at once**, making it ideal for large-scale applications. Understanding how they work will help you build high-performance applications that can process vast amounts of data seamlessly.

What is a Buffer in Node.js?

A **Buffer** is a temporary storage space for binary data. Since JavaScript was originally designed for browser-based applications, it did not include built-in support for handling raw binary data. However, **Node.js introduced Buffers** to allow JavaScript to handle binary data **directly in memory**.

Buffers are commonly used when:

Reading or writing files

Processing binary data from network connections

Handling data streams (such as audio and video processing)

A Buffer **acts like an array of bytes**, but unlike regular JavaScript arrays, it is specifically designed to handle **raw binary data**.

Creating and Using Buffers

To create a Buffer, you use the **Buffer class** provided by Node.js.

Here's a simple example:

```
const buffer = Buffer.from("Hello, Node.js");
console.log(buffer);
```

Running this script will output the raw binary representation of the string:

```
<Buffer 48 65 6c 6c 6f 2c 20 4e 6f 64 65 2e 6a 73>
```
Each value in the output represents a **hexadecimal** byte, which corresponds to the ASCII representation of each character in the string.

To convert this Buffer back to a readable string, use:

```
console.log(buffer.toString());
```
This will output:

```
Hello, Node.js
```
Buffers allow developers to **store and manipulate binary data** efficiently, which is particularly useful when dealing with **file systems and network communication**.

Modifying Buffers

Since Buffers work similarly to arrays, you can modify individual bytes.

For example:

```
const buffer = Buffer.from("ABC");
buffer[0] = 65; // 'A' in ASCII
buffer[1] = 66; // 'B' in ASCII
buffer[2] = 67; // 'C' in ASCII

console.log(buffer.toString()); // Output: ABC
```

If you change one of the values, the buffer content will change accordingly. Buffers give you **direct access to binary data**, making them much faster than regular JavaScript strings or arrays when working with raw data.

Buffers are essential when working with **large amounts of data**. Without them, Node.js would have to **load an entire file into memory before processing it**, which is inefficient for large files. By using buffers, Node.js processes data in chunks, significantly reducing memory usage.

For example, when reading a **500MB file**, using a Buffer allows you to **process it in small chunks** instead of loading the entire file into memory at once. This ensures your application remains fast and responsive.

What is a Stream in Node.js?

A **Stream** is a continuous flow of data that is **processed in chunks** rather than being loaded all at once. Think of it like watching a YouTube video—**you don't need to download the entire video before you start watching it**. Instead, the video plays as it loads.

Streams are useful when:

Reading large files

Writing data to files

Processing HTTP requests and responses

Handling real-time data processing (e.g., video/audio streaming)

Unlike Buffers, which store data **all at once**, Streams process data **piece by piece**, making them much more efficient.

Types of Streams in Node.js

Node.js provides four types of streams:

Readable Streams – Used for reading data (e.g., file input, network requests).

Writable Streams – Used for writing data (e.g., saving a file, sending a network response).

Duplex Streams – Can read and write data (e.g., network sockets).

Transform Streams – Modify data while reading or writing (e.g., compressing a file).

Each of these stream types allows data to be processed **incrementally**, reducing memory usage and improving performance.

Reading a File Using Streams

Instead of loading an entire file into memory, Node.js allows you to **read it in chunks using a stream**.

Example: Reading a Large File with Streams

Let's say you have a large text file named `largeFile.txt`. Instead of using `fs.readFile()`, which loads the entire file into memory, you can use **streams**:

```
const fs = require("fs");

const readStream =
fs.createReadStream("largeFile.txt", "utf8");

readStream.on("data", (chunk) => {
    console.log("Received chunk:", chunk);
});

readStream.on("end", () => {
    console.log("Finished reading the file.");
});

readStream.on("error", (err) => {
    console.error("Error reading file:", err);
});
```

What Happens in This Code?

A **readable stream** is created using `fs.createReadStream()`, specifying the file and encoding (`utf8` for text files).

The `data` event is triggered every time a new chunk of data is received.

The `end` event is fired once the entire file has been read.

The `error` event handles any errors that may occur.

This method is far more efficient than loading the entire file at once, especially for **large files**.

Writing to a File Using Streams

Just as you can read a file in chunks, you can also **write to a file in chunks** using a writable stream.

Example: Writing Data to a File Using a Stream

```
const fs = require("fs");

const writeStream =
fs.createWriteStream("output.txt");

writeStream.write("This is the first line.\n");
writeStream.write("This is the second line.\n");
writeStream.end("Final line."); // Signals the end
of writing

writeStream.on("finish", () => {
    console.log("File writing completed.");
});

writeStream.on("error", (err) => {
    console.error("Error writing file:", err);
});
```

In this example, Node.js **writes data in chunks** rather than storing everything in memory first. This is especially useful for large files, **log files**, or **real-time data processing**.

Piping Streams for Efficient Processing

One of the most powerful features of streams is **piping**—where the output of one stream is directly sent to another. This eliminates the need for temporary buffers, improving performance.

For example, if you want to **copy a file**, you can do it efficiently using streams:

```
const fs = require("fs");
```

```
const readStream =
fs.createReadStream("source.txt");
const writeStream =
fs.createWriteStream("destination.txt");

readStream.pipe(writeStream);

writeStream.on("finish", () => {
    console.log("File copied successfully.");
});
```

This method is much **faster and memory-efficient** compared to reading and writing the entire file manually.

Buffers and Streams are critical concepts in Node.js for handling **data efficiently**.

Buffers store binary data temporarily, allowing direct access to memory.

Streams allow data to be processed in chunks, reducing memory usage and improving performance.

Readable and Writable streams help with handling large files and network requests efficiently.

Piping streams further optimizes performance by eliminating unnecessary data storage.

By mastering Buffers and Streams, you can build **fast, scalable applications** capable of handling **large amounts of data** while keeping memory usage low. Whether you're working with **file systems, real-time data, or network requests**, these tools will help you create **efficient and high-performance applications** in Node.js.

Asynchronous Programming

When working with **Node.js**, you will frequently deal with **asynchronous operations**. These are tasks that do not execute sequentially but instead allow other operations to continue while waiting for their completion. This is particularly important for handling tasks such as **reading files, making API requests, querying databases, and managing network connections**.

In a **synchronous** program, each operation must complete before the next one begins, which can slow down the entire application. However, in **asynchronous** programming, tasks are executed independently, ensuring that the application remains responsive and efficient.

To manage asynchronous behavior, Node.js provides three key techniques: **callbacks, promises, and async/await**. Understanding how these work will help you write better, more efficient, and maintainable code.

By default, JavaScript is **single-threaded**, meaning it executes code **line by line**. However, Node.js introduces an **event loop** that allows it to handle multiple tasks concurrently without blocking execution.

Let's look at a simple example of asynchronous execution:

```
console.log("Start");

setTimeout(() => {
    console.log("Inside setTimeout");
}, 2000);

console.log("End");
```

When you run this script, you might expect the output to be:

```
Start
Inside setTimeout
End
```

However, the actual output is:

```
Start
End
Inside setTimeout
```

This happens because `setTimeout()` is **asynchronous**. Instead of blocking execution for 2 seconds, it **schedules the task** and moves on to the next statement. When the timer completes, the callback function is executed.

This is the **core principle of asynchronous programming** in Node.js: **non-blocking execution** that keeps the application responsive while waiting for certain tasks to complete.

Working with Callbacks

A **callback** is a function passed as an argument to another function, which gets executed **after** the operation completes. Callbacks were the original way of handling asynchronous operations in JavaScript.

Here's an example of a callback in action:

```
function fetchData(callback) {
    setTimeout(() => {
        callback("Data fetched successfully!");
    }, 2000);
}

function handleData(response) {
    console.log(response);
}

fetchData(handleData);
```

When you run this script, it prints:

```
(Data is fetched after 2 seconds)
Data fetched successfully!
```

The `fetchData()` function **does not return the result immediately**. Instead, it uses a `setTimeout()` to simulate a delay and then **calls the callback function (`handleData`) once the operation is done**.

Nested Callbacks and the Callback Hell Problem

Callbacks are useful, but they can quickly lead to **callback hell**—a situation where multiple nested callbacks make the code difficult to read and maintain.

Consider a scenario where you need to **fetch user details, fetch their posts, and then fetch comments on a post**, all in sequence:

```
getUser(1, (user) => {
    getPosts(user.id, (posts) => {
```

```
    getComments(posts[0].id, (comments) => {
        console.log(comments);
    });
  });
});
```

This nested structure is called **callback hell** because it creates deeply indented, unreadable code. Managing errors also becomes more difficult.

To solve this, JavaScript introduced **Promises**.

Using Promises

A **Promise** is an object that represents the eventual completion (or failure) of an asynchronous operation. Instead of passing a callback, a Promise provides **methods to handle success and failure** in a cleaner way.

A Promise has three states:

Pending: The operation has started but is not yet complete.

Fulfilled: The operation completed successfully.

Rejected: The operation failed.

Here's how you create and use a Promise:

```
function fetchData() {
    return new Promise((resolve, reject) => {
        setTimeout(() => {
            resolve("Data fetched successfully!");
        }, 2000);
    });
}

fetchData()
    .then((data) => {
        console.log(data);
    })
    .catch((error) => {
        console.error("Error:", error);
    });
```

In this example, `fetchData()` returns a **Promise**. When the asynchronous task completes, `resolve()` is called, and `.then()` handles the result. If an error occurs, `reject()` is called, and `.catch()` handles the error.

Chaining Promises to Avoid Callback Hell

One of the biggest advantages of Promises is **chaining**, which eliminates deeply nested callbacks.

Here's an improved version of the previous callback hell example:

```
getUser(1)
    .then((user) => getPosts(user.id))
    .then((posts) => getComments(posts[0].id))
    .then((comments) => console.log(comments))
    .catch((error) => console.error("Error:",
error));
```

Each `.then()` method handles the **result of the previous Promise**, making the code much cleaner and easier to read.

However, there is an even better way to handle asynchronous code—**async/await**.

Using Async/Await

Async/Await is a modern way to write asynchronous code that looks and behaves like synchronous code but still executes asynchronously. It is built on top of **Promises** but provides a cleaner, more readable syntax.

Writing an Async Function

To use `async/await`, you define a function using the `async` keyword, and within that function, you use `await` to wait for asynchronous operations to complete.

Here's an example:

```
function fetchData() {
    return new Promise((resolve, reject) => {
        setTimeout(() => {
            resolve("Data fetched successfully!");
        }, 2000);
```

```
    });
}

async function getData() {
    try {
        const data = await fetchData();
        console.log(data);
    } catch (error) {
        console.error("Error:", error);
    }
}

getData();
```

How It Works

The `fetchData()` function returns a Promise.

The `getData()` function is declared as **async**, which allows the use of `await` inside it.

`await fetchData();` pauses execution until the Promise resolves.

If an error occurs, it is caught by the `try...catch` block.

The biggest advantage of `async/await` is **readability**. Instead of chaining `.then()`, you write code that looks sequential but remains asynchronous under the hood.

Async/Await in Real-World Use Case

Consider fetching **user details, posts, and comments** using `async/await`:

```
async function getUserData() {
    try {
        const user = await getUser(1);
        const posts = await getPosts(user.id);
        const comments = await
getComments(posts[0].id);

        console.log(comments);
    } catch (error) {
        console.error("Error:", error);
```

69

```
    }
}

getUserData();
```

This version **reads like synchronous code** but executes asynchronously, making it much easier to follow.

Which One Should You Use?

Callbacks are the most basic form of handling asynchronous code but can lead to callback hell.

Promises improve readability and avoid deeply nested structures.

Async/Await provides the cleanest, most readable syntax while still leveraging Promises.

For modern JavaScript applications, **async/await is the preferred choice** due to its clarity and simplicity.

Asynchronous programming is essential for building **scalable, efficient applications** in Node.js. Understanding **callbacks, promises, and async/await** allows you to write non-blocking code that can handle **file operations, database queries, API calls, and real-time events** smoothly.

Chapter 4: Modern JavaScript for Node.js

JavaScript has evolved significantly over the years, and with **ES6+ (ECMAScript 2015 and later)**, it has become more powerful and expressive. These modern JavaScript features are essential for writing **cleaner, more efficient, and maintainable code** in Node.js.

ES6+ Features You Need to Know

JavaScript has undergone significant improvements since the release of **ECMAScript 2015 (ES6)**, introducing features that make code **more concise, readable, and efficient**. These modern additions are particularly useful in **Node.js**, where clean and optimized code is essential for building scalable applications.

If you've been working with JavaScript for a while, you might have used older syntax and patterns that require more effort to maintain. With ES6+, those outdated approaches are no longer necessary. **Arrow functions, destructuring, template literals, object shorthand, spread and rest operators, and modern module imports** are just a few examples of improvements that simplify development.

Let and Const – Replacing Var

Before ES6, JavaScript only had `var` for declaring variables. However, `var` has **functional scoping** and can introduce unintended bugs due to **hoisting**.

To solve this, ES6 introduced `let` and `const`.

Using `let` for Block Scope

A variable declared with `let` **only exists within the block** where it is defined.

```
if (true) {
    let message = "Hello!";
    console.log(message); // Works fine inside the block
}
```

```
console.log(message); // ReferenceError: message is
not defined
```

Unlike `var`, which leaks out of the block, `let` keeps variables contained where they belong.

Using `const` for Constants

If a value should **never change**, use `const`.

```
const API_URL = "https://api.example.com";
API_URL = "https://newapi.com"; // Error:
Assignment to constant variable
```

Once assigned, a `const` variable cannot be reassigned, ensuring **data integrity** in your application.

Arrow Functions – Cleaner and More Concise

Traditional function expressions can be **verbose**, especially when dealing with callbacks. Arrow functions provide a **shorter syntax** and also automatically bind `this`, which is helpful in certain cases.

Converting a Traditional Function to an Arrow Function

```
// Regular function
function greet(name) {
    return "Hello, " + name;
}

// Arrow function
const greet = (name) => "Hello, " + name;

console.log(greet("Alice"));
```

If the function has a **single parameter**, the parentheses can be omitted.

```
const square = num => num * num;
console.log(square(4)); // Output: 16
```

For functions with **multiple parameters** or **multiple lines**, use curly braces:

```
const add = (a, b) => {
    const sum = a + b;
    return sum;
};
console.log(add(3, 5)); // Output: 8
```

Template Literals – Easier String Handling

String concatenation using + can get messy, especially when inserting variables into text. **Template literals** solve this by allowing embedded expressions.

Without Template Literals

```
const name = "Alice";
const greeting = "Hello, " + name + "! Welcome to
Node.js.";
console.log(greeting);
```

With Template Literals

```
const name = "Alice";
const greeting = `Hello, ${name}! Welcome to
Node.js.`;
console.log(greeting);
```

Template literals use **backticks ()** instead of quotes and allow **multi-line strings** without needing \n`.

```
const message = `This is a
multi-line string in ES6.`;
console.log(message);
```

Destructuring – Extracting Values Easily

Object Destructuring

Accessing object properties traditionally requires dot notation:

```
const user = { name: "Alice", age: 25 };

const name = user.name;
const age = user.age;
```

```
console.log(name, age);
```
With **destructuring**, you can extract values **directly** from an object:

```
const user = { name: "Alice", age: 25 };

const { name, age } = user;

console.log(name, age);
```

If an object contains **nested properties**, destructuring works on them too:

```
const user = {
    name: "Alice",
    address: {
        city: "New York",
        zip: "10001"
    }
};

const { address: { city, zip } } = user;
console.log(city, zip); // Output: New York 10001
```

Array Destructuring

You can also destructure arrays:

```
const numbers = [1, 2, 3];

const [first, second] = numbers;

console.log(first, second); // Output: 1 2
```

You can skip elements:

```
const [, , third] = numbers;
console.log(third); // Output: 3
```

Spread and Rest Operators (...)

Spread Operator (...)

The **spread operator** is used to expand arrays or objects into individual elements.

Copying an Array

```
const numbers = [1, 2, 3];
const newNumbers = [...numbers, 4, 5];

console.log(newNumbers); // Output: [1, 2, 3, 4, 5]
```

Merging Objects

```
const user = { name: "Alice", age: 25 };
const updatedUser = { ...user, location: "New York"
};

console.log(updatedUser);
// Output: { name: "Alice", age: 25, location: "New
York" }
```

Rest Operator (...)

The **rest operator** collects multiple values into an array.

```
function sum(...numbers) {
    return numbers.reduce((acc, curr) => acc +
curr, 0);
}

console.log(sum(1, 2, 3, 4)); // Output: 10
```

Object Shorthand – Writing Less Code

If a variable name matches an object property name, you can use **shorthand syntax**.

```
const name = "Alice";
const age = 25;

const user = { name, age };

console.log(user); // Output: { name: "Alice", age:
25 }
```

Without shorthand, you would need:

```
const user = { name: name, age: age };
```

Object shorthand makes **code cleaner and easier to read**.

Default Function Parameters

Functions can now define **default values** for parameters.

```
function greet(name = "Guest") {
    return `Hello, ${name}!`;
}

console.log(greet()); // Output: Hello, Guest!
console.log(greet("Alice")); // Output: Hello,
Alice!
```

This prevents errors when arguments are **not provided**.

Modules – Import and Export

Instead of using `require()` in CommonJS, ES6 introduces **import/export** syntax for modular code.

Exporting from a Module (`math.js`)

```
export function add(a, b) {
    return a + b;
}
```

Importing the Module (`app.js`)

```
import { add } from "./math.js";

console.log(add(2, 3)); // Output: 5
```

To enable ES6 modules in Node.js, add `"type"`: `"module"` to `package.json`.

These ES6+ features **greatly improve** how JavaScript is written in Node.js. They make code **more efficient, readable, and scalable**.

Arrow functions simplify function expressions.

Template literals improve string handling.

Destructuring allows extracting data from objects and arrays efficiently.

Spread and rest operators enhance array and object operations.

Object shorthand reduces repetitive code.

Modules (`import`/`export`) organize code better.

Mastering these modern features will help you **write cleaner, faster, and more maintainable Node.js applications**.

Arrow Functions, Spread & Rest Operators

Modern JavaScript has introduced several features that make code more **concise, readable, and efficient**. Among them, **arrow functions, the spread operator (...), and the rest operator (...)** stand out as essential tools for writing cleaner, more expressive code.

Whether you're working with **functions, arrays, or objects**, these features will help you **reduce unnecessary boilerplate** and **improve performance** in your Node.js applications.

Arrow Functions – A More Concise Way to Write Functions

Traditional JavaScript functions require using the `function` keyword and, in many cases, explicit `return` statements. Arrow functions offer a **shorter syntax**, eliminating the need for these elements when they are not necessary.

Besides improving readability, arrow functions **do not create their own `this` context**, which makes them particularly useful inside object methods, event handlers, and callback functions.

Basic Arrow Function Syntax

A regular function written using the traditional approach looks like this:

```
function greet(name) {
    return "Hello, " + name;
}
```

With an arrow function, the same function can be rewritten in a more compact form:

```
const greet = (name) => "Hello, " + name;
```

If the function has a **single parameter**, the parentheses around it can be omitted:

```
const greet = name => "Hello, " + name;
```

If the function contains **multiple parameters**, they must be enclosed in parentheses:

```
const add = (a, b) => a + b;
```

When the function has **multiple statements**, curly braces {} are required, and you must explicitly use return:

```
const multiply = (a, b) => {
    const result = a * b;
    return result;
};
```

Using Arrow Functions in Callbacks

One of the most common uses of arrow functions is inside **higher-order functions**, such as .map(), .filter(), and .reduce().

For example, if you have an array of numbers and want to square each number, the traditional function approach looks like this:

```
const numbers = [1, 2, 3, 4, 5];

const squared = numbers.map(function (num) {
    return num * num;
});

console.log(squared); // Output: [1, 4, 9, 16, 25]
```

Using an arrow function simplifies this code significantly:

```
const squared = numbers.map(num => num * num);
```

The code is now easier to read while maintaining the same functionality.

Arrow Functions and the `this` Keyword

One major difference between **arrow functions and regular functions** is how they handle this.

Traditional functions bind `this` dynamically depending on **how they are called**. This can sometimes lead to unexpected behavior.

For example, consider the following object with a method:

```
const user = {
    name: "Alice",
    greet: function() {
        setTimeout(function() {
            console.log("Hello, " + this.name);
        }, 1000);
    }
};

user.greet();
```

In this case, `this.name` inside the `setTimeout` function **does not refer to `user.name`**, but instead refers to the global object (`undefined` in strict mode).

To fix this issue, an arrow function can be used because it **inherits `this` from its surrounding scope**:

```
const user = {
    name: "Alice",
    greet: function() {
        setTimeout(() => {
            console.log("Hello, " + this.name);
        }, 1000);
    }
};

user.greet(); // Output: Hello, Alice
```

This behavior makes arrow functions particularly useful in **event handlers, object methods, and class constructors** where maintaining the correct `this` context is important.

The Spread Operator (. . .) – Expanding Arrays and Objects

The spread operator (...) is a powerful feature that allows you to **expand** elements of an array or object into individual values. This is particularly useful for working with arrays and objects in a flexible and concise way.

Copying and Merging Arrays

A common operation in JavaScript is copying an array. Before ES6, this required using `.slice()`:

```
const original = [1, 2, 3];
const copy = original.slice();
```

With the spread operator, copying an array is much simpler:

```
const copy = [...original];
```

The spread operator can also be used to **merge arrays**:

```
const arr1 = [1, 2, 3];
const arr2 = [4, 5, 6];

const merged = [...arr1, ...arr2];

console.log(merged); // Output: [1, 2, 3, 4, 5, 6]
```

This is much cleaner than using `.concat()`, which was the old way of merging arrays.

Using Spread in Function Arguments

Some functions accept a variable number of arguments. The spread operator can be used to pass an **array as separate arguments** to such functions.

For example, the `Math.max()` function expects separate numbers, not an array:

```
const numbers = [10, 5, 8, 12];

console.log(Math.max(...numbers)); // Output: 12
```

Without spread, you would have to use `apply()`:

```
console.log(Math.max.apply(null, numbers)); //
Output: 12
```

The spread operator makes this process **much simpler and more intuitive**.

Merging and Copying Objects

In addition to arrays, the spread operator can be used with **objects**.

```
const user = { name: "Alice", age: 25 };
const updatedUser = { ...user, location: "New York"
};

console.log(updatedUser);
// Output: { name: "Alice", age: 25, location: "New
York" }
```

If a property exists in both objects, the **newest value replaces the old one**:

```
const user = { name: "Alice", age: 25 };
const updatedUser = { ...user, age: 30 };

console.log(updatedUser); // Output: { name:
"Alice", age: 30 }
```

This makes updating objects **much easier** than using `Object.assign()`.

The Rest Operator (...) – Gathering Values into an Array

The rest operator (...) looks identical to the spread operator, but it works differently. Instead of **expanding values**, it **collects multiple values** into an array.

Using Rest in Function Parameters

Rest parameters allow functions to accept **an unlimited number of arguments**.

```
function sum(...numbers) {
    return numbers.reduce((acc, curr) => acc +
curr, 0);
}

console.log(sum(1, 2, 3, 4)); // Output: 10
```

Instead of passing a fixed number of parameters, `...numbers` gathers all provided arguments into an **array**, which can then be processed using `.reduce()`.

Extracting Values from Arrays with Rest

When destructuring an array, the rest operator can be used to collect remaining elements:

```
const [first, second, ...rest] = [10, 20, 30, 40,
50];

console.log(first); // Output: 10
console.log(second); // Output: 20
console.log(rest); // Output: [30, 40, 50]
```

This is useful when handling arrays where **only the first few values are needed**, but the rest should still be accessible.

Arrow functions, the spread operator, and the rest operator are powerful **ES6+ features** that simplify JavaScript code significantly.

Arrow functions provide a cleaner syntax and resolve `this` binding issues.

The spread operator makes working with arrays and objects more flexible.

The rest operator helps handle dynamic function arguments and destructuring.

By integrating these features into your **Node.js applications**, you can write more **efficient, readable, and maintainable code**.

Destructuring, Template Literals, and Object Shorthand

JavaScript has evolved significantly over the years, introducing **modern syntax improvements** that make code **cleaner, more readable, and easier to maintain**. Among these, three essential features stand out:

Destructuring – A way to extract values from arrays and objects efficiently.

Template Literals – A more intuitive way to work with strings and embed expressions dynamically.

Object Shorthand – A technique to simplify object property assignments and function declarations.

82

Each of these features reduces **boilerplate code** and enhances **developer productivity**. Whether you're building APIs in Node.js, handling data from a database, or passing values between functions, these techniques will help you write **concise, maintainable, and expressive JavaScript**.

Destructuring – Extracting Values with Ease

Destructuring allows you to **unpack values from arrays or objects** into separate variables in a single step. This eliminates the need for **repetitive dot notation** or manual element assignments, making the code more elegant and readable.

Array Destructuring

In traditional JavaScript, extracting values from an array requires accessing each element individually:

```
const colors = ["red", "green", "blue"];

const first = colors[0];
const second = colors[1];
const third = colors[2];

console.log(first, second, third); // Output: red
green blue
```

With **destructuring**, the same result can be achieved in a single line:

```
const [first, second, third] = ["red", "green",
"blue"];

console.log(first, second, third); // Output: red
green blue
```

This is particularly useful when working with **function return values**.

Skipping Elements While Destructuring

If you only need certain values, you can skip elements using commas:

```
const [, second, third] = ["red", "green", "blue"];

console.log(second, third); // Output: green blue
```

This makes it easy to **extract only relevant data** without unnecessary variable assignments.

Using Default Values

If a value is **undefined**, a default value can be assigned:

```
const [first, second, third = "default"] = ["red",
"green"];

console.log(third); // Output: default
```

This prevents errors when working with **incomplete datasets**.

Object Destructuring

Objects are a fundamental part of JavaScript, and destructuring makes **extracting properties** much more convenient.

Consider an object representing a user:

```
const user = {
    name: "Alice",
    age: 25,
    location: "New York"
};

// Traditional way
const name = user.name;
const age = user.age;
const location = user.location;

console.log(name, age, location);
```

With destructuring, you can **extract multiple properties at once**:

```
const { name, age, location } = user;

console.log(name, age, location); // Output: Alice
25 New York
```

This is especially useful when working with **API responses**, where you may receive large objects but only need specific properties.

Renaming Variables While Destructuring

If you want to assign properties to **variables with different names**, you can rename them:

```
const { name: userName, age: userAge } = user;

console.log(userName, userAge); // Output: Alice 25
```

This is helpful when avoiding **naming conflicts** in a function scope.

Destructuring Nested Objects

Objects often contain **nested structures**, which can be destructured as well:

```
const person = {
    name: "Bob",
    address: {
        city: "Los Angeles",
        zip: "90001"
    }
};

const { address: { city, zip } } = person;

console.log(city, zip); // Output: Los Angeles 90001
```

With this approach, you can **extract deeply nested values** without repetitive dot notation.

Template Literals – Writing Strings the Right Way

JavaScript previously required **string concatenation** using the + operator, which made working with dynamic content **messy and error-prone**.

The Old Way – String Concatenation

```
const name = "Alice";
const age = 25;

const message = "Hello, my name is " + name + " and
I am " + age + " years old.";
```

```
console.log(message);
```

This approach is cumbersome, especially when dealing with **multi-line strings**.

The Modern Way – Using Template Literals

Template literals solve this by allowing **embedded expressions** inside **backticks (`)**:

```
const message = `Hello, my name is ${name} and I am
${age} years old.`;

console.log(message);
```

This approach improves **readability** and removes the need for manual concatenation.

Multi-Line Strings Without \n

Before ES6, multi-line strings required **escape characters**:

```
const text = "This is line one.\nThis is line
two.";
```

With **template literals**, multi-line strings are natural and easier to manage:

```
const text = `This is line one.
This is line two.`;

console.log(text);
```

This is particularly useful when **generating HTML templates** inside JavaScript:

```
const title = "Welcome";
const html = `
    <div>
        <h1>${title}</h1>
        <p>This is a dynamic template.</p>
    </div>
`;

console.log(html);
```

With template literals, HTML templates in **Node.js server responses** become much cleaner.

Object Shorthand – Writing Less Code with More Meaning

Shorthand Property Names

In ES5 and earlier, when defining objects, the key and value had to be explicitly assigned:

```
const name = "Alice";
const age = 25;

const user = { name: name, age: age };

console.log(user); // Output: { name: "Alice", age:
25 }
```

With **object shorthand**, if a variable name **matches the property name**, you can omit the redundant assignment:

```
const user = { name, age };

console.log(user); // Output: { name: "Alice", age:
25 }
```

This is particularly useful when **returning objects from functions** or **working with API payloads**.

Shorthand Method Definitions

Functions inside objects no longer need the `function` keyword:

```
const user = {
    name: "Alice",
    greet() {
        return `Hello, my name is ${this.name}`;
    }
};

console.log(user.greet()); // Output: Hello, my
name is Alice
```

This syntax improves **readability and reduces clutter**.

Using These Features in Real-World Scenarios

Processing API Responses

When working with APIs in Node.js, responses often contain large objects. **Destructuring** makes extracting relevant data much easier.

```
async function fetchUserData() {
    const response = await
fetch("https://jsonplaceholder.typicode.com/users/1
");
    const { name, email, address: { city } } =
await response.json();

    console.log(`User: ${name}, Email: ${email},
City: ${city}`);
}

fetchUserData();
```

Here, **only the required data is extracted**, making the function **cleaner and more efficient**.

Building Configuration Objects Dynamically

When constructing objects dynamically, **object shorthand** simplifies assignments:

```
function createUser(name, age, location) {
    return { name, age, location };
}

console.log(createUser("Alice", 25, "New York"));
// Output: { name: "Alice", age: 25, location: "New
York" }
```

By avoiding redundant key-value assignments, the function is more **concise and expressive**.

Modern JavaScript features such as **destructuring, template literals, and object shorthand** allow developers to **write less code while maintaining clarity and efficiency**.

Working with Fetch, Axios, and APIs

In modern web development, interacting with APIs is essential. Whether you're building a **server-side application** with Node.js or handling data requests on the **frontend**, making HTTP requests is a fundamental task.

JavaScript provides **two primary ways** to handle HTTP requests:

`fetch()`, a built-in browser API (also available in Node.js with external libraries).

Axios, a popular third-party library that simplifies HTTP requests.

Both methods allow you to **send and receive data** from web servers, interact with APIs, and integrate external services. Understanding **how to use them effectively** ensures you can work with real-world data efficiently, handle errors properly, and write cleaner code.

Using `fetch()` for API Requests

The `fetch()` function is a **built-in JavaScript API** for making HTTP requests. It returns a **Promise**, meaning it works asynchronously and does not block code execution.

Here's a **simple GET request** to fetch data from an API:

```
fetch("https://jsonplaceholder.typicode.com/users")
    .then(response => response.json()) // Convert
response to JSON
    .then(data => console.log(data))   // Handle the
data
    .catch(error => console.error("Error:",
error)); // Handle errors
```

How This Works

`fetch()` sends a request to the API.

The response is returned as a **Promise**, which means it doesn't immediately contain the data.

`.json()` extracts the JSON body from the response.

The extracted data is processed inside `.then()`.

If an error occurs (e.g., network failure), it is caught in `.catch()`.

Handling Errors in `fetch()`

One common mistake is assuming that `fetch()` throws an error when a request **fails** (e.g., a **404 Not Found** response). However, `fetch()` only rejects **on network errors**, not on HTTP errors.

To handle API errors properly, always check `response.ok`:

```
fetch("https://jsonplaceholder.typicode.com/users/9
99") // Invalid user ID
    .then(response => {
        if (!response.ok) {
            throw new Error(`HTTP Error! Status:
${response.status}`);
        }
        return response.json();
    })
    .then(data => console.log(data))
    .catch(error => console.error("Error:",
error));
```

If the request fails, `response.ok` will be **false**, triggering an error with the HTTP status code.

Using `fetch()` with `async/await`

Using `.then()` can result in **nested callbacks**, making code harder to read. Instead, `async/await` provides a more **synchronous-looking syntax** while maintaining non-blocking behavior.

Here's how you rewrite the previous example using `async/await`:

```
async function fetchUsers() {
    try {
        const response = await
fetch("https://jsonplaceholder.typicode.com/users")
;
```

```
        if (!response.ok) {
            throw new Error(`HTTP Error! Status:
${response.status}`);
        }

        const data = await response.json();
        console.log(data);
    } catch (error) {
        console.error("Error:", error);
    }
}

fetchUsers();
```

Why `async/await` is Better?

More readable – Code runs **top to bottom** without `.then()` chaining.

Easier error handling – Uses `try/catch`, making it more intuitive.

Better debugging – Errors are caught like in synchronous code.

Making a POST Request with `fetch()`

When sending data to a server, a **POST request** is required. This involves passing a **request body**, usually in JSON format.

Example: Sending Data with `fetch()`

```
async function createUser() {
    const newUser = {
        name: "John Doe",
        email: "john@example.com"
    };

    try {
        const response = await
fetch("https://jsonplaceholder.typicode.com/users",
{
            method: "POST",
            headers: {
                "Content-Type": "application/json"
```

```
        },
        body: JSON.stringify(newUser)
    });

    if (!response.ok) {
        throw new Error(`HTTP Error! Status:
${response.status}`);
    }

    const data = await response.json();
    console.log("User created:", data);
    } catch (error) {
        console.error("Error:", error);
    }
}

createUser();
```

Key Features in a POST Request

`method: "POST"` specifies the request type.

Headers include `"Content-Type": "application/json"` to indicate JSON data.

`body: JSON.stringify(newUser)` converts the object into JSON format.

Using Axios for API Requests

While `fetch()` is built-in, **Axios** provides additional benefits:

Automatic JSON parsing – No need to call `.json()`.

Better error handling – Axios throws errors for HTTP failures.

Easier syntax – Uses a simpler, more intuitive API.

Installing Axios in Node.js

Axios is **not built-in**, so you must install it first:

```
npm install axios
```

Then, import it into your script:

```
const axios = require("axios");
```

Making a GET Request with Axios

Example: Fetching Data

```
const axios = require("axios");

async function fetchUsers() {
    try {
        const response = await
axios.get("https://jsonplaceholder.typicode.com/use
rs");
        console.log(response.data);
    } catch (error) {
        console.error("Error:", error);
    }
}

fetchUsers();
```

Why Axios is Easier than `fetch()`?

Automatic JSON Parsing – No need for `.json()`.

Better Error Handling – Throws errors on failed HTTP responses.

Shorter Syntax – `axios.get(url)` instead of `fetch(url).then(response.json())`.

Making a POST Request with Axios

Example: Sending Data with Axios

```
const axios = require("axios");

async function createUser() {
    const newUser = {
        name: "John Doe",
        email: "john@example.com"
    };

    try {
```

```
        const response = await
axios.post("https://jsonplaceholder.typicode.com/us
ers", newUser);
        console.log("User created:",
response.data);
    } catch (error) {
        console.error("Error:", error);
    }
}

createUser();
```

Advantages of Axios for POST Requests

No need for `JSON.stringify(newUser)` – Axios handles it automatically.

Shorter Syntax – No need for extra headers; Axios **assumes JSON format by default**.

Handling Errors with Axios

Axios provides more **detailed error messages** than `fetch()`.

```
async function fetchUserData() {
    try {
        const response = await
axios.get("https://jsonplaceholder.typicode.com/use
rs/999"); // Invalid user ID
        console.log(response.data);
    } catch (error) {
        console.error("Error Message:",
error.message);
        console.error("Response Status:",
error.response?.status);
        console.error("Response Data:",
error.response?.data);
    }
}

fetchUserData();
```

If the request fails, Axios provides:

The **error message** (`error.message`).

The **HTTP status code** (`error.response.status`).

The **server response** (`error.response.data`).

Fetching data from APIs is a critical part of modern JavaScript development. Both `fetch()` and **Axios** allow you to:

Retrieve data using GET requests.

Send data using POST requests.

Handle errors efficiently.

While `fetch()` is **built-in and lightweight**, **Axios provides a cleaner, more feature-rich experience**. Choosing the right tool depends on **your project's needs**, but mastering both will make you a **more versatile developer**.

Error Handling and Debugging in Node.js

Errors are an inevitable part of software development. No matter how carefully you write your code, bugs and unexpected conditions will arise. What truly separates a professional developer from an inexperienced one is the **ability to handle errors gracefully and debug efficiently**.

In **Node.js**, error handling is particularly crucial because it runs on a **single-threaded event loop**. If an error is not handled properly, it can crash the entire application. That's why understanding **how to catch, manage, and log errors effectively** is essential for building reliable and maintainable applications.

Errors in Node.js generally fall into three main categories:

Operational Errors – These are expected failures that occur due to external factors, such as:

Database connection failures

Network issues

File not found errors

Request timeouts

Programming Errors (Bugs) – These occur due to mistakes in the code itself, such as:

Undefined variables

Incorrect function calls

Infinite loops

Syntax errors

System Errors – These occur when Node.js itself encounters an issue, such as:

Running out of memory

System-level failures

Each type of error should be handled differently to prevent application crashes and provide meaningful responses to users or logs for developers.

Using Try...Catch for Synchronous Errors

When working with **synchronous code**, the `try...catch` block is the simplest way to handle errors.

```
try {
    const result = JSON.parse("invalid JSON
string"); // This will throw an error
    console.log(result);
} catch (error) {
    console.error("An error occurred:",
error.message);
}
```

Here, `JSON.parse()` fails because the input is not valid JSON. Without `try...catch`, the error would **crash the application**. Instead, the error is caught and handled gracefully, preventing an abrupt failure.

Handling Errors in Asynchronous Code

Error handling in **asynchronous** code is different because errors don't always occur immediately. A common mistake developers make is assuming that `try...catch` will work for **callbacks or promises**—but it won't.

Error Handling in Callbacks

Node.js follows a convention where **the first argument in a callback is the error object**. If there is no error, this argument is `null`.

```
const fs = require("fs");

fs.readFile("nonexistent.txt", "utf8", (err, data)
=> {
    if (err) {
        console.error("Error reading file:",
err.message);
        return;
    }
    console.log(data);
});
```

If the file doesn't exist, `err` will contain the error details. By checking `if (err)`, we can handle the error properly instead of letting it crash the application.

Error Handling in Promises

When working with **Promises**, errors should be handled using `.catch()`.

```
const fetchData = () => {
    return new Promise((resolve, reject) => {
        setTimeout(() => {
            reject(new Error("Failed to fetch
data"));
        }, 1000);
    });
};

fetchData()
    .then(data => console.log(data))
    .catch(error => console.error("Error:",
error.message));
```

If `fetchData()` encounters an error, `.catch()` will handle it instead of letting it go unhandled.

Error Handling with Async/Await

When using `async/await`, errors should be handled with **try...catch** to prevent unhandled rejections.

```
const fetchData = async () => {
    try {
        throw new Error("Something went wrong");
    } catch (error) {
        console.error("Error:", error.message);
    }
};

fetchData();
```

By wrapping the `await` statement inside `try...catch`, we ensure that any errors are caught and handled properly.

Global Error Handling in Node.js

Some errors **escape local handling** and may cause the process to crash. Node.js provides two global event listeners that can help manage these cases.

Handling Uncaught Exceptions

If an error occurs outside of a `try...catch` block, it becomes an **uncaught exception**. These can be captured using:

```
process.on("uncaughtException", (error) => {
    console.error("Uncaught Exception:",
error.message);
    process.exit(1); // Exit the process to avoid
unexpected behavior
});
```

However, this should only be used as a **last resort**, since keeping the application running in an unknown state could lead to further issues.

Handling Unhandled Promise Rejections

If a Promise is rejected but no `.catch()` is provided, it results in an **unhandled promise rejection**.

```
process.on("unhandledRejection", (reason, promise)
=> {
```

98

```
        console.error("Unhandled Rejection:",
reason.message);
});
```

With this listener, you can **log unhandled rejections** and investigate them instead of letting them go unnoticed.

Logging Errors for Debugging

Logging errors properly helps developers **understand issues and track down bugs**. Instead of just printing errors to the console, use a logging system like **Winston or Bunyan** for better insights.

Using Winston for Logging

Winston is a popular logging library that allows you to log messages to **files, databases, or remote monitoring tools**.

Installing Winston

```
npm install winston
```

Setting Up a Logger

```
const winston = require("winston");

const logger = winston.createLogger({
    level: "error",
    format: winston.format.json(),
    transports: [
        new winston.transports.File({ filename:
"error.log" }),
        new winston.transports.Console()
    ]
});

try {
    throw new Error("Something went wrong");
} catch (error) {
    logger.error(error.message);
}
```

This ensures that **errors are logged both to the console and a file**, allowing you to analyze them later.

Using the Node.js Debugger

Built-in Debugger (`node inspect`)

Node.js includes a built-in debugger that allows you to **step through code execution**, inspect variables, and track errors.

To start debugging, run:

```
node inspect app.js
```

Use commands like:

c (Continue execution)

n (Next line)

s (Step into function)

o (Step out of function)

This is useful for **tracking logic errors** that may not be obvious from logs.

Using Chrome DevTools for Debugging

You can also debug Node.js code using **Chrome DevTools** by running:

```
node --inspect app.js
```

Then, open Chrome and go to:

```
chrome://inspect
```

This provides a **graphical interface** to set breakpoints, inspect variables, and execute code interactively.

Graceful Error Recovery

Handling errors properly isn't just about catching them—it's also about deciding **how to recover from them**.

For example, if a **database connection fails**, you might **retry** the connection instead of crashing the app:

```
const mongoose = require("mongoose");

const connectWithRetry = () => {

mongoose.connect("mongodb://localhost:27017/test",
{ useNewUrlParser: true })
        .then(() => console.log("Database
connected"))
        .catch(err => {
            console.error("Database connection
failed, retrying in 5 seconds...");
            setTimeout(connectWithRetry, 5000);
        });
};

connectWithRetry();
```

This ensures that **temporary failures** do not cause permanent downtime.

Error handling and debugging are **critical skills** for any Node.js developer. By **catching errors early**, **logging them properly**, and **debugging effectively**, you can build applications that are **more reliable, maintainable, and resilient**.

Chapter 5: Creating a Web Server with Node.js

Node.js is widely used for building **scalable, high-performance web applications**, and one of its core strengths is the ability to create a web server **without relying on external frameworks**. Unlike traditional backend environments like Apache or Nginx, where the web server is a separate software component, **Node.js allows you to handle HTTP requests natively** with its built-in `http` module.

HTTP and the Request-Response Cycle

Whenever you visit a website, send a message on a chat app, or interact with an online service, your device is communicating with a **server** over the internet. This communication happens using **HTTP (Hypertext Transfer Protocol)**, which defines how requests and responses are exchanged between a client (your browser or an app) and a server.

To build **Node.js web applications and APIs**, understanding HTTP and the **request-response cycle** is essential. This knowledge allows you to handle user requests effectively, return the right data, and ensure your application runs smoothly.

HTTP (Hypertext Transfer Protocol) is the **foundation of the web**. It defines how messages are formatted and transmitted between **clients** (such as browsers, mobile apps, or other systems) and **servers** (the machines hosting websites and applications).

Every time you enter a URL, **your browser is making an HTTP request** to fetch the corresponding web page from a server. The server processes this request, finds the appropriate content, and **sends back an HTTP response**.

For example, when you type:

```
https://example.com
```

Your browser sends a request to `example.com`'s server. The server then **responds** with an HTML document, which the browser renders into the webpage you see.

This **request-response cycle** happens within milliseconds, making the internet feel instantaneous.

The Request-Response Cycle

The **request-response cycle** is the fundamental interaction between a client and a server. It consists of **three key steps**:

Client Sends an HTTP Request

This request contains information such as the URL, HTTP method, headers, and (sometimes) a body with additional data.

Server Processes the Request

The server reads the request, determines what is being asked for, processes any logic (such as fetching database records), and prepares a response.

Server Sends an HTTP Response

The response includes a **status code** (e.g., 200 OK, 404 Not Found), **headers**, and **a body containing data** (such as an HTML page or JSON).

Let's look at how this works in **a real-world example**.

Understanding an HTTP Request

When a client sends a request, it includes **several important components**:

1. HTTP Method (Request Type)

An **HTTP method** tells the server what kind of action the client wants to perform. The most common methods are:

GET → Requests data from the server (e.g., loading a webpage).

POST → Sends data to the server (e.g., submitting a form).

PUT → Updates existing data on the server.

DELETE → Removes data from the server.

For example, if you want to fetch a list of users, your browser or application might send this **GET request**:

```
GET /users HTTP/1.1
Host: example.com
User-Agent: Mozilla/5.0
Accept: application/json
```

This tells the server:

The client wants to fetch data (GET).

The request is for the /users endpoint.

The client expects the response in **JSON format** (Accept: application/json).

2. URL (Uniform Resource Locator)

The **URL** (e.g., https://example.com/users) tells the server **where to find the requested resource**.

Breaking it down:

https:// → The protocol (HTTP or HTTPS).

example.com → The domain (the server's address).

/users → The specific resource being requested.

The **path** (/users) tells the server to return **a list of users**. If the request were sent to /users/1, the server would return **user with ID 1**.

3. Headers (Metadata About the Request)

Headers provide **additional information** about the request. For example:

```
User-Agent: Mozilla/5.0
Accept: application/json
Authorization: Bearer <token>
```

User-Agent tells the server what kind of browser or app is making the request.

Accept specifies the expected response format (JSON, HTML, etc.).

Authorization is used when authentication is required.

4. Request Body (For Sending Data)

Some requests (like **POST and PUT**) send data in the **body** of the request.

For example, when submitting a login form, the client sends:

```
POST /login HTTP/1.1
Content-Type: application/json

{
    "username": "alice",
    "password": "securepassword"
}
```

Here, the **Content-Type** header indicates that the body contains JSON data. The server extracts the `username` and `password` to authenticate the user.

Understanding an HTTP Response

Once the server processes the request, it **sends back an HTTP response** with three key parts:

1. HTTP Status Code (Success or Failure Indicator)

The status code tells the client whether the request was **successful or not**. Common status codes include:

200 OK → Request was successful.

201 Created → A new resource was successfully created (e.g., a new user).

400 Bad Request → The request was invalid (e.g., missing data).

401 Unauthorized → Authentication failed.

403 Forbidden → The client doesn't have permission to access the resource.

404 Not Found → The requested resource does not exist.

500 Internal Server Error → A server-side error occurred.

If a user requests a non-existent page, the server might return:

```
HTTP/1.1 404 Not Found
Content-Type: text/plain
```

2. Response Headers (Metadata About the Response)

Headers provide additional details about the response.

```
Content-Type: application/json
Date: Mon, 04 Mar 2024 12:00:00 GMT
Cache-Control: no-cache
```

`Content-Type` specifies the format of the response (`text/html`, `application/json`, etc.).

`Date` indicates when the response was generated.

`Cache-Control` tells the client whether to cache the response or fetch fresh data.

3. Response Body (The Actual Data)

The response body contains **the actual data** the client requested.

For example, if a client requested user data from `/users/1`, the server might return:

```
{
    "id": 1,
    "name": "Alice",
    "email": "alice@example.com"
}
```

If the request was for an HTML page, the response might contain:

```
<!DOCTYPE html>
<html>
<head><title>Home</title></head>
<body><h1>Welcome to Our Website!</h1></body>
</html>
```

Bringing It All Together in Node.js

Now that you understand the request-response cycle, let's **implement a simple Node.js server** that handles HTTP requests.

```
const http = require("http");

const server = http.createServer((req, res) => {
    if (req.url === "/users" && req.method ===
"GET") {
        res.writeHead(200, { "Content-Type":
"application/json" });
        res.end(JSON.stringify([{ id: 1, name:
"Alice" }, { id: 2, name: "Bob" }]));
    } else {
        res.writeHead(404, { "Content-Type":
"text/plain" });
        res.end("Page Not Found");
    }
});

server.listen(3000, () => {
    console.log("Server running on
http://localhost:3000");
});
```

When you visit **http://localhost:3000/users**, the server responds with JSON data. If you request any other URL, you get a `404 Not Found` message.

Understanding the **HTTP request-response cycle** is fundamental to building **web servers and APIs**. Every interaction on the internet follows this cycle, whether you're browsing a website or using a mobile app.

Creating a Simple HTTP Server in Node.js

A web server is the backbone of any modern application, handling incoming requests and sending responses to users. Whether you're loading a webpage, retrieving data from an API, or submitting a form, a web server is responsible for processing these interactions.

Node.js allows you to **create a fully functional web server without needing third-party software** like Apache or Nginx. Instead of depending on external servers, Node.js gives you complete control, allowing you to build, configure, and optimize your own server using just JavaScript.

Every web server **listens for incoming requests**, processes them, and **sends back responses**. Node.js makes this process straightforward using the `http` module, which provides everything needed to create and manage an HTTP server.

Step 1: Import the `http` Module

To begin, create a new file called `server.js` and import the `http` module:

```
const http = require("http");
```

This module allows you to create an HTTP server **without any additional dependencies**. Since `http` is a **core module** in Node.js, there's no need to install anything extra.

Step 2: Creating a Server Instance

Next, create the HTTP server using `http.createServer()`.

```
const server = http.createServer((req, res) => {
    res.writeHead(200, { "Content-Type":
"text/plain" });
    res.end("Hello, World!");
});
```

Here's what's happening in this code:

`http.createServer()` : Creates a server instance.

Callback Function `(req, res) => {}`: This function runs every time the server receives a request.

`res.writeHead(200, { "Content-Type": "text/plain" })` : Sets the HTTP status to `200 OK` and specifies that the response will be plain text.

`res.end("Hello, World!")` : Sends the response body and closes the connection.

Step 3: Listening for Requests

After defining the server, it needs to listen for incoming connections.

```
server.listen(3000, () => {
    console.log("Server running at
http://localhost:3000");
});
```

The `.listen(3000)` method tells the server to listen on **port 3000**. The callback function logs a message to indicate that the server is running.

Step 4: Running the Server

Save `server.js` and start the server by running:

```
node server.js
```
You should see the message:

```
Server running at http://localhost:3000
```

Now, **open your browser** and visit http://localhost:3000. You will see:

```
Hello, World!
```

Congratulations! You've just created a **fully functional HTTP server** in Node.js.

Understanding the Server Code in Detail

Handling Requests (`req`)

The `req` (request) object contains **information about the client's request**, such as:

The **HTTP method** (GET, POST, etc.).

The **requested URL** (e.g., /, /about, etc.).

Headers, query parameters, and request body (for POST requests).

To inspect an incoming request, modify `server.js` to log details:

```
const server = http.createServer((req, res) => {
    console.log(`Received request: ${req.method}
${req.url}`);
```

```
    res.writeHead(200, { "Content-Type":
"text/plain" });
    res.end("Hello, World!");
});
```

Restart the server, refresh the browser, and check your terminal. You'll see:

```
Received request: GET /
```

This confirms that **the server is correctly receiving and logging requests**.

Serving Different Routes

Most web applications serve **multiple routes**. Let's modify the server to handle different URLs.

```
const server = http.createServer((req, res) => {
    if (req.url === "/") {
        res.writeHead(200, { "Content-Type":
"text/plain" });
        res.end("Welcome to the Homepage!");
    } else if (req.url === "/about") {
        res.writeHead(200, { "Content-Type":
"text/plain" });
        res.end("This is the About page.");
    } else {
        res.writeHead(404, { "Content-Type":
"text/plain" });
        res.end("404 Page Not Found");
    }
});

server.listen(3000, () => {
    console.log("Server running at
http://localhost:3000");
});
```

Now, test the following URLs:

http://localhost:3000/ → Displays: Welcome to the Homepage!

http://localhost:3000/about → Displays: This is the About page.

http://localhost:3000/contact → Displays: 404 Page Not Found

This allows the server to **respond differently based on the requested URL**.

Handling POST Requests (Receiving Data from Clients)

Most web applications **accept data from users**. This could be form submissions, API requests, or file uploads.

Let's modify the server to **accept POST requests** and process incoming data.

```
const server = http.createServer((req, res) => {
    if (req.method === "POST" && req.url ===
"/submit") {
        let body = "";

        req.on("data", chunk => {
            body += chunk.toString();
        });

        req.on("end", () => {
            res.writeHead(200, { "Content-Type":
"application/json" });
            res.end(JSON.stringify({ message: "Data
received", data: body }));
        });
    } else {
        res.writeHead(404, { "Content-Type":
"text/plain" });
        res.end("404 Page Not Found");
    }
});

server.listen(3000, () => {
    console.log("Server running at
http://localhost:3000");
});
```

Testing the POST Request

Use **Postman** or **cURL** to send data:

```
curl -X POST -H "Content-Type: application/json" -d
'{"name": "Alice"}' http://localhost:3000/submit
```

The server will respond with:

```
{
```

```
    "message": "Data received",
    "data": "{\"name\": \"Alice\"}"
}
```

This demonstrates how a **Node.js server can process incoming data**, a fundamental part of building APIs.

Graceful Error Handling

A real-world server needs **error handling** to avoid unexpected crashes. Let's modify the server to catch errors properly.

```
const server = http.createServer((req, res) => {
    try {
        if (req.url === "/error") {
            throw new Error("Intentional error!");
        }

        res.writeHead(200, { "Content-Type":
"text/plain" });
        res.end("Request processed successfully.");
    } catch (error) {
        console.error("Server error:",
error.message);
        res.writeHead(500, { "Content-Type":
"text/plain" });
        res.end("Internal Server Error");
    }
});

server.listen(3000, () => {
    console.log("Server running at
http://localhost:3000");
});
```

Now, visiting http://localhost:3000/error triggers an **intentional error**, which is properly handled, preventing the server from crashing.

This knowledge **forms the foundation** for building more advanced web applications and REST APIs using frameworks like **Express.js**. But before moving on, mastering how **Node.js itself handles HTTP** is essential for understanding how web servers truly work.

Handling Requests and Responses in Node.js

When a client—such as a **browser, mobile app, or another server**—connects to your **Node.js** server, it sends a **request**. Your server reads this request, processes the necessary logic, and sends back an appropriate **response**. This **request-response cycle** is at the core of web development, and understanding how to handle it properly is what enables you to build everything from **simple web pages** to **complex APIs**.

Why Handling Requests and Responses Matters

If your server doesn't **properly interpret requests**, it might:

Send the **wrong data** or fail to process user input.

Return a **generic response** for everything, making the app **non-interactive**.

Lack **proper error handling**, causing unexpected crashes.

Similarly, if responses are not handled **correctly**, users might:

Receive **incorrect or incomplete data**.

Experience **slow responses**, making your application feel unresponsive.

Encounter **unexpected behavior**, like a **404 Page Not Found** error when the requested resource actually exists.

To avoid these issues, we must handle **requests and responses correctly**.

Understanding Incoming HTTP Requests

Whenever a client sends an HTTP request to your server, it consists of **several key parts**:

The HTTP Method – Defines the type of request (e.g., GET, POST, PUT, DELETE).

The URL (Path/Route) – Specifies which resource the client is trying to access.

113

Headers – Provide metadata about the request (e.g., `Content-Type`, `Authorization`).

Body (For Some Requests) – Contains data sent by the client, usually in JSON format.

Reading the Request in Node.js

Let's start by creating a **basic Node.js server** that **logs incoming requests** so we can see their details.

1. Setting Up the Server

```
const http = require("http");

const server = http.createServer((req, res) => {
    console.log(`Received ${req.method} request for
${req.url}`);

    res.writeHead(200, { "Content-Type":
"text/plain" });
    res.end("Request received");
});

server.listen(3000, () => {
    console.log("Server running on
http://localhost:3000");
});
```

2. Running the Server

Save the file as `server.js` and run:

```
node server.js
```
Now, open your **browser** and visit:

```
http://localhost:3000
```
Or send a request using **cURL**:

```
curl -X GET http://localhost:3000
```
Every time a request is received, it will be logged in the terminal:

```
Received GET request for /
```

This confirms that **the server is capturing HTTP requests properly**.

Handling Different HTTP Methods

In real applications, servers must support different **types of requests**.

Handling GET Requests

GET requests are used to **retrieve data**. Let's modify our server to handle different **routes**:

```
const http = require("http");

const server = http.createServer((req, res) => {
    if (req.method === "GET" && req.url === "/") {
        res.writeHead(200, { "Content-Type":
"text/plain" });
        res.end("Welcome to the homepage!");
    } else if (req.method === "GET" && req.url ===
"/about") {
        res.writeHead(200, { "Content-Type":
"text/plain" });
        res.end("This is the About page.");
    } else {
        res.writeHead(404, { "Content-Type":
"text/plain" });
        res.end("Page Not Found");
    }
});

server.listen(3000, () => {
    console.log("Server running on
http://localhost:3000");
});
```

Now, test it by visiting:

http://localhost:3000/ → Displays: `Welcome to the homepage!`

http://localhost:3000/about → Displays: `This is the About page.`

http://localhost:3000/contact → Displays: `Page Not Found`

This ensures that the **server correctly identifies different URLs and sends appropriate responses**.

Handling POST Requests (Receiving Data from Clients)

POST requests are used when **sending data to the server**. This is common when handling **form submissions, API requests, and user authentication**.

When a POST request is sent, **the data is included in the request body**. Let's modify our server to handle **POST data**:

```
const http = require("http");

const server = http.createServer((req, res) => {
    if (req.method === "POST" && req.url ===
"/submit") {
        let body = "";

        // Read data chunks
        req.on("data", chunk => {
            body += chunk.toString();
        });

        // Process data when request ends
        req.on("end", () => {
            res.writeHead(200, { "Content-Type":
"application/json" });
            res.end(JSON.stringify({ message: "Data
received", data: JSON.parse(body) }));
        });
    } else {
        res.writeHead(404, { "Content-Type":
"text/plain" });
        res.end("Page Not Found");
    }
});

server.listen(3000, () => {
    console.log("Server running on
http://localhost:3000");
});
```

Testing the POST Request

Send data using **cURL**:

```
curl -X POST -H "Content-Type: application/json" -d
'{"name": "Alice"}' http://localhost:3000/submit
```

What Happens Here?

The server **listens for incoming data** (`req.on("data")`).

Data chunks are **combined** into a full string.

Once **all data is received**, the server **parses it as JSON** and responds with a confirmation message.

This ensures that **our server can process incoming user data properly**.

Handling Response Headers

Headers provide **additional information** about the response. Let's modify our server to send **custom headers**.

```
const server = http.createServer((req, res) => {
    res.writeHead(200, {
        "Content-Type": "text/plain",
        "X-Custom-Header": "CustomHeaderValue"
    });
    res.end("Headers set successfully!");
});

server.listen(3000, () => {
    console.log("Server running on
http://localhost:3000");
});
```

Now, test it using cURL:

```
curl -i http://localhost:3000
```

You'll see something like this in the response headers:

```
HTTP/1.1 200 OK
Content-Type: text/plain
X-Custom-Header: CustomHeaderValue
```

Headers help **manage caching, security, and content negotiation** in web applications.

Graceful Error Handling

A robust server should **handle errors** properly. If an error occurs, the server should **return a meaningful response** instead of crashing.

Let's modify our server to catch **unexpected errors**:

```
const server = http.createServer((req, res) => {
    try {
        if (req.url === "/error") {
            throw new Error("Intentional error!");
        }

        res.writeHead(200, { "Content-Type":
"text/plain" });
        res.end("Request processed successfully.");
    } catch (error) {
        console.error("Server error:",
error.message);
        res.writeHead(500, { "Content-Type":
"text/plain" });
        res.end("Internal Server Error");
    }
});

server.listen(3000, () => {
    console.log("Server running on
http://localhost:3000");
});
```

Now, visit http://localhost:3000/error, and the server will **catch and handle the error gracefully** instead of crashing.

Understanding **how to handle requests and responses** properly is essential for building reliable web applications.

Chapter 6: Building APIs with Express.js

APIs (Application Programming Interfaces) are the backbone of modern web applications, enabling communication between clients and servers. Whether you're building a **RESTful API** for a frontend application or a **backend service** for a mobile app, **Express.js** simplifies the process.

Express.js is a **fast, lightweight, and flexible web framework** for Node.js. It abstracts many complexities of handling **HTTP requests and responses**, allowing you to build scalable web applications with minimal effort.

Introduction to Express.js

When building a web application or an API, one of the biggest challenges is **handling HTTP requests and responses efficiently**. While Node.js provides a built-in `http` module for creating web servers, it requires a lot of **boilerplate code** just to handle basic routing, request processing, and middleware. This is where **Express.js** comes in.

Express.js is a **minimalist and flexible web framework for Node.js** that simplifies server-side development. It provides a **clean and structured way** to create web applications and APIs, allowing developers to handle requests, define routes, and implement middleware with ease. Whether you're **building a simple website, a REST API, or a full-fledged web application**, Express.js makes the process significantly **faster and more maintainable**.

If you've worked with **raw Node.js HTTP servers**, you may have noticed that handling routes, parsing request bodies, and managing headers **can get messy quickly**. Express.js is built to **reduce complexity** and provide a more **intuitive way** to handle these tasks.

Express.js Simplifies Web Development

With Express.js, you can:

Create a web server with minimal code

Define routes easily to handle different URLs

Use middleware to process requests efficiently

Serve static files like images, CSS, and JavaScript

Handle JSON and form data out of the box

Integrate databases like MongoDB or PostgreSQL seamlessly

Instead of writing **hundreds of lines of code** to create a basic API with Node.js's `http` module, Express.js lets you accomplish the same task with just **a few lines of code**.

To better understand **why Express.js is so useful**, let's start by looking at a **basic HTTP server** in raw Node.js and compare it to an Express.js version.

Creating a Basic Server: Node.js vs. Express.js

Building a Server with Raw Node.js

Let's start by creating a simple HTTP server using **only the built-in `http` module**:

```
const http = require("http");

const server = http.createServer((req, res) => {
    if (req.method === "GET" && req.url === "/") {
        res.writeHead(200, { "Content-Type":
"text/plain" });
        res.end("Welcome to our homepage!");
    } else if (req.method === "GET" && req.url ===
"/about") {
        res.writeHead(200, { "Content-Type":
"text/plain" });
        res.end("This is the About page.");
    } else {
        res.writeHead(404, { "Content-Type":
"text/plain" });
        res.end("Page Not Found");
    }
});

server.listen(3000, () => {
```

```
    console.log("Server running on
http://localhost:3000");
});
```

This approach works, but it's **verbose**, and adding **more routes and features** quickly becomes **cumbersome**.

Building the Same Server with Express.js

Now, let's rewrite the same functionality using **Express.js**:

```
const express = require("express");
const app = express();

app.get("/", (req, res) => {
    res.send("Welcome to our homepage!");
});

app.get("/about", (req, res) => {
    res.send("This is the About page.");
});

app.use((req, res) => {
    res.status(404).send("Page Not Found");
});

app.listen(3000, () => {
    console.log("Server running on
http://localhost:3000");
});
```

Key Differences

Cleaner and More Readable Code

Express allows us to define routes with `app.get()` instead of manually checking `req.method` and `req.url`.

Automatic Response Handling

Instead of manually setting response headers, `res.send()` automatically determines the correct content type.

Built-in Middleware Support

Express makes it easy to add **custom middleware** for logging, authentication, or error handling.

This is why **Express.js is the preferred choice** for **web applications and APIs**—it removes unnecessary complexity and lets you focus on your application logic.

How Express.js Works

To understand **how Express.js handles requests and responses**, let's break it down into three main components:

Routes – Define different URLs that the server responds to.

Middleware – Functions that process requests before they reach the final response handler.

Request & Response Objects – The core objects that Express provides for handling HTTP requests and responses.

Defining Routes in Express.js

In Express, **routes** determine how the server responds to different requests. Each route consists of:

A **path** (e.g., /, /about, /users)

A **method** (e.g., GET, POST, PUT, DELETE)

A **callback function** that runs when the request is received

Example: Handling Different Routes

```
app.get("/", (req, res) => {
    res.send("Welcome to the homepage!");
});

app.get("/users", (req, res) => {
    res.json([{ id: 1, name: "Alice" }, { id: 2,
name: "Bob" }]);
});

app.post("/submit", (req, res) => {
    res.send("Form submitted successfully!");
```

```
});
```

Now:

A GET request to / returns "Welcome to the homepage!"

A GET request to /users returns a **JSON response**

A POST request to /submit returns "Form submitted successfully!"

Understanding Middleware in Express.js

Middleware functions in Express are executed **before the final request handler**. They can:

Modify the request object

Perform authentication

Log request details

Handle errors

Example: Logging Middleware

```
app.use((req, res, next) => {
    console.log(`${req.method} request to
${req.url}`);
    next(); // Proceed to the next function
});
```

This logs every incoming request to the terminal:

```
GET request to /
POST request to /submit
```

Middleware is one of **Express.js's most powerful features**, enabling everything from **security** to **data validation**.

Real-World Use Cases for Express.js

1. Creating RESTful APIs

Express is widely used for **building APIs** that serve data to frontend applications.

```
app.get("/api/products", (req, res) => {
    res.json([{ id: 1, name: "Laptop" }, { id: 2,
name: "Phone" }]);
});
```

2. Handling Form Submissions

Express can **process form data** and save it to a database.

```
app.use(express.urlencoded({ extended: true }));

app.post("/register", (req, res) => {
    const { username, password } = req.body;
    res.send(`User registered: ${username}`);
});
```

3. Serving Static Files (HTML, CSS, Images)

Express can **serve frontend assets** like images and stylesheets.

```
app.use(express.static("public"));
```

Now, you can **access static files** from the `public` folder directly in your browser.

By using Express.js, you can **build scalable applications faster** while keeping your code **organized and maintainable**. Whether you're creating a **simple website**, a **REST API**, or a **full-stack application**, Express.js will help you **deliver efficient and reliable web services**.

Setting Up an Express.js Project

Before building any web application or API, you need to have a structured project setup. **Express.js**, being a lightweight and flexible framework for Node.js, allows you to create a fully functional server with minimal effort. However, setting up the project properly ensures that your application is scalable, maintainable, and easy to develop.

Step 1: Install Node.js (If Not Installed)

Before setting up Express.js, you need to have **Node.js** installed. You can check if Node.js is installed on your system by running the following command in your terminal or command prompt:

```
node -v
```

If Node.js is installed, this command will return the installed version, such as:

```
v18.16.0
```

If it's not installed, download it from nodejs.org and follow the installation instructions. Node.js comes with **npm (Node Package Manager)**, which we will use to manage dependencies.

To check if **npm** is installed, run:

```
npm -v
```

Step 2: Create a New Project Folder

Let's start by creating a dedicated folder for our Express.js project. Open your terminal or command prompt and run:

```
mkdir my-express-app
cd my-express-app
```

This will create a new folder called `my-express-app` and move into it.

Step 3: Initialize a New Node.js Project

Inside the project folder, initialize a **package.json** file, which keeps track of project dependencies and configurations. Run the following command:

```
npm init -y
```

The `-y` flag automatically generates a `package.json` file with default values, so you don't have to answer multiple prompts.

If you open `package.json`, you'll see something like this:

```
{
  "name": "my-express-app",
  "version": "1.0.0",
  "description": "",
  "main": "index.js",
  "scripts": {
```

```
    "test": "echo \"Error: no test specified\" &&
exit 1"
  },
  "dependencies": {},
  "devDependencies": {},
  "author": "",
  "license": "ISC"
}
```

This file will be automatically updated as we install packages.

Step 4: Install Express.js

Now that our project is initialized, we need to install **Express.js** as a dependency. Run the following command:

```
npm install express
```

This command will:

Download Express.js into the `node_modules` folder

Update the `package.json` file to include Express under the `dependencies` section

If you check `package.json`, you'll now see Express listed under `dependencies`:

```
"dependencies": {
  "express": "^4.18.2"
}
```

Step 5: Create the Main Server File

Inside your project folder, create a new file called `server.js`:

```
touch server.js   # For macOS/Linux
type nul > server.js   # For Windows (Command
Prompt)
```

Open `server.js` in your code editor and add the following code:

```
const express = require("express");

const app = express();
const PORT = 3000;
```

```
app.get("/", (req, res) => {
    res.send("Welcome to your Express.js server!");
});

app.listen(PORT, () => {
    console.log(`Server running on
http://localhost:${PORT}`);
});
```

Breaking Down the Code

Importing Express.js → `const express = require("express");`

This imports the Express.js module so we can use it.

Creating an Express App → `const app = express();`

This initializes an Express application.

Defining a Route (GET /) → `app.get("/", (req, res) => {...});`

This defines a **route** that listens for GET requests on / and responds with `"Welcome to your Express.js server!"`.

Starting the Server → `app.listen(PORT, () => {...});`

This tells Express to **listen for incoming requests on port 3000** and logs a message once the server is running.

Step 6: Run the Express Server

Now that our server is set up, we can start it using:

```
node server.js
```
You should see this output in your terminal:

```
Server running on http://localhost:3000
```
Now, open your browser and visit:

```
http://localhost:3000
```
You will see:

```
Welcome to your Express.js server!
```
This confirms that your **Express.js server is running successfully**.

Step 7: Install Nodemon for Automatic Restarts

During development, restarting the server manually every time you make changes is inefficient. **Nodemon** automatically restarts your server whenever you update the code.

To install Nodemon, run:

```
npm install --save-dev nodemon
```

This installs Nodemon as a **development dependency**.

Now, modify your `package.json` file to add a **start script**:

```
"scripts": {
  "start": "node server.js",
  "dev": "nodemon server.js"
}
```

Now, you can run your server with:

```
npm run dev
```

Now, any changes you make to your server **will automatically restart it**, making development much smoother.

Step 8: Organizing Your Project Structure

As your project grows, keeping files organized is crucial. A well-structured Express.js project follows a **modular approach**.

Here's a recommended folder structure:

```
my-express-app/
|— node_modules/
|— public/          # Static files (CSS, JS, images)
|— routes/          # Route handlers
|— controllers/     # Business logic
|— models/          # Database models
|— middleware/      # Custom middleware functions
|— views/            # HTML templates (if using templating engines)
|— server.js        # Main entry point
```

|— package.json   # Project metadata

Refactoring Routes for Better Organization

Instead of defining all routes in `server.js`, move them to a **separate file** inside the `routes/` directory.

1. Create a Routes Folder

```
mkdir routes
touch routes/home.js
```

2. Define Routes in `routes/home.js`

```
const express = require("express");
const router = express.Router();

router.get("/", (req, res) => {
    res.send("Welcome to the Home Page!");
});

router.get("/about", (req, res) => {
    res.send("About Us Page");
});

module.exports = router;
```

3. Use the Routes in `server.js`

Modify `server.js` to **import the routes**:

```
const express = require("express");
const homeRoutes = require("./routes/home");

const app = express();
const PORT = 3000;

app.use("/", homeRoutes);

app.listen(PORT, () => {
    console.log(`Server running on
http://localhost:${PORT}`);
});
```

Now, when you visit http://localhost:3000/about, it responds with:

```
About Us Page
```

This modular approach keeps the project **organized and maintainable**.

This **structured approach** ensures that your Express.js project is **scalable, easy to maintain, and ready for further development**. From here, you can add **middleware, connect to a database, or build a REST API** with ease.

Routing and Middleware in Express.js

When building an **Express.js** application, two of the most fundamental concepts you'll work with are **routing** and **middleware**. Routing allows your server to handle different HTTP requests efficiently, while middleware enables you to **process and modify requests and responses** before they reach their final destination.

If you've ever visited a website and navigated between different pages or interacted with an API that fetches specific data, you were using **routes**. Behind the scenes, middleware was likely handling **logging, authentication, validation, error handling**, and more.

What is Routing?

Routing determines how an Express application **responds to client requests** based on the request's URL and HTTP method. When a client (such as a browser or a mobile app) sends a request to the server, the server uses routing logic to **decide which function should handle that request**.

Each route consists of:

A **URL path** (e.g., `/home`, `/users`, `/products/123`)

An **HTTP method** (`GET`, `POST`, `PUT`, `DELETE`)

A **callback function** that executes when the route is matched

Creating Basic Routes in Express.js

Let's start by setting up a basic Express application and defining a few routes.

1. Install Express.js (If Not Installed)

If you haven't already installed Express, run:

```
npm install express
```

2. Create a Basic Express Server

Create a file called `server.js` and add the following code:

```
const express = require("express");

const app = express();
const PORT = 3000;

// Define routes
app.get("/", (req, res) => {
    res.send("Welcome to the Homepage!");
});

app.get("/about", (req, res) => {
    res.send("This is the About page.");
});

// Start the server
app.listen(PORT, () => {
    console.log(`Server running at
http://localhost:${PORT}`);
});
```

Now, start the server:

```
node server.js
```

Visit `http://localhost:3000/` → Displays `"Welcome to the Homepage!"`

Visit `http://localhost:3000/about` → Displays `"This is the About page."`

This is **basic routing**, where the server **listens for requests at specific paths** and sends a response.

Handling Different HTTP Methods

Express allows handling **various HTTP methods**, which are commonly used in **RESTful APIs**:

GET → Retrieve data

POST → Send new data

PUT → Update existing data

DELETE → Remove data

Modify server.js to handle different request types:

```
app.post("/submit", (req, res) => {
    res.send("Data has been submitted!");
});

app.put("/update", (req, res) => {
    res.send("Data has been updated!");
});

app.delete("/delete", (req, res) => {
    res.send("Data has been deleted!");
});
```

Now, test these endpoints using **cURL** or Postman:

```
curl -X POST http://localhost:3000/submit

curl -X PUT http://localhost:3000/update

curl -X DELETE http://localhost:3000/delete
```

Each request triggers a **different response**, demonstrating how Express **handles multiple HTTP methods efficiently**.

Using Route Parameters

Sometimes, you need to handle **dynamic values** in URLs. Express allows you to capture **route parameters** using a : before a variable name.

Modify server.js to handle **dynamic user profiles**:

```
app.get("/users/:id", (req, res) => {
    const userId = req.params.id;
    res.send(`User Profile for ID: ${userId}`);
```

```
});
```
Now, if you visit:
```
http://localhost:3000/users/123
```
The response will be:
```
User Profile for ID: 123
```
This is incredibly useful for handling **user profiles, product details, and API resources** dynamically.

Handling Query Parameters

Apart from route parameters, Express also allows handling **query parameters** in URLs, which are useful for filtering or sorting data.

Modify `server.js` to process query parameters:
```
app.get("/search", (req, res) => {
    const keyword = req.query.keyword;
    res.send(`Search results for: ${keyword}`);
});
```
Now, if you visit:
```
http://localhost:3000/search?keyword=express
```
The response will be:
```
Search results for: express
```
Query parameters allow users to **pass data through the URL** without modifying the route itself.

Middleware in Express.js

Middleware functions **intercept** incoming requests **before they reach the final route handler**. They are used for:

Logging requests

Authenticating users

Parsing request data

Handling errors

Every request in Express passes through **a series of middleware functions**, which **can modify the request or response** before reaching its final destination.

Using Middleware for Logging

Let's create **a simple logging middleware** that prints details of every request.

Modify `server.js`:

```
app.use((req, res, next) => {
    console.log(`${req.method} request to
${req.url}`);
    next(); // Proceed to the next function
});
```

Now, every request will be logged in the terminal:

```
GET request to /

POST request to /submit

GET request to /users/123
```

The `next()` function ensures that **the request moves to the next middleware or route handler**.

Using Built-in Middleware for JSON and Form Data

Express provides built-in middleware to **parse incoming data** from JSON and forms.

Enable JSON and URL-encoded body parsing:

```
app.use(express.json());
app.use(express.urlencoded({ extended: true }));
```

Now, create a **POST endpoint** that accepts JSON data:

```
app.post("/register", (req, res) => {
    const { username, email } = req.body;
    res.send(`User registered: ${username}
(${email})`);
});
```

Send a request using cURL:

```
curl -X POST -H "Content-Type: application/json" -d
'{"username":"Alice", "email":"alice@example.com"}'
http://localhost:3000/register
```
Response:

```
User registered: Alice (alice@example.com)
```
This shows how middleware allows Express to **handle incoming data seamlessly**.

Error Handling Middleware

To prevent your application from **crashing due to unexpected errors**, Express allows you to define **error-handling middleware**.

```
app.use((err, req, res, next) => {
    console.error("Error:", err.message);
    res.status(500).send("Internal Server Error");
});
```
Now, any unhandled error will be caught, logged, and a **500 Internal Server Error** response will be sent instead of crashing the server.

Routing and middleware are the **backbone** of any Express.js application.

Routing allows you to handle **different URLs and HTTP methods**, enabling users to interact with your server.

Middleware provides a way to **process requests, authenticate users, log activity, and handle errors** efficiently.

By mastering these concepts, you'll be able to build **scalable, structured, and high-performance applications** with Express.js.

Handling Query Parameters and Request Bodies

When a client sends a request to a server, it often includes **additional data**—whether it's filtering search results, submitting a form, or sending JSON data from a frontend application. In Express.js, handling this data properly ensures that your application **processes user input efficiently and securely**.

There are two primary ways clients send data to a server:

Query Parameters – Data sent in the **URL**, usually for filtering, searching, or pagination.

Request Bodies – Data sent in the **body of the request**, typically in POST, PUT, or PATCH requests.

What are Query Parameters?

Query parameters are **key-value pairs** sent in the URL after a ?. They allow clients to pass data to the server **without modifying the URL structure**.

For example, when searching for products on an e-commerce website, the URL might look like this:

```
https://example.com/products?category=electronics&p
rice=100-500
```

Here:

category=electronics filters products by category.

price=100-500 filters products by price range.

The server reads these parameters and returns **only the matching products**.

Extracting Query Parameters in Express.js

Express provides an easy way to **access query parameters** using req.query. Let's set up a basic server that extracts and logs query parameters.

1. Install Express.js (If Not Installed)

If you haven't installed Express, run:

```
npm install express
```

2. Create a Basic Server (server.js)

```
const express = require("express");
const app = express();
const PORT = 3000;

app.get("/search", (req, res) => {
    const query = req.query.query;
    const category = req.query.category;
```

```
    res.send(`Search results for: ${query},
Category: ${category}`);
});

app.listen(PORT, () => {
    console.log(`Server running at
http://localhost:${PORT}`);
});
```

3. Testing Query Parameters

Start the server:

```
node server.js
```
Now, visit the following URLs:

http://localhost:3000/search?query=laptop&category=electronics

Response: "`Search results for: laptop, Category: electronics`"

http://localhost:3000/search?query=phone

Response: "`Search results for: phone, Category: undefined`"

If a query parameter is **missing**, its value will be `undefined`.

Handling Multiple Query Parameters Dynamically

Instead of extracting specific keys, you can retrieve **all query parameters dynamically** using `req.query`.

```
app.get("/filter", (req, res) => {
    res.json({ receivedParams: req.query });
});
```

Now, if you visit:

```
http://localhost:3000/filter?brand=Apple&color=blac
k&price=1000
```
You'll receive a **JSON response** with all parameters:

```
{
    "receivedParams": {
        "brand": "Apple",
        "color": "black",
```

```
        "price": "1000"
    }
}
```

This makes **handling dynamic filtering and search features** much easier.

Handling Request Bodies in Express.js

A **request body** contains data sent from the client to the server in POST, PUT, or PATCH requests.

For example, when a user **submits a form**, the browser sends the data in the **request body**, not in the URL. Similarly, when a frontend **sends JSON data to an API**, it is sent in the request body.

Unlike **query parameters**, which are part of the URL, request bodies are **not visible** in the address bar.

Extracting JSON Data from a Request Body

By default, Express **does not parse request bodies**. You need to enable the express.json() middleware to handle **incoming JSON data**.

1. Setting Up the Server

Modify server.js to handle JSON request bodies:

```
const express = require("express");
const app = express();
const PORT = 3000;

// Middleware to parse JSON body
app.use(express.json());

app.post("/submit", (req, res) => {
    const { name, email } = req.body;
    res.json({ message: `User registered: ${name},
Email: ${email}` });
});

app.listen(PORT, () => {
    console.log(`Server running at
http://localhost:${PORT}`);
});
```

2. Sending a POST Request

To test this, use **Postman** or **cURL**.

With **cURL**:

```
curl -X POST -H "Content-Type: application/json" -d
'{"name":"Alice", "email":"alice@example.com"}'
http://localhost:3000/submit
```

The server responds with:

```
{
    "message": "User registered: Alice, Email:
alice@example.com"
}
```

Now, the server **correctly processes JSON request bodies**!

Handling Form Data in Express.js

If your application processes **form submissions**, the data is usually sent as **URL-encoded form data**, not JSON. Express provides built-in middleware to handle this:

```
app.use(express.urlencoded({ extended: true }));
```

Example: Handling Form Submissions

Modify `server.js` to accept form data:

```
app.post("/register", (req, res) => {
    const { username, password } = req.body;
    res.send(`User registered: ${username}`);
});
```

Now, test it using **cURL**:

```
curl -X POST -H "Content-Type: application/x-www-
form-urlencoded" -d
"username=Alice&password=secret"
http://localhost:3000/register
```

The response will be:

```
User registered: Alice
```

This ensures **your server can handle traditional form submissions**.

Combining Query Parameters and Request Bodies

Some APIs use **both query parameters and request bodies** to process requests. For example, a **user filtering system** might accept query parameters for searching and a request body for additional filters.

Modify `server.js`:

```
app.post("/users", (req, res) => {
    const { age, country } = req.body;
    const search = req.query.search;

    res.json({
        message: `Searching for users with:
${search}`,
        filters: { age, country }
    });
});
```

Now, test it with **both query parameters and a request body**:

```
curl -X POST -H "Content-Type: application/json" -d
'{"age":30, "country":"USA"}'
"http://localhost:3000/users?search=developer"
```
Response:

```
{
    "message": "Searching for users with:
developer",
    "filters": {
        "age": 30,
        "country": "USA"
    }
}
```

This **flexible approach** allows you to **process complex requests dynamically**, making your APIs more powerful.

By mastering these techniques, you can **build powerful APIs** that efficiently process user input while maintaining clean, maintainable code.

Serving Static Files in Express.js

A **static file** is any file that **doesn't change dynamically on the server**. These files are pre-written and sent to the browser exactly as they are. Examples include:

HTML files → Webpages (`index.html`, `about.html`)

CSS files → Stylesheets (`styles.css`)

JavaScript files → Client-side scripts (`app.js`)

Images → Logos, icons, and photos (`logo.png`, `background.jpg`)

Fonts → Custom typography files (`Roboto.woff2`)

Documents → PDFs, Excel sheets, and text files

When a browser requests a static file, the server simply **fetches the file and delivers it**, without modifying its content. This is different from **dynamic files**, where the server **generates content dynamically**, such as fetching data from a database.

Setting Up a Basic Static File Server

Before we serve static files, let's set up an **Express.js project**.

1. Create a New Express Project

If you haven't already installed Express, create a new project and install it:

```
mkdir express-static
cd express-static
npm init -y
npm install express
```

2. Create a Public Directory

Inside your project folder, create a directory called `public`. This will store your **static files**.

```
mkdir public
```

Now, create three files inside the `public` directory:

```
public/index.html
<!DOCTYPE html>
```

```html
<html lang="en">
<head>
    <meta charset="UTF-8">
    <meta name="viewport" content="width=device-
width, initial-scale=1.0">
    <title>Express Static Files</title>
    <link rel="stylesheet" href="styles.css">
</head>
<body>
    <h1>Welcome to Express Static File Serving</h1>
    <img src="logo.png" alt="Logo" width="200">
    <script src="script.js"></script>
</body>
</html>
```

```css
public/styles.css
body {
    font-family: Arial, sans-serif;
    text-align: center;
    background-color: #f4f4f4;
}

h1 {
    color: #333;
}
```

```javascript
public/script.js
console.log("Static JavaScript file loaded
successfully!");
```

Add an Image (`public/logo.png`)

Place an image file inside the `public` folder. It can be any image you want.

3. Serve Static Files Using Express

Now, create `server.js` and add the following code:

```javascript
const express = require("express");
const path = require("path");

const app = express();
const PORT = 3000;

// Serve static files from the "public" directory
```

```
app.use(express.static(path.join(__dirname,
"public")));

app.listen(PORT, () => {
    console.log(`Server running on
http://localhost:${PORT}`);
});
```

4. Run the Server

Start the server using:

```
node server.js
```

Now, open your browser and visit:

```
http://localhost:3000/
```

You should see the **HTML page with the styled text and logo**, and if you check your browser's console (F12 → Console), you'll see:

```
Static JavaScript file loaded successfully!
```

How Express Serves Static Files

The line:

```
app.use(express.static(path.join(__dirname,
"public")));
```

Tells Express to **serve all files inside the public folder** automatically.

Now:

`http://localhost:3000/` → Serves `public/index.html`

`http://localhost:3000/styles.css` → Serves `public/styles.css`

`http://localhost:3000/script.js` → Serves `public/script.js`

`http://localhost:3000/logo.png` → Serves `public/logo.png`

Express automatically maps **files in the public folder** to their respective URLs without needing additional routes.

Serving Files from Multiple Folders

Sometimes, you may want to serve static files **from multiple directories**.

143

Modify `server.js` to allow this:

```
app.use(express.static(path.join(__dirname,
"public")));
app.use(express.static(path.join(__dirname,
"assets")));
```

Now, create another folder called `assets` and add a new image (`assets/banner.jpg`).

You can now access:

```
http://localhost:3000/banner.jpg
```

Express will **search multiple directories** for the requested file and serve the first match it finds.

Restricting Access to Static Files

By default, all files in the `public` directory are **publicly accessible**. If you want to restrict access to certain files, you can create **custom middleware**.

For example, **blocking access to .pdf files**:

```
app.use((req, res, next) => {
    if (req.url.endsWith(".pdf")) {
        return res.status(403).send("Access to PDF
files is restricted.");
    }
    next();
});
```

Now, if someone tries to access:

```
http://localhost:3000/secret.pdf
```

They will receive a **403 Forbidden** response.

Adding Caching for Performance

By default, Express serves static files **without caching headers**, meaning browsers fetch a new copy each time. To enable caching, modify `express.static()` like this:

```
app.use(express.static(path.join(__dirname,
"public"), {
    maxAge: "1d" // Cache files for 1 day
```

```
}));
```

Now, the browser **caches static files**, improving page load speed.

Handling 404 for Missing Static Files

If a requested file doesn't exist, Express simply responds with:

```
Cannot GET /nonexistent-file.js
```

To customize this behavior, add a **404 handler**:

```
app.use((req, res) => {
    res.status(404).send("File Not Found");
});
```

Now, missing files return a **user-friendly error message** instead of a generic Express response.

Serving static files in Express.js is **straightforward and powerful**. By using `express.static()`, you can efficiently:

Serve **HTML, CSS, JavaScript, images, fonts, and other assets**.

Organize content into **public directories**.

Configure caching to **improve performance**.

Restrict access to **certain file types**.

Handle **404 errors for missing files**.

This capability is crucial for building **fast and responsive web applications**, ensuring that assets are delivered **quickly and efficiently** to users.

Chapter 7: Connecting Node.js to Databases

A web application is only as useful as the data it stores and retrieves. Whether you're building a **simple blog**, a **real-time chat application**, or a **large-scale e-commerce platform**, your Node.js application needs a **database** to manage data efficiently.

In this chapter, we'll explore how to **connect Node.js to databases**, covering both **SQL and NoSQL databases**, and demonstrating **real-world implementations** using MongoDB (NoSQL) and PostgreSQL (SQL). We'll also discuss **best practices for optimizing database performance** to ensure your applications run efficiently.

Introduction to SQL and NoSQL Databases

When developing applications, data plays a crucial role. Whether you're building an **e-commerce website**, a **social media platform**, or a **real-time analytics dashboard**, you need a **database** to store, manage, and retrieve information efficiently.

Databases fall into two primary categories:

SQL (Structured Query Language) Databases – Traditional relational databases that store data in structured tables.

NoSQL (Not Only SQL) Databases – Flexible, non-relational databases that store data in various formats, such as key-value pairs, documents, or graphs.

Choosing between **SQL and NoSQL** depends on your application's needs. Some applications require **strict data consistency** (banking, inventory management), while others prioritize **scalability and flexibility** (social media, IoT).

What is a SQL Database?

A **SQL (Structured Query Language) database** is a **relational database** that stores data in structured **tables** consisting of **rows and columns**. Each

146

row represents a **record**, and each column represents a **field** (attribute) within that record.

SQL databases follow the **ACID (Atomicity, Consistency, Isolation, Durability) principles**, ensuring **data integrity and reliability**.

Key Features of SQL Databases

Structured and organized data → Data is stored in tables with predefined schemas.

Uses SQL for queries → Allows powerful querying with commands like SELECT, INSERT, UPDATE, and DELETE.

Supports relationships → Tables can be linked using **foreign keys**.

Ensures data integrity → Uses constraints like PRIMARY KEY, FOREIGN KEY, and UNIQUE to maintain consistency.

Ideal for transactional applications → Perfect for banking, financial systems, and inventory management.

Example: A Users Table in a SQL Database

id	name	email	age
1	Alice	alice@email.com	25
2	Bob	bob@email.com	30

This structured approach ensures that each record is uniquely identified and related data can be retrieved efficiently.

Common SQL Databases

Some of the most popular **SQL databases** include:

PostgreSQL → Open-source, highly scalable, supports JSON and advanced querying.

MySQL → Widely used for web applications (e.g., WordPress, e-commerce).

SQLite → Lightweight database used in mobile apps and embedded systems.

Microsoft SQL Server → Enterprise-level database for large-scale applications.

Each SQL database has its own **features and optimizations**, but they all follow the **relational model**.

How SQL Queries Work

SQL uses **structured queries** to interact with data.

1. Creating a Table

```
CREATE TABLE users (
    id SERIAL PRIMARY KEY,
    name VARCHAR(100),
    email VARCHAR(100) UNIQUE,
    age INT
);
```

2. Inserting Data

```
INSERT INTO users (name, email, age)
VALUES ('Alice', 'alice@email.com', 25);
```

3. Retrieving Data

```
SELECT * FROM users;
```

4. Updating Data

```
UPDATE users
SET age = 26
WHERE name = 'Alice';
```

5. Deleting Data

```
DELETE FROM users
WHERE name = 'Alice';
```

SQL databases excel in scenarios where **data relationships and integrity are critical**. However, they require a **predefined schema**, making them **less flexible** when dealing with rapidly changing data structures.

What is a NoSQL Database?

A **NoSQL (Not Only SQL) database** is a **non-relational database** that stores data in **various flexible formats**, such as **documents, key-value pairs, graphs, or wide-column stores**.

NoSQL databases **do not require a fixed schema**, making them ideal for applications that handle **large-scale, unstructured, or semi-structured data**.

Key Features of NoSQL Databases

Schema-less and flexible → No predefined table structure; data can change dynamically.

Highly scalable → Designed for high availability and horizontal scaling.

Optimized for large datasets → Handles **big data** and **real-time analytics** efficiently.

Faster write speeds → Great for applications with frequent data inserts (e.g., IoT, logs, social media).

Common NoSQL Databases

Some of the most widely used **NoSQL databases** include:

MongoDB → Document-based, stores data in **JSON-like format**, widely used in web apps.

Redis → In-memory key-value store, great for caching and real-time applications.

Cassandra → Wide-column store, optimized for high availability and scalability.

Firebase (Firestore) → Cloud-based NoSQL database used in mobile applications.

Each NoSQL database has a **unique structure** suited for different use cases.

Example: Storing User Data in MongoDB (NoSQL Document)

Instead of tables, **MongoDB stores data as documents (JSON-like format)**:

```
{
    "_id": "1234567890",
```

```
    "name": "Alice",
    "email": "alice@email.com",
    "age": 25
}
```

This flexibility allows **data fields to change dynamically** without requiring schema migrations.

How NoSQL Queries Work

Instead of SQL, NoSQL databases use **their own query languages**.

1. Inserting a Document in MongoDB

```
db.users.insertOne({
    name: "Alice",
    email: "alice@email.com",
    age: 25
});
```

2. Retrieving Data

```
db.users.find({ age: 25 });
```

3. Updating Data

```
db.users.updateOne(
    { name: "Alice" },
    { $set: { age: 26 } }
);
```

4. Deleting a Document

```
db.users.deleteOne({ name: "Alice" });
```

NoSQL databases excel when **data structures frequently change**, and high scalability is required.

SQL vs. NoSQL: Key Differences

Feature	SQL Databases (Relational)	NoSQL Databases (Non-Relational)
Data Structure	Tables with rows & columns	Flexible documents, key-value pairs, graphs

Feature	SQL Databases (Relational)	NoSQL Databases (Non-Relational)
Schema	Predefined, rigid	Schema-less, flexible
Query Language	SQL (Structured Query Language)	Varies (Mongo Query Language, Cassandra Query Language)
Relationships	Uses Foreign Keys	Stores data in self-contained documents
Scalability	Vertical scaling (adding more power to a single server)	Horizontal scaling (adding more servers)
Use Cases	Banking, e-commerce, inventory management	Real-time analytics, IoT, social media, logs

Both SQL and NoSQL databases have their strengths and are used in different scenarios.

SQL databases provide **structured, relational data storage**, ensuring **data integrity and consistency**.

NoSQL databases offer **flexibility, scalability, and high-performance data handling**, making them perfect for modern web applications.

Choosing the right database depends on **your application's requirements**, **data structure**, and **scalability needs**. In some cases, a **hybrid approach** using both SQL and NoSQL can be the best solution for handling different types of data efficiently.

Using MongoDB with Mongoose

MongoDB is one of the most widely used **NoSQL databases**, offering **scalability, flexibility, and high performance** for applications that need to store and process vast amounts of **unstructured or semi-structured data**. Unlike SQL databases, where data is stored in tables, MongoDB stores data in

JSON-like documents, making it an excellent choice for **JavaScript and Node.js applications**.

However, directly interacting with MongoDB using its native driver can lead to **repetitive and complex queries**, especially when handling **data validation, schema management, and relationships**. This is where **Mongoose** comes in.

Mongoose is an **Object Data Modeling (ODM) library for MongoDB and Node.js**. It provides a structured way to define schemas, interact with MongoDB, and enforce data validation while still allowing **flexibility in data modeling**.

Step 1: Install and Set Up MongoDB

Installing MongoDB Locally

If you haven't already installed MongoDB, download it from MongoDB's official website and follow the installation instructions for your operating system.

After installation, start MongoDB by running:

```
mongod --dbpath /path/to/data/db
```

Or, if using **MongoDB Atlas (cloud database)**, create an account at MongoDB Atlas and get a **connection string**.

Step 2: Create a New Node.js Project and Install Dependencies

Create a new folder for your project:

```
mkdir mongoose-app
cd mongoose-app
```

Initialize a **Node.js project**:

```
npm init -y
```

Now, install **Express.js, Mongoose, and dotenv** (for environment variables):

```
npm install express mongoose dotenv
```

Step 3: Connect Node.js to MongoDB Using Mongoose

Create a `.env` file in your project and add your MongoDB connection string:

```
MONGO_URI=mongodb://localhost:27017/mydatabase
```

Now, create a file `server.js` and set up the connection:

```
require("dotenv").config();
const express = require("express");
const mongoose = require("mongoose");

const app = express();
const PORT = 3000;

// Connect to MongoDB
mongoose.connect(process.env.MONGO_URI, {
    useNewUrlParser: true,
    useUnifiedTopology: true
})
.then(() => console.log("MongoDB Connected"))
.catch(err => console.error("MongoDB Connection
Error:", err));

app.listen(PORT, () => {
    console.log(`Server running on
http://localhost:${PORT}`);
});
```

Start your server:

```
node server.js
```

If the connection is successful, you'll see:

```
MongoDB Connected
Server running on http://localhost:3000
```

Step 4: Define a Mongoose Schema and Model

Mongoose requires a **schema** to define the structure of documents in a MongoDB collection.

Create a folder `models/` and inside it, create a file `User.js`:

```
const mongoose = require("mongoose");
```

```
const userSchema = new mongoose.Schema({
    name: { type: String, required: true },
    email: { type: String, required: true, unique:
true },
    age: { type: Number, required: true },
    createdAt: { type: Date, default: Date.now }
});

const User = mongoose.model("User", userSchema);

module.exports = User;
```

Breaking Down the Schema

name → A **required string**

email → A **unique email field**

age → A **required number**

createdAt → A **timestamp** that defaults to the current date

Now, we can use this model to interact with MongoDB.

Step 5: Perform CRUD Operations in Mongoose

1. Create a New User (POST Request)

Modify server.js to **handle user creation**:

```
const User = require("./models/User");

app.use(express.json()); // Middleware to parse
JSON body

app.post("/users", async (req, res) => {
    try {
        const newUser = new User(req.body);
        await newUser.save();
        res.status(201).json(newUser);
    } catch (error) {
        res.status(400).json({ error: error.message
});
```

```
        }
});
```

Now, test it with **cURL or Postman**:

```
curl -X POST -H "Content-Type: application/json" -d
'{"name":"Alice","email":"alice@email.com","age":25
}' http://localhost:3000/users
```

The response should be:

```
{
    "_id": "6512c0d52f36b98f3a4a1a12",
    "name": "Alice",
    "email": "alice@email.com",
    "age": 25,
    "createdAt": "2023-09-27T12:00:00.000Z",
    "__v": 0
}
```

This confirms the user was **successfully stored in MongoDB**.

2. Retrieve All Users (GET Request)

Modify `server.js` to **fetch all users**:

```
app.get("/users", async (req, res) => {
    try {
        const users = await User.find();
        res.json(users);
    } catch (error) {
        res.status(500).json({ error: error.message
});
    }
});
```

Test it with:

```
curl -X GET http://localhost:3000/users
```

This will return **all users stored in MongoDB**.

3. Update a User (PUT Request)

Modify `server.js` to **update a user's age**:

```
app.put("/users/:id", async (req, res) => {
```

```
    try {
        const updatedUser = await
User.findByIdAndUpdate(req.params.id, req.body, {
new: true });
        res.json(updatedUser);
    } catch (error) {
        res.status(400).json({ error: error.message
});
    }
});
```

Test it with:

```
curl -X PUT -H "Content-Type: application/json" -d
'{"age":30}'
http://localhost:3000/users/6512c0d52f36b98f3a4a1a1
2
```

4. Delete a User (DELETE Request)

Modify `server.js` to **delete a user**:

```
app.delete("/users/:id", async (req, res) => {
    try {
        await
User.findByIdAndDelete(req.params.id);
        res.json({ message: "User deleted" });
    } catch (error) {
        res.status(400).json({ error: error.message
});
    }
});
```

Test it with:

```
curl -X DELETE
http://localhost:3000/users/6512c0d52f36b98f3a4a1a1
2
```

This removes the user from the database.

Mongoose **simplifies MongoDB operations**, ensuring **structured data handling, schema validation, and better maintainability**. Whether you're building a **REST API, e-commerce platform, or a social media application**, this approach provides a **scalable and flexible** database solution.

Using PostgreSQL with Sequelize

PostgreSQL is a **powerful, open-source relational database** that is widely used in **web applications, financial systems, and data analytics** due to its **scalability, data integrity, and advanced features**. Unlike NoSQL databases, PostgreSQL follows the **relational model**, meaning it organizes data into **tables** with strict relationships, ensuring data consistency.

However, interacting with raw SQL queries can become **verbose and error-prone**, especially as the database grows. This is where **Sequelize** comes in.

Sequelize is an **ORM (Object Relational Mapper) for Node.js**, allowing developers to:

Define models instead of writing raw SQL

Easily perform CRUD operations

Handle relationships between tables

Migrate and seed databases programmatically

In this section, we'll **set up PostgreSQL with Sequelize**, create **models**, perform **database operations**, and implement **best practices** for handling data efficiently.

Step 1: Install PostgreSQL and Sequelize

Before we begin, ensure PostgreSQL is installed on your system.

If you haven't installed PostgreSQL, download it from **postgresql.org** and follow the installation instructions.

After installation, start PostgreSQL and create a new database using `psql`:

```
psql -U postgres
```

Create a new database named `mydatabase`:

```
CREATE DATABASE mydatabase;
```

157

Now, exit `psql` and install Sequelize along with the PostgreSQL driver:

`npm install sequelize pg pg-hstore`

`sequelize` → The ORM for interacting with PostgreSQL.

`pg` → The PostgreSQL database driver for Node.js.

`pg-hstore` → Required for handling JSON data types in PostgreSQL.

Step 2: Set Up Sequelize and Connect to PostgreSQL

Create a **Node.js project** and initialize it:

```
mkdir sequelize-app
cd sequelize-app
npm init -y
```

Now, create a new file named `database.js` inside a `config` folder to manage the database connection:

```
const { Sequelize } = require("sequelize");

const sequelize = new Sequelize("mydatabase",
"postgres", "your_password", {
    host: "localhost",
    dialect: "postgres",
    logging: false, // Disables SQL logging in the
console
});

sequelize.authenticate()
    .then(() => console.log("PostgreSQL
Connected"))
    .catch((err) => console.error("PostgreSQL
Connection Error:", err));

module.exports = sequelize;
```

Replace `"your_password"` with your actual **PostgreSQL password**.

Run this file using:

```
node config/database.js
```
If the connection is successful, you'll see:

```
PostgreSQL Connected
```

Step 3: Define a Sequelize Model

Now, create a `models` folder and inside it, a `User.js` file to define the database schema.

```
const { Sequelize, DataTypes } =
require("sequelize");
const sequelize = require("../config/database");

const User = sequelize.define("User", {
    id: {
        type: DataTypes.UUID,
        defaultValue: Sequelize.UUIDV4,
        primaryKey: true
    },
    name: {
        type: DataTypes.STRING,
        allowNull: false
    },
    email: {
        type: DataTypes.STRING,
        allowNull: false,
        unique: true,
        validate: {
            isEmail: true
        }
    },
    age: {
        type: DataTypes.INTEGER,
        allowNull: false
    }
}, {
    timestamps: true
});

module.exports = User;
```

Breaking Down the Schema

`id` → A **UUID** is used instead of an integer to ensure unique identifiers.

`name` → A **required string** that stores the user's name.

`email` → A **unique string** with built-in email validation.

`age` → A **required integer**.

`timestamps: true` → Automatically adds **createdAt** and **updatedAt** fields.

Now, create an `index.js` file inside `models/` to **sync models** with the database:

```
const sequelize = require("../config/database");
const User = require("./User");

sequelize.sync({ force: false })
    .then(() => console.log("Database synced"))
    .catch(err => console.error("Error syncing
database:", err));

module.exports = { User };
```

Run the sync command:

```
node models/index.js
```
This **creates the Users table** in PostgreSQL based on the defined schema.

Step 4: Perform CRUD Operations in Sequelize

Now, create an `api.js` file and add the following Express.js routes for user management:

1. Setting Up the Express Server

```
const express = require("express");
const { User } = require("./models");

const app = express();
const PORT = 3000;

app.use(express.json()); // Middleware to parse
JSON
```

```
app.listen(PORT, () => {
    console.log(`Server running on
http://localhost:${PORT}`);
});
```

2. Create a New User (POST Request)

```
app.post("/users", async (req, res) => {
    try {
        const user = await User.create(req.body);
        res.status(201).json(user);
    } catch (error) {
        res.status(400).json({ error: error.message
});
    }
});
```

Test with **cURL or Postman**:

```
curl -X POST -H "Content-Type: application/json" -d
'{"name":"Alice","email":"alice@email.com","age":25
}' http://localhost:3000/users
```

The response will be:

```
{
    "id": "7f4d9f12-3c57-4e3a-a6b5-d1423b5b69e9",
    "name": "Alice",
    "email": "alice@email.com",
    "age": 25,
    "createdAt": "2023-09-27T12:00:00.000Z",
    "updatedAt": "2023-09-27T12:00:00.000Z"
}
```

3. Retrieve All Users (GET Request)

```
app.get("/users", async (req, res) => {
    try {
        const users = await User.findAll();
        res.json(users);
    } catch (error) {
        res.status(500).json({ error: error.message
});
    }
```

```
});
```

Test with:

```
curl -X GET http://localhost:3000/users
```

4. Update a User (PUT Request)

```
app.put("/users/:id", async (req, res) => {
    try {
        const updatedUser = await
User.update(req.body, {
            where: { id: req.params.id }
        });
        res.json(updatedUser);
    } catch (error) {
        res.status(400).json({ error: error.message
});
    }
});
```

Test with:

```
curl -X PUT -H "Content-Type: application/json" -d
'{"age":30}' http://localhost:3000/users/7f4d9f12-
3c57-4e3a-a6b5-d1423b5b69e9
```

5. Delete a User (DELETE Request)

```
app.delete("/users/:id", async (req, res) => {
    try {
        await User.destroy({ where: { id:
req.params.id } });
        res.json({ message: "User deleted" });
    } catch (error) {
        res.status(400).json({ error: error.message
});
    }
});
```

Test with:

```
curl -X DELETE
http://localhost:3000/users/7f4d9f12-3c57-4e3a-
a6b5-d1423b5b69e9
```

Sequelize **simplifies SQL operations**, making database interactions in Node.js **efficient, readable, and well-structured**. Whether you're building **a small application or a large enterprise system**, this approach ensures **data integrity and high performance**.

Best Practices for Database Optimization

Databases are the **core of every application** that handles data. Whether you're building an **e-commerce platform, social media site, or financial system**, an optimized database is crucial for **performance, scalability, and reliability**. Poorly designed databases lead to **slow queries, bottlenecks, and increased infrastructure costs**, which can degrade the user experience.

Optimizing a database **isn't just about making queries faster**—it's about **efficiently storing, retrieving, and maintaining data** while ensuring that the system remains responsive under heavy load.

In this section, we'll explore **practical and effective techniques** for optimizing SQL and NoSQL databases. These best practices apply whether you're using **PostgreSQL, MySQL, MongoDB, or any other database system**.

1. Design Your Database Schema Carefully

A well-designed schema ensures **efficient queries and easy scalability**. Poor schema design can lead to **redundant data, slow lookups, and excessive storage use**.

Use Proper Data Types

Choosing the right data type **reduces storage size and improves performance**.

Example (PostgreSQL Table Creation with Optimal Data Types)

```
CREATE TABLE users (
    id SERIAL PRIMARY KEY,          -- Uses auto-
incrementing integer for efficiency
    name VARCHAR(100) NOT NULL,   -- Limits string
length to optimize indexing
```

```
    email VARCHAR(255) UNIQUE,    -- Ensures email
uniqueness
    age SMALLINT CHECK (age > 0), -- Uses SMALLINT
instead of INT to save space
    created_at TIMESTAMP DEFAULT CURRENT_TIMESTAMP
);
```

Why this is optimized:

VARCHAR(100) is better than TEXT for name as it reduces unnecessary space allocation.

SMALLINT instead of INT saves space for storing ages.

CHECK (age > 0) ensures data integrity.

2. Use Indexing for Faster Queries

Indexes **speed up data retrieval** by allowing the database to find rows **without scanning the entire table**.

Example: Adding an Index to Speed Up Searches

```
CREATE INDEX idx_email ON users(email);
```
Now, when querying users by email:

```
SELECT * FROM users WHERE email =
'alice@email.com';
```
Instead of scanning **every row**, the database **jumps directly to the relevant record**, improving speed significantly.

⚠ **Be careful**: Too many indexes **slow down inserts and updates**, as each index must be updated when modifying data.

3. Optimize Queries with EXPLAIN and ANALYZE

Before optimizing queries, you need to **understand how they run**. Most databases provide tools to analyze query execution plans.

Using EXPLAIN ANALYZE in PostgreSQL

```
EXPLAIN ANALYZE SELECT * FROM users WHERE email =
'alice@email.com';
```

This command **shows how PostgreSQL processes the query**, helping identify bottlenecks such as **sequential scans** (full table scans).

If you see:

```
Seq Scan on users    (cost=0.00..100.00 rows=1
width=100)
```

It means **the database is scanning the whole table**, which is inefficient. Adding an **index** can convert this into a **fast index scan**.

4. Normalize and Denormalize Data as Needed

When to Normalize

Normalization **removes duplicate data** and ensures **data consistency** by breaking large tables into related ones.

Example (Splitting User and Orders Tables to Avoid Redundant Data)

```
CREATE TABLE users (
    id SERIAL PRIMARY KEY,
    name VARCHAR(100),
    email VARCHAR(255) UNIQUE
);

CREATE TABLE orders (
    id SERIAL PRIMARY KEY,
    user_id INT REFERENCES users(id),
    total_price DECIMAL(10,2),
    created_at TIMESTAMP DEFAULT CURRENT_TIMESTAMP
);
```

This prevents **repeating user data** in every order. Instead, `orders.user_id` **references** the `users` table.

When to Denormalize

Sometimes, **denormalization** (storing redundant data) is better for **read-heavy applications** where **performance matters more than storage efficiency**.

For example, in an **analytics dashboard**, precomputed **summary tables** reduce **complex JOIN operations**.

```
CREATE TABLE user_order_summary AS
SELECT user_id, COUNT(*) AS total_orders,
SUM(total_price) AS total_spent
FROM orders
GROUP BY user_id;
```

Instead of recalculating totals **each time a user checks their order history**, the system **fetches data instantly** from user_order_summary.

5. Optimize Joins and Use Proper Relationships

Optimizing Joins with Indexes

If your queries involve **joining tables**, indexes improve efficiency.

Example: Indexing Foreign Keys for Faster Joins

```
CREATE INDEX idx_orders_user_id ON orders(user_id);
```
Now, when executing:

```
SELECT users.name, orders.total_price
FROM users
JOIN orders ON users.id = orders.user_id
WHERE users.id = 1;
```

The database **efficiently matches records** instead of performing a costly full table scan.

6. Use Connection Pooling for Scalability

Opening and closing database connections **is expensive**. Connection pooling allows applications to **reuse database connections**, reducing overhead.

Example: Using Sequelize with Connection Pooling (PostgreSQL)

```
const { Sequelize } = require("sequelize");

const sequelize = new Sequelize("mydatabase",
"postgres", "password", {
    host: "localhost",
    dialect: "postgres",
    pool: {
        max: 10,   // Maximum connections
```

```
        min: 2,    // Minimum connections
        acquire: 30000, // Maximum time to try to
get a connection
        idle: 10000  // Time before releasing an
idle connection
    }
});

module.exports = sequelize;
```

This prevents **overloading the database** when handling multiple user requests.

7. Cache Frequently Accessed Data

For data that doesn't change frequently, **caching** improves performance significantly. Instead of querying the database every time, the system **stores the results in memory**.

Using Redis for Query Caching

```
const redis = require("redis");
const client = redis.createClient();

app.get("/users/:id", async (req, res) => {
    const userId = req.params.id;

    // Check if data is cached
    client.get(userId, async (err, cachedData) => {
        if (cachedData) {
            return
res.json(JSON.parse(cachedData));
        }

        // Fetch from database if not in cache
        const user = await User.findByPk(userId);
        client.setex(userId, 3600,
JSON.stringify(user)); // Cache for 1 hour
        res.json(user);
    });
});
```

Now, if a user requests their profile **multiple times**, it is served from **Redis** instead of hitting the database.

8. Regularly Archive or Delete Old Data

Storing **huge amounts of old data** slows queries. Periodically **archiving or deleting unnecessary records** improves performance.

Example: Archiving Old Orders into a Separate Table

```sql
INSERT INTO orders_archive SELECT * FROM orders
WHERE created_at < NOW() - INTERVAL '1 year';
DELETE FROM orders WHERE created_at < NOW() -
INTERVAL '1 year';
```

This keeps the `orders` table **small and fast** while preserving historical data.

By following these best practices, you ensure that your database remains **fast, scalable, and reliable**, no matter how much data it handles.

Chapter 8: Authentication & Authorization

In any modern application, **authentication and authorization** are fundamental. Without them, your system is vulnerable to unauthorized access, data breaches, and security threats. Whether you're building a **web application, REST API, or microservices architecture**, ensuring that users are properly authenticated and have the right level of access is critical.

Implementing User Authentication with JWT

Securing user access to applications is one of the most critical aspects of modern software development. **Authentication** ensures that only legitimate users can access certain resources, while **authorization** controls what they are allowed to do.

One of the most widely used authentication mechanisms today is **JWT (JSON Web Token)**, a **stateless, scalable, and secure** method for authenticating users in **web and mobile applications**.

JWT (**JSON Web Token**) is a compact, self-contained token that is **digitally signed** and used to verify a user's identity. It is commonly used for **stateless authentication**, meaning **no session storage is required on the server**.

How JWT Authentication Works

User logs in by providing valid credentials (email and password).

The server verifies the credentials and, if valid, generates a **JWT token**.

The client **stores the token** (in **local storage, session storage, or cookies**).

For every subsequent request, the **client sends the token in the Authorization header**.

The server **verifies the token** before allowing access to protected resources.

JWT consists of **three parts**:

Header → Contains metadata about the token and signing algorithm.

Payload → Contains user information (e.g., `id`, `email`, `role`).

Signature → A cryptographic signature that ensures the token **has not been tampered with**.

A JWT token looks like this:

```
eyJhbGciOiJIUzI1NiIsInR5cCI6IkpXVCJ9
.eyJlc2VySWQiOiIxMjM0NTY3ODkwIiwiZW1haWwiOiJhbGljZU
BtYWlsLmNvbSIsImlhdCI6MTY1Nzg5MDAwMH0
.LQmsFJvJKzYo-BTqK1A6zFNNG_K7Z6Cd5m98HRU6IC0
```

Let's now implement a **secure authentication system** using JWT in **Node.js and Express**.

Step 1: Set Up a Node.js Project

First, create a new project directory and initialize it:

```
mkdir jwt-auth-app
cd jwt-auth-app
npm init -y
```

Now, install the required dependencies:

```
npm install express jsonwebtoken bcryptjs dotenv
cors
```

express → Web framework for handling routes and requests.

jsonwebtoken → Library for creating and verifying JWT tokens.

bcryptjs → Securely hashes and verifies passwords.

dotenv → Manages environment variables.

cors → Enables cross-origin requests for APIs.

Step 2: Create an Express Server

Inside the project folder, create a file named `server.js` and set up a basic Express server:

```
require("dotenv").config();
```

```
const express = require("express");

const app = express();
const PORT = process.env.PORT || 3000;

// Middleware
app.use(express.json()); // Allows Express to parse
JSON request bodies

// Home Route
app.get("/", (req, res) => {
    res.send("JWT Authentication System is
Running!");
});

app.listen(PORT, () => {
    console.log(`Server running on
http://localhost:${PORT}`);
});
```

Run the server:

```
node server.js
```

Open a browser and go to **http://localhost:3000/**. You should see:

```
JWT Authentication System is Running!
```

Step 3: Create User Authentication Routes

1. User Registration with Password Hashing

To securely store passwords, we will **hash them using bcryptjs** before saving them in the database.

Modify `server.js` to include a registration route:

```
const bcrypt = require("bcryptjs");

const users = []; // Simulated database

// User Registration Route
app.post("/register", async (req, res) => {
    try {
        const { name, email, password } = req.body;
```

```
        // Check if user already exists
        if (users.some(user => user.email ===
email)) {
                return res.status(400).json({ message:
"User already exists" });
        }

        // Hash password
        const hashedPassword = await
bcrypt.hash(password, 10);

        // Save user
        const newUser = { id: users.length + 1,
name, email, password: hashedPassword };
        users.push(newUser);

        res.status(201).json({ message: "User
registered successfully!" });
    } catch (error) {
        res.status(500).json({ message: "Internal
Server Error" });
    }
});
```

Now, register a new user using **Postman or cURL**:

```
curl -X POST -H "Content-Type: application/json" -d
'{"name":"Alice","email":"alice@example.com","passw
ord":"secret"}' http://localhost:3000/register
```

2. User Login and JWT Token Generation

Modify `server.js` to add a **login route that issues a JWT token**:

```
const jwt = require("jsonwebtoken");

app.post("/login", async (req, res) => {
    try {
        const { email, password } = req.body;
        const user = users.find(user => user.email
=== email);
```

```
        if (!user || !(await
bcrypt.compare(password, user.password))) {
            return res.status(401).json({ message:
"Invalid email or password" });
        }

        // Generate JWT Token
        const token = jwt.sign(
            { id: user.id, email: user.email },
            process.env.JWT_SECRET,
            { expiresIn: "1h" }
        );

        res.json({ token });
    } catch (error) {
        res.status(500).json({ message: "Internal
Server Error" });
    }
});
```

To log in and obtain a JWT token:

```
curl -X POST -H "Content-Type: application/json" -d
'{"email":"alice@example.com","password":"secret"}'
http://localhost:3000/login
```

Response:

```
{
    "token": "your-generated-jwt-token"
}
```

3. Protecting Routes with JWT Authentication

To protect certain API endpoints, we create a **middleware function** to verify JWT tokens.

Add this middleware function to `server.js`:

```
function authenticateToken(req, res, next) {
    const token =
req.header("Authorization")?.split(" ")[1];
```

```
    if (!token) return res.status(401).json({
message: "Access Denied" });

    jwt.verify(token, process.env.JWT_SECRET, (err,
user) => {
        if (err) return res.status(403).json({
message: "Invalid Token" });
        req.user = user;
        next();
    });
}
```

Now, protect the `/dashboard` route:

```
app.get("/dashboard", authenticateToken, (req, res)
=> {
    res.json({ message: "Welcome to the
dashboard!", user: req.user });
});
```

Test it by sending a request **without a token**:

```
curl -X GET http://localhost:3000/dashboard
```
Response:

```
{
    "message": "Access Denied"
}
```
Now, send the request **with the token**:

```
curl -H "Authorization: Bearer your-generated-jwt-
token" http://localhost:3000/dashboard
```
Response:

```
{
    "message": "Welcome to the dashboard!",
    "user": {
        "id": 1,
        "email": "alice@example.com"
    }
}
```

You have now implemented a **secure user authentication system using JWT in Node.js**.

This authentication system is **scalable and stateless**, making it ideal for **RESTful APIs, microservices, and distributed applications**.

Using Passport.js for Authentication Strategies

Passport.js is a **popular authentication middleware** for Node.js that simplifies integrating authentication mechanisms, including:

Local authentication (username & password)

OAuth authentication (Google, Facebook, GitHub, Twitter, etc.)

JWT authentication

Session-based authentication

By using Passport.js, you can implement **secure authentication systems** that work across different platforms with minimal effort.

How Passport.js Works

Passport.js follows a **strategy-based authentication approach**, meaning you can plug in **different authentication mechanisms** without modifying core application logic.

User provides credentials (e.g., username & password).

Passport processes the authentication strategy (local, JWT, OAuth, etc.).

If credentials are valid, **Passport creates a session** or **returns a token**.

The user is now **authenticated** and can access protected resources.

Setting Up Passport.js in an Express.js Application

Before we implement various authentication strategies, let's set up a **Node.js and Express application** with Passport.js.

Step 1: Install Required Dependencies

Create a new project and install Passport.js along with required dependencies:

```
mkdir passport-auth
cd passport-auth
npm init -y
npm install express passport passport-local
bcryptjs jsonwebtoken dotenv express-session
```

passport → Core Passport.js authentication library.

passport-local → Strategy for username/password authentication.

bcryptjs → Securely hashes passwords.

jsonwebtoken → Issues JWT tokens.

dotenv → Manages environment variables.

express-session → Enables session management for storing login states.

Implementing Local Authentication with Passport.js

Local authentication verifies users **with a username (or email) and password**. This is the **most common authentication method** used in web applications.

Step 2: Set Up the Express Server

Create a new file `server.js` and initialize an Express.js application:

```
require("dotenv").config();
const express = require("express");
const session = require("express-session");
const passport = require("passport");

const app = express();
const PORT = process.env.PORT || 3000;

app.use(express.json());
app.use(express.urlencoded({ extended: true }));

// Configure session management
app.use(session({
    secret: "supersecretkey",
    resave: false,
    saveUninitialized: true
```

```
}));

// Initialize Passport
app.use(passport.initialize());
app.use(passport.session());

app.listen(PORT, () => {
    console.log(`Server running on
http://localhost:${PORT}`);
});
```

Now, run the server:

```
node server.js
```

Step 3: Set Up User Authentication

Create a `users` array to act as a **temporary database**:

```
const users = []; // Simulated database
```

Create a new file `passport-config.js` and configure **Passport Local Strategy**:

```
const LocalStrategy = require("passport-
local").Strategy;
const bcrypt = require("bcryptjs");

module.exports = function(passport) {
    passport.use(new LocalStrategy(
        { usernameField: "email" }, // We use email
instead of username
        async (email, password, done) => {
            const user = users.find(u => u.email
=== email);
            if (!user) return done(null, false, {
message: "User not found" });

            // Compare password
            if (!(await bcrypt.compare(password,
user.password))) {
                return done(null, false, { message:
"Incorrect password" });
            }
```

```
            return done(null, user);
        }
    ));

    passport.serializeUser((user, done) => {
        done(null, user.email);
    });

    passport.deserializeUser((email, done) => {
        const user = users.find(u => u.email ===
email);
        done(null, user);
    });
};
```

Now, modify `server.js` to **initialize Passport.js with this strategy**:

```
require("./passport-config")(passport);
```

Step 4: Implement User Registration and Login Routes

Modify `server.js` to add **user registration**:

```
const bcrypt = require("bcryptjs");

// User Registration
app.post("/register", async (req, res) => {
    const { name, email, password } = req.body;

    if (users.find(user => user.email === email)) {
        return res.status(400).json({ message:
"User already exists" });
    }

    const hashedPassword = await
bcrypt.hash(password, 10);
    users.push({ id: users.length + 1, name, email,
password: hashedPassword });

    res.json({ message: "User registered
successfully!" });
});
```

178

Now, add **user login with Passport.js**:

```
app.post("/login", passport.authenticate("local", {
    successRedirect: "/dashboard",
    failureRedirect: "/login-failure"
}));

app.get("/dashboard", (req, res) => {
    if (!req.isAuthenticated()) {
        return res.status(401).json({ message:
"Unauthorized access" });
    }
    res.json({ message: "Welcome to the
dashboard!", user: req.user });
});

app.get("/login-failure", (req, res) => {
    res.json({ message: "Login failed. Check your
credentials." });
});
```

Step 5: Logging Out

To **log out a user**, destroy their session:

```
app.post("/logout", (req, res) => {
    req.logout(err => {
        if (err) return res.status(500).json({
message: "Logout failed" });
        res.json({ message: "Logged out
successfully" });
    });
});
```

Using JWT with Passport.js

Instead of **session-based authentication**, we can use **JWT authentication** with Passport.js. This is useful for **stateless APIs**.

Step 1: Install Passport JWT Strategy

```
npm install passport-jwt
```
Step 2: Configure Passport for JWT Authentication

Modify `passport-config.js`:

```
const { Strategy: JwtStrategy, ExtractJwt } =
require("passport-jwt");

module.exports = function(passport) {
    passport.use(new JwtStrategy({
        jwtFromRequest:
ExtractJwt.fromAuthHeaderAsBearerToken(),
        secretOrKey: process.env.JWT_SECRET
    }, (jwt_payload, done) => {
        const user = users.find(u => u.email ===
jwt_payload.email);
        return user ? done(null, user) : done(null,
false);
    }));
};
```

Step 3: Modify Login to Issue JWT Token

Modify `/login` in `server.js`:

```
const jwt = require("jsonwebtoken");

app.post("/jwt-login", (req, res) => {
    passport.authenticate("local", { session: false
}, (err, user) => {
        if (!user) return res.status(401).json({
message: "Invalid credentials" });

        const token = jwt.sign({ email: user.email
}, process.env.JWT_SECRET, { expiresIn: "1h" });
        res.json({ token });
    })(req, res);
});
```

Step 4: Protect Routes with JWT

Modify `server.js` to protect the dashboard route:

```
app.get("/jwt-dashboard",
passport.authenticate("jwt", { session: false }),
(req, res) => {
    res.json({ message: "Welcome to the protected
JWT route!", user: req.user });
```

```
});
```

Passport.js **simplifies authentication** by providing a **plug-and-play strategy-based approach**, making it ideal for **scalable and secure applications**.

Role-Based Access Control (RBAC)

Controlling access to different parts of an application is essential for maintaining security and enforcing **user permissions**. In a **multi-user system**, not all users should have the same level of access. Some may be able to **view data but not modify it**, while others may have **administrative privileges**.

This is where **Role-Based Access Control (RBAC)** comes in. RBAC ensures that users can only perform **actions that align with their assigned roles**.

For example, in an **e-commerce platform**:

A **customer** can **view products** and **place orders**.

A **vendor** can **add and manage products**.

An **admin** can **modify all data, including user accounts**.

RBAC enforces **access control policies** based on user roles.

How RBAC Works

Users are assigned roles during registration or by an administrator.

Each role has a predefined set of permissions (e.g., `admin`, `editor`, `user`).

When a user logs in, their role is **encoded in a JWT token**.

Before accessing protected routes, middleware **checks if the user has the correct role**.

If the role matches the required permission, **access is granted**; otherwise, the request is **denied**.

Setting Up RBAC in a Node.js Application

Let's implement **RBAC** in an **Express.js** application using **JWT-based authentication**.

181

Step 1: Install Dependencies

If you haven't already, create a new project and install the required packages:

```
mkdir rbac-auth
cd rbac-auth
npm init -y
npm install express jsonwebtoken bcryptjs dotenv
cors
```

express → Web framework.

jsonwebtoken → Generates and verifies JWT tokens.

bcryptjs → Hashes passwords securely.

dotenv → Manages environment variables.

cors → Handles cross-origin requests for APIs.

Step 2: Set Up the Express Server

Create a file named `server.js` and set up the **Express server**:

```
require("dotenv").config();
const express = require("express");

const app = express();
const PORT = process.env.PORT || 3000;

app.use(express.json());

app.listen(PORT, () => {
    console.log(`Server running on
http://localhost:${PORT}`);
});
```

Step 3: Create User Authentication with Roles

We will now create **user authentication** with predefined roles:

`admin` → Full access to all operations.

`editor` → Can modify content but not manage users.

`user` → Can only access basic content.

Modify `server.js` to add **user authentication and role assignment**:

```
const jwt = require("jsonwebtoken");
const bcrypt = require("bcryptjs");

const users = []; // Simulated database

// User Registration
app.post("/register", async (req, res) => {
    const { name, email, password, role } =
req.body;

    if (!["admin", "editor",
"user"].includes(role)) {
        return res.status(400).json({ message:
"Invalid role assigned" });
    }

    const hashedPassword = await
bcrypt.hash(password, 10);
    users.push({ id: users.length + 1, name, email,
password: hashedPassword, role });

    res.json({ message: "User registered
successfully!" });
});

// User Login
app.post("/login", async (req, res) => {
    const { email, password } = req.body;
    const user = users.find(user => user.email ===
email);

    if (!user || !(await bcrypt.compare(password,
user.password))) {
        return res.status(401).json({ message:
"Invalid credentials" });
    }

    const token = jwt.sign(
```

```
    { id: user.id, email: user.email, role:
user.role },
        process.env.JWT_SECRET,
        { expiresIn: "1h" }
    );

    res.json({ token });
});
```

Now, register a user using **Postman or cURL**:

```
curl -X POST -H "Content-Type: application/json" -d
'{"name":"Alice","email":"alice@example.com","passw
ord":"secret","role":"admin"}'
http://localhost:3000/register
```

Then, log in to receive a **JWT token**:

```
curl -X POST -H "Content-Type: application/json" -d
'{"email":"alice@example.com","password":"secret"}'
http://localhost:3000/login
```

Response:

```
{
    "token": "your-generated-jwt-token"
}
```

This token will be **used for authentication** in protected routes.

Step 4: Implement Middleware for Role-Based Access Control

Now, create a **middleware function** that **restricts access based on user roles**.

```
function authenticateToken(req, res, next) {
    const token =
req.header("Authorization")?.split(" ")[1];

    if (!token) return res.status(401).json({
message: "Access Denied" });

    jwt.verify(token, process.env.JWT_SECRET, (err,
user) => {
        if (err) return res.status(403).json({
message: "Invalid Token" });
        req.user = user;
        next();
```

```
        });
}

function authorizeRoles(...allowedRoles) {
    return (req, res, next) => {
        if (!allowedRoles.includes(req.user.role))
{
            return res.status(403).json({ message:
"Access Denied: Insufficient Permissions" });
        }
        next();
    };
}
```

Step 5: Protect Routes with Role-Based Access Control

Now, let's define **protected API routes** that only allow access based on user roles.

```
// Admin-only Route
app.get("/admin", authenticateToken,
authorizeRoles("admin"), (req, res) => {
    res.json({ message: "Welcome, Admin! You have
full access." });
});

// Editor and Admin Access
app.get("/editor", authenticateToken,
authorizeRoles("admin", "editor"), (req, res) => {
    res.json({ message: "Welcome, Editor! You can
modify content." });
});

// All Users Can Access This Route
app.get("/user", authenticateToken,
authorizeRoles("admin", "editor", "user"), (req,
res) => {
    res.json({ message: "Welcome, User! You have
basic access." });
});
```

Step 6: Testing the Role-Based Access Control System

1. Log in as an Admin to Get a JWT Token

```
curl -X POST -H "Content-Type: application/json" -d
'{"email":"alice@example.com","password":"secret"}'
http://localhost:3000/login
```

Use the received token for authorization.

2. Try Accessing the Admin Route

```
curl -H "Authorization: Bearer your-generated-jwt-
token" http://localhost:3000/admin
```
Response:

```
{
    "message": "Welcome, Admin! You have full
access."
}
```

3. Try Accessing the Editor Route with a Regular User Token

If a regular user (role: "user") tries to access the **editor route**, the response will be:

```
{
    "message": "Access Denied: Insufficient
Permissions"
}
```

This confirms that **RBAC is working correctly**.

RBAC **improves security and maintainability**, ensuring that only **authorized users** can perform specific actions. Whether you're building an **admin panel, multi-user SaaS platform, or an enterprise-grade system**, RBAC is an essential part of securing your application.

Securing APIs with OAuth

APIs are the backbone of modern web applications, enabling seamless communication between services, applications, and users. However, APIs must be **secured** to prevent **unauthorized access, data breaches, and abuse**. One of the most robust and widely adopted security protocols for API authentication and authorization is **OAuth (Open Authorization)**.

OAuth allows applications to **securely access resources** on behalf of users without exposing their credentials. Whether you're integrating with **Google, Facebook, GitHub**, or building a **third-party API**, OAuth provides a **standardized, scalable, and secure** authentication method.

OAuth is an **open standard for access delegation** that allows users to grant applications **limited access to their data** without exposing their credentials.

Instead of **directly sharing a password**, OAuth issues **access tokens**, which applications use to authenticate API requests.

How OAuth Works (Step-by-Step)

User requests access → A user tries to log in to an application via a third-party service (e.g., Google).

Authorization request → The application redirects the user to the **OAuth provider** (e.g., Google).

User grants permission → The user logs in and grants access.

OAuth provider issues a token → The provider sends back an **access token** to the application.

Application accesses API with token → The application uses the **token** to request data from the provider's API (e.g., retrieving user profile details).

OAuth 2.0 Grant Types

OAuth 2.0 defines different **grant types** based on the authentication flow. The most commonly used are:

Grant Type	Use Case
Authorization Code	Used for **web applications** where the user logs in via an OAuth provider (e.g., Google, GitHub).
Client Credentials	Used for **machine-to-machine authentication** (e.g., internal services, microservices).
Implicit Grant	Used for **browser-based apps** (less secure, rarely recommended).

Grant Type	Use Case
Password Grant	Used when a user **directly provides a username & password** (not recommended for public apps).
Refresh Token	Used to **renew an expired access token** without re-authenticating.

Now that we understand OAuth, let's **implement OAuth 2.0 in a Node.js API**.

Setting Up OAuth in a Node.js API

We'll secure an **Express API** using **Google OAuth 2.0** with **Passport.js**, a popular authentication middleware.

Step 1: Install Required Dependencies

```
mkdir oauth-api
cd oauth-api
npm init -y
npm install express passport passport-google-
oauth20 jsonwebtoken dotenv cors
```

passport → Authentication middleware.

passport-google-oauth20 → OAuth 2.0 strategy for Google authentication.

jsonwebtoken → Generates and verifies OAuth access tokens.

dotenv → Manages environment variables.

cors → Enables cross-origin requests.

Step 2: Set Up the Express Server

Create a `server.js` file and configure the Express server:

```
require("dotenv").config();
const express = require("express");
const passport = require("passport");
const jwt = require("jsonwebtoken");
```

```
const app = express();
const PORT = process.env.PORT || 3000;

app.use(express.json());
app.use(passport.initialize());

app.get("/", (req, res) => {
    res.send("OAuth Authentication with Google");
});

app.listen(PORT, () => {
    console.log(`Server running on
http://localhost:${PORT}`);
});
```

Step 3: Configure Google OAuth Strategy

To authenticate users with Google, create **OAuth credentials** in Google Cloud Console:

Go to Google Developers Console

Create a new project

Enable **Google OAuth API**

Set up **OAuth 2.0 credentials** with the following:

Redirect URI: `http://localhost:3000/auth/google/callback`

Allowed scopes: `profile`, `email`

Once done, **copy your** `CLIENT_ID` and `CLIENT_SECRET`.

Now, configure **Passport.js for Google authentication** in `passport-config.js`:

```
const passport = require("passport");
const GoogleStrategy = require("passport-google-
oauth20").Strategy;
const jwt = require("jsonwebtoken");

passport.use(
    new GoogleStrategy(
```

```
        {
            clientID: process.env.GOOGLE_CLIENT_ID,
            clientSecret:
process.env.GOOGLE_CLIENT_SECRET,
            callbackURL: "/auth/google/callback"
        },
        (accessToken, refreshToken, profile, done)
=> {
            // Generate a JWT token
            const token = jwt.sign(
                { id: profile.id, email:
profile.emails[0].value, name: profile.displayName
},
                process.env.JWT_SECRET,
                { expiresIn: "1h" }
            );

            return done(null, { token });
        }
    )
);

passport.serializeUser((user, done) => {
    done(null, user);
});

passport.deserializeUser((user, done) => {
    done(null, user);
});
```

Step 4: Implement Google OAuth Login

Modify `server.js` to add OAuth authentication routes:

```
require("./passport-config");

app.get("/auth/google",
passport.authenticate("google", { scope:
["profile", "email"] }));

app.get("/auth/google/callback",
passport.authenticate("google", { session: false
}), (req, res) => {
```

```
    res.json({ message: "Google authentication
successful", token: req.user.token });
});
```

Step 5: Secure API Routes with OAuth Token

Create **middleware to protect routes** using JWT verification:

```
function authenticateToken(req, res, next) {
    const token =
req.header("Authorization")?.split(" ")[1];

    if (!token) return res.status(401).json({
message: "Access Denied" });

    jwt.verify(token, process.env.JWT_SECRET, (err,
user) => {
        if (err) return res.status(403).json({
message: "Invalid Token" });
        req.user = user;
        next();
    });
}
```

Now, protect an API route:

```
app.get("/dashboard", authenticateToken, (req, res)
=> {
    res.json({ message: "Welcome to the
dashboard!", user: req.user });
});
```

Testing OAuth 2.0 Authentication

1. Start the Server

```
node server.js
```

2. Authenticate via Google

Visit:

```
http://localhost:3000/auth/google
```

This will redirect you to **Google's login page**. After successful login, you'll receive a **JWT token** in the response.

3. Access Protected Route with Token

Copy the token from the Google OAuth response and use it to access the protected route:

```
curl -H "Authorization: Bearer your-jwt-token"
http://localhost:3000/dashboard
```

If the token is valid, you'll receive:

```
{
    "message": "Welcome to the dashboard!",
    "user": {
        "id": "123456789",
        "email": "user@example.com",
        "name": "John Doe"
    }
}
```

Best Practices for Securing APIs with OAuth

- **Use HTTPS** → Always encrypt data in transit to prevent token interception.
- **Implement refresh tokens** → Allow users to stay authenticated without re-logging in frequently.
- **Limit token lifetime** → Short-lived tokens reduce security risks.
- **Scope-based permissions** → Restrict API access based on user roles and required actions.
- **Store tokens securely** → Never expose OAuth credentials in client-side code.

By integrating **OAuth with JWT**, you create a **scalable and secure authentication system** suitable for **modern web and mobile applications**.

Chapter 9: Building a RESTful API

APIs (Application Programming Interfaces) are the foundation of **modern web and mobile applications**, enabling different systems to **communicate seamlessly**. A **RESTful API** follows **REST (Representational State Transfer) principles**, making it **scalable, stateless, and easy to integrate**.

REST API Design Principles

A well-designed REST API is **predictable, scalable, and easy to use**. Whether you're building an API for **a web application, a mobile app, or a microservices architecture**, following RESTful design principles ensures that your API is **efficient, maintainable, and developer-friendly**.

A **REST API (Representational State Transfer API)** follows a set of architectural constraints that make web services **lightweight, scalable, and maintainable**. REST APIs communicate using **HTTP** and rely on standard methods such as `GET`, `POST`, `PUT`, and `DELETE` to perform operations.

Characteristics of a Well-Designed REST API

Statelessness → Each request contains all necessary information; the server does not store session data.

Uniform Interface → APIs follow predictable conventions for URL structures, HTTP methods, and responses.

Resource-Based → Everything is represented as a **resource** with a unique identifier (URI).

Cacheable → Responses should be cacheable for performance optimization.

1. Structuring RESTful Endpoints

A RESTful API should be **resource-centric**, meaning that it should **expose entities (resources)** rather than actions.

Example: Managing Users

`GET /users` → Retrieve all users

`GET /users/{id}` → Retrieve a specific user

`POST /users` → Create a new user

`PUT /users/{id}` → Update user details

`DELETE /users/{id}` → Delete a user

Bad API Design (Action-Based URLs)

`GET /getUsers` ✖

`POST /createNewUser` ✖

`PUT /editUserDetails` ✖

These are **not RESTful** because they rely on action-based verbs instead of resources. Instead, **use HTTP methods to describe the action** and **use resource names in the path**.

2. Using HTTP Methods Correctly

Each HTTP method has a specific purpose:

HTTP Method Purpose

GET	Retrieve a resource
POST	Create a new resource
PUT	Update an existing resource
PATCH	Partially update an existing resource
DELETE	Remove a resource

Example: API for a Blog System

`GET /articles` → Fetch all articles

`POST /articles` → Create a new article

`GET /articles/{id}` → Fetch a specific article

`PUT /articles/{id}` → Update an article (entire object)

`PATCH /articles/{id}` → Partially update an article (e.g., update title only)

`DELETE /articles/{id}` → Delete an article

Using **correct HTTP methods** makes an API more **intuitive and predictable**.

3. Implementing Status Codes for Clear Communication

Clients interacting with an API need **clear feedback**. HTTP status codes help define the outcome of a request.

Commonly Used HTTP Status Codes

Status Code	Meaning
200 OK	Request was successful
201 Created	Resource was successfully created
204 No Content	Request was successful, but no response body needed
400 Bad Request	The request was malformed or contained invalid data
401 Unauthorized	Authentication required
403 Forbidden	User does not have permission to access the resource
404 Not Found	The requested resource does not exist
500 Internal Server Error	A server-side issue occurred

Example: Handling API Responses Properly

```
app.get("/users/:id", async (req, res) => {
    try {
```

```
        const user = await
User.findById(req.params.id);
        if (!user) {
            return res.status(404).json({ message:
"User not found" });
        }
        res.status(200).json(user);
    } catch (error) {
        res.status(500).json({ message: "Server
error", error: error.message });
    }
});
```

Returns **200** OK if the user exists

Returns **404** Not Found if the user does not exist

Returns **500** Internal Server Error if something goes wrong

4. Handling Query Parameters, Pagination, and Filtering

Using Query Parameters for Filtering and Sorting

Instead of creating multiple endpoints for filtering, use **query parameters**:

GET /products?category=electronics → Filter products by category

GET /products?sort=price → Sort products by price

GET /products?price_min=100&price_max=500 → Filter products within a price range

Implementing Pagination for Large Datasets

APIs returning **large amounts of data** should use **pagination** to improve performance.

Example: Paginating API Responses

```
app.get("/products", async (req, res) => {
    const page = parseInt(req.query.page) || 1;
    const limit = parseInt(req.query.limit) || 10;
```

```
    const skip = (page - 1) * limit;

    const products = await
Product.find().skip(skip).limit(limit);
    res.json({ page, limit, products });
});
```

GET /products?page=2&limit=10 → Fetch the second page of results with 10 products per page.

5. Versioning APIs for Backward Compatibility

When an API evolves, older versions should remain available to avoid breaking existing applications.

Common API Versioning Approaches

URL Versioning (Recommended)

GET /v1/users → API Version 1

GET /v2/users → API Version 2

Header Versioning

Clients pass Accept: application/vnd.myapp.v1+json in the header

Query Parameter Versioning

GET /users?version=1

Using **URL versioning** makes it **clear and intuitive** for API consumers.

6. Securing the API with Authentication and Authorization

Using JWT for API Authentication

Most REST APIs use **JWT (JSON Web Token)** to authenticate users.

Example: Protecting API Routes with JWT

```
const jwt = require("jsonwebtoken");

function authenticateToken(req, res, next) {
    const token =
req.header("Authorization")?.split(" ")[1];
```

```
    if (!token) return res.status(401).json({
message: "Access Denied" });

    jwt.verify(token, process.env.JWT_SECRET, (err,
user) => {
        if (err) return res.status(403).json({
message: "Invalid Token" });
        req.user = user;
        next();
    });
}

app.get("/dashboard", authenticateToken, (req, res)
=> {
    res.json({ message: "Welcome to the
dashboard!", user: req.user });
});
```

Now, the `/dashboard` route **can only be accessed with a valid JWT token**.

By following these **RESTful API design principles**, you can build **robust APIs** that provide a **seamless developer experience while maintaining high performance and security**.

CRUD Operations with Express.js and MongoDB/PostgreSQL

CRUD (**Create, Read, Update, Delete**) operations form the foundation of any application that interacts with a database. Whether you're working with **MongoDB (NoSQL)** or **PostgreSQL (SQL)**, implementing these operations efficiently ensures that your API is **reliable, scalable, and easy to maintain**.

Setting Up Express.js

Before implementing CRUD operations, let's set up a basic **Express.js server** that will handle our API requests.

1. Initialize a Node.js Project

First, create a new project directory and install dependencies:

```
mkdir express-crud
cd express-crud
npm init -y
```

Now, install the necessary packages:

```
npm install express mongoose pg pg-hstore sequelize
dotenv cors body-parser
```

express → Web framework for handling API routes

mongoose → MongoDB ORM for managing database interactions

pg, pg-hstore, sequelize → PostgreSQL ORM and database drivers

dotenv → Loads environment variables

cors → Enables cross-origin requests

body-parser → Parses incoming request bodies

Connecting Express.js to a Database

We will implement CRUD operations using **both MongoDB (Mongoose) and PostgreSQL (Sequelize)**. Choose the one that fits your project requirements.

MongoDB Setup (Using Mongoose)

Step 1: Configure Database Connection

Create a `config/database.js` file:

```
const mongoose = require("mongoose");

mongoose.connect(process.env.MONGO_URI, {
    useNewUrlParser: true,
    useUnifiedTopology: true
})
.then(() => console.log("MongoDB Connected"))
.catch(err => console.error("MongoDB Connection
Error:", err));

module.exports = mongoose;
```

In your `.env` file, add:

```
MONGO_URI=mongodb://localhost:27017/express_crud
```

PostgreSQL Setup (Using Sequelize)

Step 1: Configure Database Connection

Create a `config/database.js` file:

```
const { Sequelize } = require("sequelize");

const sequelize = new
Sequelize(process.env.DB_NAME, process.env.DB_USER,
process.env.DB_PASS, {
    host: process.env.DB_HOST,
    dialect: "postgres",
    logging: false
});

sequelize.authenticate()
    .then(() => console.log("PostgreSQL
Connected"))
    .catch(err => console.error("PostgreSQL
Connection Error:", err));

module.exports = sequelize;
```

In your `.env` file, add:

```
DB_NAME=express_crud
DB_USER=postgres
DB_PASS=yourpassword
DB_HOST=localhost
```

Defining the User Model

Now, define a **User model** that will be used for CRUD operations.

MongoDB Model (Using Mongoose)

Create `models/User.js`:

```
const mongoose = require("mongoose");
```

```
const userSchema = new mongoose.Schema({
    name: { type: String, required: true },
    email: { type: String, required: true, unique:
true },
    age: { type: Number, required: true }
});

module.exports = mongoose.model("User",
userSchema);
```

PostgreSQL Model (Using Sequelize)

Create models/User.js:

```
const { Sequelize, DataTypes } =
require("sequelize");
const sequelize = require("../config/database");

const User = sequelize.define("User", {
    name: { type: DataTypes.STRING, allowNull:
false },
    email: { type: DataTypes.STRING, allowNull:
false, unique: true },
    age: { type: DataTypes.INTEGER, allowNull:
false }
});

sequelize.sync(); // Ensure table is created

module.exports = User;
```

Implementing CRUD Operations

Now, let's create an **Express Router** that handles **CRUD operations** for our User model.

Create routes/userRoutes.js:

```
const express = require("express");
const User = require("../models/User");
const router = express.Router();
```

1. Create a New User (POST Request)

MongoDB (Mongoose)

```
router.post("/", async (req, res) => {
    try {
        const user = new User(req.body);
        await user.save();
        res.status(201).json(user);
    } catch (error) {
        res.status(400).json({ error: error.message
});
    }
});
```

PostgreSQL (Sequelize)

```
router.post("/", async (req, res) => {
    try {
        const user = await User.create(req.body);
        res.status(201).json(user);
    } catch (error) {
        res.status(400).json({ error: error.message
});
    }
});
```

2. Retrieve All Users (GET Request)

MongoDB (Mongoose)

```
router.get("/", async (req, res) => {
    const users = await User.find();
    res.json(users);
});
```

PostgreSQL (Sequelize)

```
router.get("/", async (req, res) => {
    const users = await User.findAll();
    res.json(users);
});
```

3. Retrieve a Single User (GET Request by ID)

MongoDB (Mongoose)

```
router.get("/:id", async (req, res) => {
    const user = await
User.findById(req.params.id);
    user ? res.json(user) : res.status(404).json({
message: "User not found" });
});
```

PostgreSQL (Sequelize)

```
router.get("/:id", async (req, res) => {
    const user = await
User.findByPk(req.params.id);
    user ? res.json(user) : res.status(404).json({
message: "User not found" });
});
```

4. Update a User (PUT Request by ID)

MongoDB (Mongoose)

```
router.put("/:id", async (req, res) => {
    const updatedUser = await
User.findByIdAndUpdate(req.params.id, req.body, {
new: true });
    res.json(updatedUser);
});
```

PostgreSQL (Sequelize)

```
router.put("/:id", async (req, res) => {
    await User.update(req.body, { where: { id:
req.params.id } });
    const updatedUser = await
User.findByPk(req.params.id);
    res.json(updatedUser);
});
```

5. Delete a User (DELETE Request by ID)

MongoDB (Mongoose)

```
router.delete("/:id", async (req, res) => {
    await User.findByIdAndDelete(req.params.id);
    res.json({ message: "User deleted" });
```

```
});
```

PostgreSQL (Sequelize)

```
router.delete("/:id", async (req, res) => {
    await User.destroy({ where: { id: req.params.id
} });
    res.json({ message: "User deleted" });
});
```

Integrating Routes in Express.js

Modify `server.js` to use the routes:

```
const express = require("express");
require("dotenv").config();
const mongoose = require("./config/database"); //
Use sequelize for PostgreSQL
const userRoutes = require("./routes/userRoutes");

const app = express();
const PORT = process.env.PORT || 3000;

app.use(express.json());
app.use("/users", userRoutes);

app.listen(PORT, () => {
    console.log(`Server running on
http://localhost:${PORT}`);
});
```

This architecture ensures **scalability, maintainability, and security**, making it suitable for **production-ready APIs**.

Handling API Errors and Validations

A well-designed API should provide **clear, meaningful error messages** and **validate incoming data** to prevent incorrect or malicious inputs from causing issues. Error handling and validation are critical for maintaining **data integrity, security, and user experience**.

Without proper error handling, your API could:

Expose sensitive internal details to users.

Return inconsistent responses, making debugging difficult.

Process invalid or incomplete data, leading to data corruption.

Errors in an API generally fall into three categories:

1. Client-Side Errors (4xx Series)

These occur when the **client sends an invalid request**. Examples include:

`400 Bad Request` → The request is malformed or missing required fields.

`401 Unauthorized` → The request lacks valid authentication credentials.

`403 Forbidden` → The authenticated user does not have permission.

`404 Not Found` → The requested resource does not exist.

2. Server-Side Errors (5xx Series)

These indicate **issues on the server** that prevent processing the request. Examples include:

`500 Internal Server Error` → An unexpected error occurred.

`503 Service Unavailable` → The server is temporarily overloaded or down for maintenance.

3. Validation Errors

These occur when **user input fails validation rules**. Instead of allowing bad data, APIs should return structured error messages.

Example:

```
{
  "error": "Validation Error",
  "details": [
    { "field": "email", "message": "Invalid email format" },
```

```
    { "field": "password", "message": "Password
must be at least 8 characters long" }
  ]
}
```

Now, let's **implement structured error handling and input validation** in Express.js.

Implementing Error Handling in Express.js

A structured error handling mechanism ensures that **all API errors are processed uniformly**.

Step 1: Create a Centralized Error Handling Middleware

Modify `server.js` to include a custom error handler:

```
const express = require("express");

const app = express();
app.use(express.json());

// Global Error Handling Middleware
app.use((err, req, res, next) => {
    console.error(err.stack);

    res.status(err.status || 500).json({
        error: err.message || "Internal Server
Error",
        details: err.details || []
    });
});

const PORT = process.env.PORT || 3000;
app.listen(PORT, () => {
    console.log(`Server running on
http://localhost:${PORT}`);
});
```

Step 2: Throw and Handle Errors Correctly

Now, modify a route to handle errors properly.

```
app.get("/user/:id", async (req, res, next) => {
```

```
    try {
        const user = await
User.findById(req.params.id);
        if (!user) {
            return next({ status: 404, message:
"User not found" });
        }
        res.json(user);
    } catch (error) {
        next({ status: 500, message: "Database
error", details: error.message });
    }
});
```

This ensures:

If the user **does not exist**, a `404 Not Found` response is returned.

If an **unexpected error** occurs, a `500 Internal Server Error` response is
returned.

Validating API Requests with Joi and Express Validator

To **prevent bad data from entering the system**, all incoming API requests
should be **validated before processing**.

Option 1: Using Joi for Validation

Joi is a powerful validation library for JavaScript applications.

Step 1: Install Joi

```
npm install joi
```

Step 2: Create Validation Schema

Modify `routes/userRoutes.js`:

```
const Joi = require("joi");

const userSchema = Joi.object({
    name: Joi.string().min(3).required(),
    email: Joi.string().email().required(),
    age:
Joi.number().integer().min(18).max(100).required()
```

```
});
```

Step 3: Apply Validation to a Route

```
app.post("/users", async (req, res, next) => {
    const { error } = userSchema.validate(req.body,
{ abortEarly: false });

    if (error) {
        return res.status(400).json({
            error: "Validation Error",
            details: error.details.map(err => ({
                field: err.path[0],
                message: err.message
            }))
        });
    }

    try {
        const user = await User.create(req.body);
        res.status(201).json(user);
    } catch (err) {
        next({ status: 500, message: "Database
error", details: err.message });
    }
});
```

Now, if a user submits an invalid request, they'll get **detailed validation errors**:

```
{
  "error": "Validation Error",
  "details": [
    { "field": "name", "message": "\"name\" is
required" },
    { "field": "email", "message": "\"email\" must
be a valid email" }
  ]
}
```

Option 2: Using Express Validator

Express Validator is another great validation library for Express applications.

Step 1: Install Express Validator

```
npm install express-validator
```

Step 2: Apply Middleware Validation

Modify `routes/userRoutes.js`:

```
const { body, validationResult } =
require("express-validator");

app.post("/users",
    [
        body("name").isLength({ min: 3
}).withMessage("Name must be at least 3 characters
long"),

body("email").isEmail().withMessage("Invalid email
format"),
        body("age").isInt({ min: 18, max: 100
}).withMessage("Age must be between 18 and 100")
    ],
    (req, res, next) => {
        const errors = validationResult(req);
        if (!errors.isEmpty()) {
            return res.status(400).json({ error:
"Validation Error", details: errors.array() });
        }
        next();
    },
    async (req, res, next) => {
        try {
            const user = await
User.create(req.body);
            res.status(201).json(user);
        } catch (err) {
            next({ status: 500, message: "Database
error", details: err.message });
        }
    }
);
```

Handling Rate Limiting and Security Measures

To **prevent API abuse**, implement rate limiting.

Step 1: Install Express Rate Limit

```
npm install express-rate-limit
```

Step 2: Apply Rate Limiting Middleware

Modify `server.js`:

```
const rateLimit = require("express-rate-limit");

const limiter = rateLimit({
    windowMs: 15 * 60 * 1000, // 15 minutes
    max: 100 // Max 100 requests per 15 minutes per
IP
});

app.use("/api", limiter);
```

Now, each IP can make **100 requests per 15 minutes**, helping **protect against brute-force attacks**.

By following these best practices, you ensure **a smooth, secure, and efficient API experience** for users and developers alike.

Rate Limiting and API Security

APIs are the backbone of modern applications, enabling data exchange between clients and servers. However, **without proper security measures**, APIs become vulnerable to **brute-force attacks, abuse, and unauthorized access**. To protect APIs from such threats, **rate limiting and security best practices** must be implemented.

Rate limiting **controls the number of API requests** a user or client can make within a specified timeframe. This prevents:

Brute-force attacks (e.g., trying thousands of passwords to break into an account).

DDoS attacks (Distributed Denial of Service, where attackers flood an API with requests).

Excessive API usage (one user consuming too many resources, affecting others).

How Rate Limiting Works

The API **tracks the number of requests** from each client (IP address, user ID, or API key).

If requests exceed the allowed limit, the server **returns a** `429 Too Many Requests` **error**.

The client must **wait** before making further requests.

Implementing Rate Limiting in Express.js

Step 1: Install Express Rate Limit

```
npm install express-rate-limit
```

Step 2: Apply Rate Limiting to the API

Modify `server.js` to include **rate limiting middleware**:

```
const express = require("express");
const rateLimit = require("express-rate-limit");

const app = express();

// Apply rate limiting
const limiter = rateLimit({
    windowMs: 15 * 60 * 1000, // 15 minutes
    max: 100, // Limit each IP to 100 requests per
windowMs
    message: "Too many requests from this IP,
please try again later."
});

app.use("/api", limiter);

app.get("/api/data", (req, res) => {
    res.json({ message: "You have access to the
API!" });
});
```

```
app.listen(3000, () => {
    console.log("Server running on
http://localhost:3000");
});
```

Now, each **IP address** can make a maximum of **100 requests per 15 minutes**. If they exceed this limit, they receive:

```
{
  "message": "Too many requests from this IP,
please try again later."
}
```

API Security Best Practices

1. Enforce Authentication and Authorization

APIs should **never be publicly accessible** unless explicitly required. Every request must be authenticated using **API keys, JWT tokens, or OAuth tokens**.

Implementing JWT Authentication

```
npm install jsonwebtoken
```
Modify server.js to use JWT authentication:

```
const jwt = require("jsonwebtoken");

function authenticateToken(req, res, next) {
    const token =
req.header("Authorization")?.split(" ")[1];

    if (!token) return res.status(401).json({
message: "Access Denied" });

    jwt.verify(token, process.env.JWT_SECRET, (err,
user) => {
        if (err) return res.status(403).json({
message: "Invalid Token" });
        req.user = user;
        next();
    });
}
```

```
// Protected API route
app.get("/api/protected", authenticateToken, (req,
res) => {
    res.json({ message: "Welcome to the protected
API!", user: req.user });
});
```

Now, API consumers must send a **valid JWT token** to access
`/api/protected`.

2. Secure API Endpoints Against SQL and NoSQL Injection

Attackers may attempt **injection attacks** by manipulating API requests to
execute unauthorized database commands.

Preventing SQL Injection in PostgreSQL (Using Sequelize)

Instead of:

```
const user = await sequelize.query(`SELECT * FROM
users WHERE email = '${req.query.email}'`);
```

Use **parameterized queries**:

```
const user = await sequelize.query(
    "SELECT * FROM users WHERE email = ?",
    { replacements: [req.query.email], type:
sequelize.QueryTypes.SELECT }
);
```

Preventing NoSQL Injection in MongoDB (Using Mongoose)

Instead of:

```
const user = await User.find({ email:
req.query.email });
```

Use **strict type checks**:

```
const user = await User.findOne({ email:
req.query.email.toString() });
```

3. Validate API Inputs to Prevent Malicious Requests

213

APIs should never **trust incoming data**. Always validate **body parameters, query parameters, and headers**.

Using Joi for Validation

```
npm install joi
```

Modify `routes/userRoutes.js` to validate requests:

```
const Joi = require("joi");

const userSchema = Joi.object({
    name: Joi.string().min(3).required(),
    email: Joi.string().email().required(),
    age:
Joi.number().integer().min(18).max(100).required()
});

router.post("/users", async (req, res) => {
    const { error } =
userSchema.validate(req.body);
    if (error) return res.status(400).json({ error:
"Validation Error", details: error.details });

    try {
        const user = await User.create(req.body);
        res.status(201).json(user);
    } catch (err) {
        res.status(500).json({ message: "Database
error", details: err.message });
    }
});
```

Now, if invalid data is sent, the API responds with **clear validation errors**.

4. Prevent Cross-Site Request Forgery (CSRF)

CSRF attacks trick authenticated users into executing **unwanted actions** on their accounts.

Step 1: Install CSRF Protection

```
npm install csurf
```

Step 2: Apply CSRF Middleware

Modify `server.js`:

```
const csrf = require("csurf");

const csrfProtection = csrf({ cookie: true });
app.use(csrfProtection);

app.get("/api/csrf-token", (req, res) => {
    res.json({ csrfToken: req.csrfToken() });
});
```

Clients must now send a **valid CSRF token** in their requests to prevent **forged requests**.

5. Use HTTPS to Encrypt API Traffic

APIs must always run on **HTTPS** to encrypt sensitive data. Never allow **HTTP** in production.

Redirect HTTP to HTTPS

Modify `server.js`:

```
app.use((req, res, next) => {
    if (req.headers["x-forwarded-proto"] !==
"https") {
        return res.redirect("https://" +
req.headers.host + req.url);
    }
    next();
});
```

6. Restrict Access Based on API Keys

Some APIs should be **accessible only via API keys**, allowing control over who can access the service.

Step 1: Generate API Keys for Clients

Assign API keys to users in your database:

```
const users = [
    { id: 1, name: "Alice", apiKey: "123abc456def"
}
```

```
];
```

Step 2: Validate API Keys in Requests

Modify `server.js`:

```
function checkApiKey(req, res, next) {
    const apiKey = req.header("x-api-key");
    const user = users.find(u => u.apiKey ===
apiKey);

    if (!user) return res.status(403).json({
message: "Invalid API Key" });
    req.user = user;
    next();
}

app.get("/api/secure-data", checkApiKey, (req, res)
=> {
    res.json({ message: "Authorized access", user:
req.user });
});
```

Now, clients must include a valid **API key** in the headers:

```
curl -H "x-api-key: 123abc456def"
http://localhost:3000/api/secure-data
```

By applying these **security best practices**, your API becomes **resistant to attacks**, ensuring **safe and efficient communication** between clients and servers.

Chapter 10: Integrating Node.js with Front-End Frameworks

Modern web applications are typically built using **a front-end framework (React, Vue, or Angular) to handle the user interface** and a **back-end server (Node.js) to manage business logic and data processing**. Understanding how these two parts communicate effectively is crucial for building **scalable, high-performance applications**.

How Frontend and Backend Communicate

In a modern web application, the **frontend** and **backend** must communicate effectively to exchange data and deliver a seamless user experience. The **frontend** is responsible for **presenting data** and interacting with users, while the **backend** handles **business logic, data storage, and security**.

To make this communication **efficient, secure, and scalable**, developers use **standardized methods and protocols** such as **REST APIs, GraphQL, WebSockets, and real-time messaging**.

What is the Frontend?

The frontend is the **user interface (UI)** that users interact with. It is built using technologies like:

HTML, CSS, JavaScript → Basic UI structure and styling.

Frontend frameworks like **React, Vue, or Angular** → Provide dynamic, interactive experiences.

The frontend is responsible for:

✓ **Displaying data** fetched from the backend.

✓ **Handling user input** (forms, buttons, events).

✓ **Sending API requests** to retrieve or modify data.

What is the Backend?

The backend is the **server-side application** that processes requests and manages data. It is built using:

Node.js, Python, Java, or PHP → Server-side programming languages.

Databases like MongoDB or PostgreSQL → Store and retrieve data.

The backend is responsible for:

✓ **Processing business logic** (e.g., authentication, payments, data analysis).

✓ **Handling database operations** (storing, updating, and deleting data).

✓ **Providing APIs** for the frontend to fetch and send data.

How APIs Enable Communication Between Frontend and Backend

An **API (Application Programming Interface)** acts as a bridge between the frontend and backend, allowing data to be exchanged using standardized methods.

RESTful APIs (Most Common Method of Communication)

RESTful APIs use **HTTP methods** to interact with the backend.

Example: REST API for a User Management System

HTTP Method	Endpoint	Purpose
GET	`/users`	Retrieve all users
GET	`/users/{id}`	Retrieve a specific user
POST	`/users`	Create a new user
PUT	`/users/{id}`	Update user details
DELETE	`/users/{id}`	Delete a user

Making API Requests from the Frontend

To fetch data from the backend, the frontend sends an **HTTP request** to an API endpoint. The backend processes the request and returns a **response**.

Example: Fetching Data from a Node.js API (Using JavaScript Fetch API)

```
fetch("http://localhost:3000/users")
    .then(response => response.json())
    .then(data => console.log(data))
    .catch(error => console.error("Error fetching
data:", error));
```

Example: A Basic Express.js API (Backend)

```
const express = require("express");
const app = express();
const PORT = 3000;

app.use(express.json());

const users = [
    { id: 1, name: "Alice", email:
"alice@example.com" },
    { id: 2, name: "Bob", email: "bob@example.com"
}
];

app.get("/users", (req, res) => {
    res.json(users);
});

app.listen(PORT, () => console.log(`Server running
on http://localhost:${PORT}`));
```

Now, when the frontend requests **GET** **/users**, the backend responds with:

```
[
    { "id": 1, "name": "Alice", "email":
"alice@example.com" },
    { "id": 2, "name": "Bob", "email":
"bob@example.com" }
]
```

The frontend can then **display this data in the UI dynamically**.

When to Use GraphQL Instead of REST

While REST APIs **return predefined responses**, GraphQL allows the frontend to **request exactly what it needs**, reducing over-fetching and under-fetching of data.

REST vs. GraphQL Example

REST API Call (Returns Full User Object)

```
{
    "id": 1,
    "name": "Alice",
    "email": "alice@example.com",
    "age": 30,
    "address": "123 Main St"
}
```

GraphQL Query (Fetch Only Needed Fields)

```
{
  user(id: 1) {
    name
    email
  }
}
```

GraphQL Response

```
{
    "user": {
        "name": "Alice",
        "email": "alice@example.com"
    }
}
```

Use GraphQL when:
✓ You need flexible data fetching.
✓ You want to avoid multiple API calls for related data.

Real-Time Communication with WebSockets

REST APIs are **request-response based**, meaning data updates only when requested. However, some applications (chat apps, live notifications) need **real-time updates**.

How WebSockets Work

WebSockets create a **persistent connection** between the frontend and backend, allowing **bi-directional communication**.

Example: Implementing WebSockets in Node.js

Step 1: Install WebSocket Library

```
npm install ws
```

Step 2: Create a WebSocket Server (Backend)

Modify `server.js`:

```
const WebSocket = require("ws");

const wss = new WebSocket.Server({ port: 8080 });

wss.on("connection", ws => {
    console.log("New client connected");

    ws.on("message", message => {
        console.log(`Received: ${message}`);
        ws.send(`Server received: ${message}`);
    });

    ws.on("close", () => {
        console.log("Client disconnected");
    });
});
```

Step 3: Connect from the Frontend

Modify `frontend.js`:

```
const socket = new
WebSocket("ws://localhost:8080");

socket.onopen = () => {
    console.log("Connected to server");
    socket.send("Hello from client!");
};

socket.onmessage = (event) => {
    console.log("Message from server:",
event.data);
```

```
};
```
Now, the frontend and backend can **send messages instantly**, enabling **real-time updates**.

Handling CORS Issues

When a frontend app (e.g., `http://localhost:3001`) tries to access an API on a different domain (e.g., `http://localhost:3000`), the browser **blocks the request** due to **Cross-Origin Resource Sharing (CORS) policy**.

Solution: Enable CORS in Node.js

Step 1: Install CORS Middleware

```
npm install cors
```
Step 2: Apply CORS Middleware in Express.js

Modify `server.js`:

```
const cors = require("cors");
app.use(cors());
```
Now, the frontend can successfully communicate with the backend **across different origins**.

With these principles and techniques, you can confidently **build and scale full-stack applications** where the frontend and backend work together seamlessly.

Connecting Node.js with React, Vue, and Angular

Modern web applications are often **built as full-stack solutions**, where a **backend (Node.js) manages data and business logic**, while a **frontend framework (React, Vue, or Angular) handles the user interface**. Ensuring **seamless communication** between the backend and frontend is crucial for building **efficient, scalable, and maintainable applications**.

Setting Up a Node.js API Backend

Before connecting to a frontend framework, we need a **backend API** that the frontend can communicate with.

Step 1: Create a Node.js Project

```
mkdir node-backend
cd node-backend
npm init -y
```

Step 2: Install Dependencies

```
npm install express cors mongoose dotenv body-parser
```

express → Web framework for handling API routes

cors → Allows cross-origin requests from frontend apps

mongoose → ORM for MongoDB (for database operations)

dotenv → Loads environment variables

body-parser → Parses incoming request bodies

Step 3: Set Up the Express Server

Create a file `server.js`:

```
require("dotenv").config();
const express = require("express");
const cors = require("cors");

const app = express();
app.use(express.json());
app.use(cors());

const PORT = process.env.PORT || 5000;

app.get("/api/users", (req, res) => {
    res.json([{ id: 1, name: "Alice" }, { id: 2,
name: "Bob" }]);
});

app.listen(PORT, () => {
```

```
    console.log(`Server running on
http://localhost:${PORT}`);
});
```

Step 4: Start the Backend Server

```
node server.js
```
Your backend is now running at `http://localhost:5000/api/users`.

Connecting Node.js with React

Step 1: Create a React App

```
npx create-react-app frontend
cd frontend
npm start
```

Step 2: Fetch Data from the Node.js API

Modify `src/App.js` to fetch user data from the backend:

```
import React, { useEffect, useState } from "react";

function App() {
    const [users, setUsers] = useState([]);

    useEffect(() => {
        fetch("http://localhost:5000/api/users")
            .then(res => res.json())
            .then(data => setUsers(data))
            .catch(error => console.error("Error
fetching data:", error));
    }, []);

    return (
        <div>
            <h1>User List</h1>
            <ul>
                {users.map(user => (
                    <li
key={user.id}>{user.name}</li>
                ))}
            </ul>
```

```
      </div>
    );
}

export default App;
```

Step 3: Run the React App

```
npm start
```

Your React app now fetches data from the Node.js backend and displays it in a **user list**.

Connecting Node.js with Vue.js

Step 1: Create a Vue App

```
npm install -g @vue/cli
vue create frontend
cd frontend
npm run serve
```

Step 2: Fetch Data in a Vue Component

Modify `src/components/UserList.vue`:

```
<template>
    <div>
        <h1>User List</h1>
        <ul>
            <li v-for="user in users"
:key="user.id">{{ user.name }}</li>
        </ul>
    </div>
</template>

<script>
export default {
    data() {
        return { users: [] };
    },
    mounted() {
        fetch("http://localhost:5000/api/users")
            .then(res => res.json())
```

```
            .then(data => { this.users = data; })
            .catch(error => console.error("Error
fetching data:", error));
    }
};
</script>
```

Step 3: Run the Vue App

```
npm run serve
```

Now, Vue will fetch and display user data from the **Node.js API**.

Connecting Node.js with Angular

Step 1: Create an Angular App

```
ng new frontend
cd frontend
ng serve
```

Step 2: Install HTTP Client for API Requests

```
npm install @angular/common
```

Step 3: Create a Service to Fetch API Data

Modify `src/app/user.service.ts`:

```
import { Injectable } from "@angular/core";
import { HttpClient } from "@angular/common/http";
import { Observable } from "rxjs";

@Injectable({ providedIn: "root" })
export class UserService {
    constructor(private http: HttpClient) {}

    getUsers(): Observable<any> {
        return
this.http.get("http://localhost:5000/api/users");
    }
}
```

Step 4: Fetch and Display Data in Angular Component

Modify `src/app/app.component.ts`:

```
import { Component, OnInit } from "@angular/core";
import { UserService } from "./user.service";

@Component({
    selector: "app-root",
    template: `
        <h1>User List</h1>
        <ul>
            <li *ngFor="let user of users">{{
user.name }}</li>
        </ul>
    `
})
export class AppComponent implements OnInit {
    users: any[] = [];

    constructor(private userService: UserService)
{}

    ngOnInit() {
        this.userService.getUsers().subscribe(data
=> {
            this.users = data;
        });
    }
}
```

Step 5: Run the Angular App

```
ng serve
```

Now, **Angular** will successfully retrieve data from **Node.js** and display it dynamically.

Best Practices for Connecting Node.js with Frontend Frameworks

1. Use Environment Variables for API URLs

Instead of hardcoding API URLs, use environment variables:

React (.env file)

```
REACT_APP_API_URL=http://localhost:5000
```
Then use it in `App.js`:

```
fetch(`${process.env.REACT_APP_API_URL}/api/users`)
```
Vue (.env file)

```
VUE_APP_API_URL=http://localhost:5000
```
Then use it in `UserList.vue`:

```
fetch(`${process.env.VUE_APP_API_URL}/api/users`)
```
Angular (environment.ts)

```
export const environment = {
  production: false,
  apiUrl: "http://localhost:5000"
};
```

Then use it in `user.service.ts`:

```
this.http.get(`${environment.apiUrl}/api/users`);
```

2. Handle API Errors Properly

Always check for errors in API requests:

```
fetch("http://localhost:5000/api/users")
    .then(res => {
        if (!res.ok) throw new Error("Failed to
fetch data");
        return res.json();
    })
    .catch(error => console.error("API Error:",
error));
```

3. Secure API Requests with Authentication

Use JWT authentication to protect API routes.

```
fetch("http://localhost:5000/api/protected", {
    headers: { Authorization: `Bearer
${localStorage.getItem("token")}` }
});
```

4. Enable CORS for Cross-Origin Requests

Modify `server.js` to allow frontend requests:

```
const cors = require("cors");
app.use(cors());
```

By integrating **Node.js with frontend frameworks**, you can build **scalable, efficient, and maintainable full-stack applications**.

Best Practices for API Consumption in Frontend Apps

When building modern frontend applications, **consuming APIs efficiently** is just as important as **building them correctly**. A well-structured frontend should fetch data from the backend **securely, efficiently, and in a user-friendly manner**.

1. Making API Requests Efficiently

Use Async/Await for Readable and Maintainable Code

Instead of using **callback-based fetch requests**, use **async/await** to make code more readable and easier to debug.

Example: Fetching Data from an API

```
async function fetchUsers() {
    try {
        const response = await
fetch("https://api.example.com/users");
        if (!response.ok) throw new Error("Network
response was not OK");
        const data = await response.json();
        console.log(data);
    } catch (error) {
        console.error("Error fetching users:",
error);
    }
}

fetchUsers();
```

✓ Handles errors properly

✓ More readable than `.then()` chaining

Use Axios for Simpler API Calls

Axios is a popular HTTP client that provides **automatic JSON parsing, request cancellation, and timeout handling**.

Step 1: Install Axios

```
npm install axios
```

Step 2: Fetch API Data Using Axios

```
import axios from "axios";

async function fetchUsers() {
    try {
        const response = await
axios.get("https://api.example.com/users");
        console.log(response.data);
    } catch (error) {
        console.error("API request failed:",
error.message);
    }
}

fetchUsers();
```

✓ Axios automatically parses JSON responses

✓ Handles request timeouts more efficiently

2. Handling API Errors and User Feedback

Check for HTTP Response Status Codes

An API request might **succeed in making a request** but fail due to issues like **authentication failure or missing data**.

Example: Handling Different Error Cases

```
async function fetchData() {
    try {
```

```
        const response = await
fetch("https://api.example.com/data");

        if (!response.ok) {
            if (response.status === 401) throw new
Error("Unauthorized: Please log in");
            if (response.status === 404) throw new
Error("Data not found");
            throw new Error("An unknown error
occurred");
        }

        const data = await response.json();
        console.log(data);
    } catch (error) {
        console.error("API Error:", error.message);
    }
}

fetchData();
```

✓ **Properly handles common HTTP errors** (401, 404, 500)

✓ **Prevents application crashes due to failed requests**

Show User-Friendly Messages Instead of Raw Errors

Instead of displaying raw error logs, **show meaningful messages to users**.

Example: Displaying Error Messages in React

```
import { useState, useEffect } from "react";
import axios from "axios";

function App() {
    const [users, setUsers] = useState([]);
    const [error, setError] = useState("");

    useEffect(() => {
        axios.get("https://api.example.com/users")
            .then(res => setUsers(res.data))
            .catch(err => setError("Failed to load
users. Please try again later."));
    }, []);
```

231

```
    return (
        <div>
            <h1>User List</h1>
            {error && <p style={{ color: "red"
}}>{error}</p>}
            <ul>
                {users.map(user => (
                    <li
key={user.id}>{user.name}</li>
                ))}
            </ul>
        </div>
    );
}

export default App;
```

✓ Provides user-friendly error messages

✓ Prevents displaying cryptic error logs to users

3. Optimizing Performance with Caching and Pagination

Use Caching to Avoid Unnecessary API Calls

If the same data is frequently requested, **cache it in local storage or memory** to **reduce API load** and improve **performance**.

Example: Using Local Storage for Caching

```
async function fetchUsers() {
    const cachedUsers =
localStorage.getItem("users");

    if (cachedUsers) {
        console.log("Using cached data:",
JSON.parse(cachedUsers));
        return;
    }

    try {
        const response = await
fetch("https://api.example.com/users");
```

```
        const data = await response.json();
        localStorage.setItem("users",
JSON.stringify(data));
        console.log("Fetched new data:", data);
    } catch (error) {
        console.error("Error fetching users:",
error);
    }
}

fetchUsers();
```

✓ Reduces redundant API requests

✓ Improves app performance and responsiveness

Use Pagination to Fetch Large Datasets in Chunks

Fetching too much data at once can slow down the frontend. Instead, use **pagination** to **load data in chunks**.

Example: Fetching Paginated Data

```
async function fetchUsers(page = 1, limit = 10) {
    try {
        const response = await
fetch(`https://api.example.com/users?page=${page}&l
imit=${limit}`);
        const data = await response.json();
        console.log(`Page ${page}:`, data);
    } catch (error) {
        console.error("Error fetching paginated
users:", error);
    }
}

fetchUsers(1, 10);
```

✓ Prevents overloading the API with unnecessary data

✓ Improves frontend rendering speed

4. Securing API Requests

Use JWT Authentication for Protected Routes

For protected routes, include **JWT tokens** in requests.

Example: Sending JWT in API Requests

```
async function fetchProtectedData() {
    const token = localStorage.getItem("token");

    if (!token) {
        console.error("User not authenticated");
        return;
    }

    try {
        const response = await
fetch("https://api.example.com/protected", {
            headers: { Authorization: `Bearer
${token}` }
        });
        const data = await response.json();
        console.log("Protected data:", data);
    } catch (error) {
        console.error("Error fetching protected
data:", error);
    }
}

fetchProtectedData();
```

Ensures only authenticated users can access protected API routes

Prevent API Abuse with Rate Limiting

APIs should **limit how often users can make requests** to **prevent abuse**.

Example: Rate Limiting in Express Backend

```
const rateLimit = require("express-rate-limit");

const limiter = rateLimit({
    windowMs: 15 * 60 * 1000, // 15 minutes
    max: 100, // Limit each IP to 100 requests per
15 minutes
```

```
     message: "Too many requests, please try again
later."
});

app.use("/api", limiter);
```

Protects APIs from brute-force attacks
Ensures fair usage across all users

By applying these **best practices**, your frontend application will interact **efficiently and securely** with APIs, ensuring **a smooth user experience** and **optimal backend performance**.

Handling CORS Issues

When developing web applications, you may have encountered the **CORS (Cross-Origin Resource Sharing) error** while making requests to an API. The **browser blocks the request** because the frontend and backend are on **different origins**.

By default, **browsers enforce the Same-Origin Policy (SOP)** to protect users from malicious scripts that try to access sensitive data from different origins.

An **origin** consists of:

Protocol (e.g., `http`, `https`)

Domain (e.g., `example.com`)

Port (e.g., `:3000`)

If a frontend running on `http://localhost:3001` makes a request to a backend at `http://localhost:3000`, the browser **blocks the request** because the origins are different.

CORS (Cross-Origin Resource Sharing) as a Solution

CORS is a **mechanism that allows servers to specify which origins are permitted to access their resources**. The backend **sends HTTP headers** instructing the browser to allow or block requests.

Recognizing CORS Errors

When a frontend application tries to make a request to a backend API from a different origin, the browser might display errors like:

```
Access to fetch at 'http://localhost:3000/api/data'
from origin 'http://localhost:3001' has been
blocked by CORS policy
```

This means the server has **not included the proper CORS headers** in the response.

Now, let's **fix this issue in a Node.js and Express application**.

Enabling CORS in Node.js and Express

Method 1: Using the CORS Middleware (Recommended)

The easiest way to handle CORS is by using the `cors` package in Express.js.

Step 1: Install the CORS Package

```
npm install cors
```

Step 2: Enable CORS in Express

Modify `server.js`:

```
const express = require("express");
const cors = require("cors");

const app = express();

// Enable CORS for all requests
app.use(cors());

app.get("/api/data", (req, res) => {
    res.json({ message: "CORS enabled API
response!" });
});

app.listen(3000, () => {
    console.log("Server running on
http://localhost:3000");
});
```

Now, the backend will **allow all origins** to access the API.

Testing the Fix

From the frontend (running on `http://localhost:3001`), make a fetch request:

```
fetch("http://localhost:3000/api/data")
    .then(response => response.json())
    .then(data => console.log(data))
    .catch(error => console.error("CORS Error:",
error));
```

If CORS is configured correctly, the response will be:

```
{ "message": "CORS enabled API response!" }
```

Method 2: Restricting Access to Specific Origins

Instead of allowing **all origins**, you can **restrict access** to only specific frontend domains.

Modify CORS Configuration to Allow Only Certain Origins

```
const corsOptions = {
    origin: "http://localhost:3001", // Only allow
requests from this frontend
    methods: "GET,POST,PUT,DELETE", // Specify
allowed HTTP methods
    allowedHeaders: "Content-Type,Authorization" //
Specify allowed headers
};

app.use(cors(corsOptions));
```

Now, only requests from **http://localhost:3001** will be allowed. Requests from any other domain will be blocked.

Method 3: Handling CORS Manually (Without Middleware)

If you don't want to use the `cors` package, you can manually set CORS headers.

Modify `server.js`:

```
app.use((req, res, next) => {
    res.header("Access-Control-Allow-Origin",
"http://localhost:3001"); // Allow only frontend
domain
    res.header("Access-Control-Allow-Methods",
"GET,POST,PUT,DELETE"); // Allowed HTTP methods
    res.header("Access-Control-Allow-Headers",
"Content-Type,Authorization"); // Allowed headers
    next();
});
```

This **manually sets CORS headers**, but using the `cors` package is recommended for flexibility.

Handling Preflight Requests (OPTIONS Method)

Some requests, like **PUT, DELETE, and requests with custom headers**, trigger a **preflight request** before sending the actual request.

To handle this, ensure the backend responds to **OPTIONS** requests:

```
app.options("*", cors()); // Handle preflight
requests
```
Or, manually set up an OPTIONS route:

```
app.options("*", (req, res) => {
    res.header("Access-Control-Allow-Origin",
"http://localhost:3001");
    res.header("Access-Control-Allow-Methods",
"GET, POST, PUT, DELETE");
    res.header("Access-Control-Allow-Headers",
"Content-Type, Authorization");
    res.sendStatus(204);
});
```
This tells the browser that the server **accepts CORS requests** and which methods/headers are allowed.

CORS with Authentication (JWT or API Keys)

If your API requires authentication, ensure the **Authorization header is allowed** in CORS settings.

Modify `corsOptions` to allow authentication headers:

```
const corsOptions = {
    origin: "http://localhost:3001",
    methods: "GET,POST,PUT,DELETE",
    allowedHeaders: "Content-Type,Authorization"
};

app.use(cors(corsOptions));
```

Now, the frontend can **send JWT tokens** in API requests:

```
fetch("http://localhost:3000/api/protected", {
    method: "GET",
    headers: {
        "Authorization": `Bearer
${localStorage.getItem("token")}`
    }
})
.then(response => response.json())
.then(data => console.log(data))
.catch(error => console.error("CORS Error:",
error));
```

Common CORS Issues and Fixes

1. The Backend Does Not Have CORS Enabled

Fix: Install the `cors` package and use `app.use(cors())`.

2. Requests Are Blocked for Specific HTTP Methods (PUT, DELETE)

Fix: Handle **preflight requests** by enabling the `OPTIONS` method.

3. Frontend Fails to Include Authentication Headers

Fix: Ensure `Authorization` is added to `Access-Control-Allow-Headers`.

4. APIs Work in Postman but Fail in the Browser

Fix: Postman doesn't enforce CORS, but browsers do. Enable CORS on the backend.

Best Practices for Handling CORS Securely

✓ **Allow only trusted origins** → Instead of *, allow specific frontend domains.

✓ **Use OPTIONS for preflight requests** → Ensure the server correctly handles them.

✓ **Allow authentication headers** → If using JWT, ensure `Authorization` is permitted.

✓ **Use HTTPS** → Secure requests to prevent security vulnerabilities.

✓ **Test CORS configurations** → Use the browser console to debug CORS errors.

By implementing **proper CORS handling**, you ensure **secure and seamless communication** between your frontend and backend, allowing users to interact with your application without errors or security risks.

Chapter 11: Real-Time Applications with WebSockets

Modern web applications are no longer just about static pages and request-response interactions. Users expect **instant updates**, whether it's in **live chat, notifications, collaborative editing, or real-time dashboards**. Traditional HTTP APIs aren't designed for continuous data flow, and that's where **WebSockets** come in.

WebSockets and the Need for Real-Time Communication

The web has evolved significantly from simple static pages to highly interactive applications that demand **instant updates**. Traditional HTTP-based communication, while effective for many tasks, is not designed for **real-time interactions**.

For applications like **live chat, stock market updates, collaborative editing, multiplayer games, and IoT**, users expect **instantaneous data exchange** without refreshing the page or making repeated requests. This is where **WebSockets** come in.

The Problem with Traditional HTTP Communication

How Traditional APIs Work

Most web applications rely on **REST APIs** or **GraphQL APIs**, which follow a **request-response model**:

The **client (frontend)** makes a request (`GET /messages`).

The **server (backend)** processes the request and returns a response.

The connection **closes** after the response is sent.

While this model works well for **static content and database operations**, it is inefficient for applications that need **real-time updates**.

Why Traditional HTTP Falls Short

Let's say we are building a **chat application** using only REST APIs. We have two options:

Option 1: Polling (Frequent API Requests)

The frontend continuously sends requests **every few seconds**:

```
setInterval(() => {
    fetch("https://api.example.com/messages")
        .then(res => res.json())
        .then(data => console.log("New messages:",
data));
}, 5000);
```

Issues with Polling:

High server load → Even if no new messages arrive, the server gets **constant requests**.

Delays in updates → New messages only appear **after the next request cycle**.

Bandwidth waste → The client fetches **duplicate data** in every request.

Option 2: Long Polling (Keeping the Connection Open)

Instead of frequent requests, the client makes a **request that stays open** until new data is available:

```
fetch("https://api.example.com/messages")
    .then(res => res.json())
    .then(data => {
        console.log("New messages:", data);
        fetchMessages(); // Make another request
immediately
    });
```

Issues with Long Polling:

More efficient than simple polling, but still inefficient.

Each request keeps a connection open, consuming server resources.

Not scalable for thousands of users.

To solve these issues, we need **WebSockets**, which enable real-time, bidirectional communication.

What Are WebSockets?

WebSockets are a **protocol that allows persistent, full-duplex communication between a client and a server**. Unlike HTTP, which follows a **request-response cycle**, WebSockets allow **both parties to send messages at any time** without closing the connection.

How WebSockets Work

The **client (browser)** sends a **WebSocket handshake request** to the server.

If the server **accepts the request**, a **persistent connection** is established.

Both the **client and server** can **send messages at any time**, without additional requests.

Benefits of WebSockets:

✓ **Real-time updates** → Data is pushed **instantly** when available.

✓ **Less server load** → No need for **constant polling requests**.

✓ **Efficient bandwidth usage** → Data is sent **only when necessary**.

✓ **Persistent connection** → Once connected, the **client and server can communicate freely**.

WebSockets vs. HTTP: Key Differences

Feature	HTTP (REST API)	WebSockets
Communication Type	Request-Response	Bidirectional
Connection	Closes after each request	Stays open
Data Flow	Client requests, server responds	Both client & server can send data anytime

Feature	HTTP (REST API)	WebSockets
Latency	Higher (Polling needed)	Low (Instant updates)
Use Case	Static pages, CRUD operations	Chat, live notifications, gaming

When to Use WebSockets

Live chat applications

Real-time dashboards (Stock prices, analytics, IoT updates)

Multiplayer online games

Live notifications

Collaborative document editing (Google Docs-style apps)

Implementing a WebSocket Server with Node.js

Now, let's build a **simple WebSocket server** using Node.js and the **ws** library.

Step 1: Install WebSockets Library

```
npm install ws
```

Step 2: Create a WebSocket Server

Modify server.js:

```
const WebSocket = require("ws");

const wss = new WebSocket.Server({ port: 8080 });

wss.on("connection", ws => {
    console.log("New client connected");

    ws.on("message", message => {
        console.log("Received:", message);
        ws.send(`Server received: ${message}`); // Send response
    });
```

```
    ws.on("close", () => {
        console.log("Client disconnected");
    });
});

console.log("WebSocket server running on
ws://localhost:8080");
```

When a **client connects**, the server logs the connection.

When a **message is received**, the server **sends a response back**.

When the **client disconnects**, the server logs it.

Step 3: Connect from a WebSocket Client

Create an `index.html` file to test the WebSocket connection:

```
<!DOCTYPE html>
<html lang="en">
<head>
    <meta charset="UTF-8">
    <title>WebSocket Test</title>
</head>
<body>
    <h1>WebSocket Connection</h1>
    <input id="message" type="text"
placeholder="Type a message">
    <button onclick="sendMessage()">Send</button>
    <ul id="messages"></ul>

    <script>
        const socket = new
WebSocket("ws://localhost:8080");

        socket.onopen = () => {
            console.log("Connected to WebSocket
server");
        };

        socket.onmessage = (event) => {
            const li =
document.createElement("li");
            li.textContent = event.data;
```

```
document.getElementById("messages").appendChild(li)
;
        };

        function sendMessage() {
            const message =
document.getElementById("message").value;
            socket.send(message);
        }
    </script>
</body>
</html>
```

Now, open **multiple browser tabs** and type messages. The messages will be **instantly sent and received** between all connected clients.

Real-World Example: Building a Real-Time Notification System

Let's extend our WebSocket server to **send notifications** to connected clients.

Modify `server.js`:

```
setInterval(() => {
    wss.clients.forEach(client => {
        if (client.readyState === WebSocket.OPEN) {
            client.send(`Notification at ${new
Date().toLocaleTimeString()}`);
        }
    });
}, 5000);
```

Now, every **5 seconds**, all connected clients receive a **real-time notification**.

With WebSockets, you can build **interactive, real-time applications** that **engage users instantly**. Whether it's **chat apps, stock updates, or live notifications**, WebSockets provide a **fast, scalable** solution for modern web applications.

Implementing Socket.io for Real-Time Features

Web applications have evolved beyond traditional **request-response interactions**. Today, users expect **instant updates** in chat applications, live notifications, real-time dashboards, and collaborative tools.

Socket.io is a powerful library that enables **real-time, bidirectional communication** between a client and a server, making it an ideal choice for building interactive web applications.

Why Use Socket.io?

Socket.io provides an abstraction over **WebSockets**, handling complexities such as:

✓ **Automatic reconnection** if the connection is lost.

✓ **Fallback mechanisms** to work even in older browsers.

✓ **Event-based communication**, making it easy to manage messages.

✓ **Room-based broadcasting**, enabling private and group interactions.

How Does Socket.io Work?

The **client connects** to the server using Socket.io.

A persistent **WebSocket connection is established**.

The **client and server can send and receive messages at any time**.

The connection remains **open**, allowing real-time updates without repeated requests.

Setting Up a Real-Time Node.js Server with Socket.io

Step 1: Install Dependencies

First, create a new project and install required packages:

```
mkdir socket-io-app
cd socket-io-app
npm init -y
npm install express socket.io cors
```

express → For creating the server.

socket.io → Enables real-time communication.

cors → Allows frontend applications to communicate with the backend.

Step 2: Create a WebSocket Server Using Socket.io

Modify `server.js`:

```
const express = require("express");
const http = require("http");
const socketIo = require("socket.io");
const cors = require("cors");

const app = express();
const server = http.createServer(app);
const io = socketIo(server, {
    cors: {
        origin: "*",
        methods: ["GET", "POST"]
    }
});

const PORT = process.env.PORT || 3000;

app.use(cors());

// Handle WebSocket connections
io.on("connection", (socket) => {
    console.log("New client connected:",
socket.id);

    // Handle incoming messages
    socket.on("message", (data) => {
        console.log("Received message:", data);
        io.emit("message", data); // Broadcast to
all clients
    });

    socket.on("disconnect", () => {
        console.log("Client disconnected:",
socket.id);
    });
});

server.listen(PORT, () => {
```

```
    console.log(`WebSocket server running on
http://localhost:${PORT}`);
});
```

✓ **Creates a WebSocket server** using Socket.io.

✓ **Listens for messages and broadcasts them to all connected clients**.

✓ **Handles client connections and disconnections**.

Step 3: Connect a Frontend to the WebSocket Server

Basic HTML Frontend for WebSocket Communication

Create an `index.html` file to test real-time messaging:

```html
<!DOCTYPE html>
<html lang="en">
<head>
    <meta charset="UTF-8">
    <title>WebSocket Chat</title>
    <script
src="https://cdn.socket.io/4.0.1/socket.io.min.js">
</script>
</head>
<body>
    <h1>WebSocket Chat</h1>
    <input id="message" type="text"
placeholder="Type a message">
    <button onclick="sendMessage()">Send</button>
    <ul id="messages"></ul>

    <script>
        const socket = io("http://localhost:3000");

        socket.on("connect", () => {
            console.log("Connected to WebSocket
server");
        });

        socket.on("message", (data) => {
            const li =
document.createElement("li");
            li.textContent = data;
```

```
document.getElementById("messages").appendChild(li)
;
        });

        function sendMessage() {
            const message =
document.getElementById("message").value;
            socket.emit("message", message);
        }
    </script>
</body>
</html>
```

✓ Allows users to send and receive messages in real time.

✓ Displays incoming messages instantly without page refresh.

Building a Real-Time Chat Application

Now, let's extend our WebSocket server to **support multiple users** and **display sender names**.

Step 1: Modify Server to Handle Usernames

Update server.js to store usernames:

```
io.on("connection", (socket) => {
    console.log("New user connected:", socket.id);

    // Set username
    socket.on("setUsername", (username) => {
        socket.username = username;
    });

    // Handle messages
    socket.on("message", (data) => {
        io.emit("message", { user: socket.username
|| "Anonymous", text: data });
    });

    socket.on("disconnect", () => {
        console.log("User disconnected:",
socket.id);
```

```
    });
});
```

Step 2: Update Frontend to Set Usernames

Modify `index.html` to ask for a username:

```html
<input id="username" type="text" placeholder="Enter
your name">
<button onclick="setUsername()">Set Name</button>

<script>
    function setUsername() {
        const username =
document.getElementById("username").value;
        socket.emit("setUsername", username);
    }
</script>
```

Now, users can **set a username**, and messages will **include the sender's name**.

Implementing Real-Time Notifications

Now, let's send **live notifications** to users when someone joins the chat.

Step 1: Update Server to Broadcast Join Notifications

Modify `server.js`:

```js
io.on("connection", (socket) => {
    console.log("User connected:", socket.id);

    // Notify all users when someone joins
    io.emit("notification", "A new user has joined
the chat");

    socket.on("disconnect", () => {
        console.log("User disconnected:",
socket.id);
        io.emit("notification", "A user has left
the chat");
    });
});
```

Step 2: Update Frontend to Listen for Notifications

Modify `index.html`:

```
socket.on("notification", (message) => {
    alert(message);
});
```

Now, when a user joins or leaves, all users **receive a real-time notification**.

Handling Reconnection and Optimization

Automatically Reconnect on Disconnection

Modify `index.html`:

```
const socket = io("http://localhost:3000", {
reconnectionAttempts: 5 });

socket.on("connect", () => {
    console.log("Connected to server");
});

socket.on("disconnect", () => {
    console.log("Disconnected. Trying to
reconnect...");
});
```

Ensures users automatically reconnect if they get disconnected.

By leveraging **Socket.io**, you can build **interactive applications** such as **live chat, real-time dashboards, collaborative tools, and multiplayer games**, bringing a **seamless experience** to your users.

Building a Live Chat Application

Live chat applications have become an essential feature in **social platforms, customer support systems, and team collaboration tools**. Unlike traditional request-response communication, chat apps require **real-time data transfer** to ensure messages are delivered instantly without delays.

To achieve this, we will use **Socket.io**, which enables **persistent, two-way communication** between users and a central server.

Before we build the frontend, we need to create a **WebSocket server** that will manage user connections and message exchanges.

Step 1: Install Dependencies

First, initialize a Node.js project and install the required packages:

```
mkdir live-chat
cd live-chat
npm init -y
npm install express socket.io cors
```

express → Manages the HTTP server.

socket.io → Handles WebSocket communication.

cors → Allows cross-origin requests from the frontend.

Step 2: Create the WebSocket Server

Now, create a `server.js` file and configure Socket.io.

```
const express = require("express");
const http = require("http");
const socketIo = require("socket.io");
const cors = require("cors");

const app = express();
const server = http.createServer(app);
const io = socketIo(server, {
    cors: {
        origin: "*",
        methods: ["GET", "POST"]
    }
});

const PORT = process.env.PORT || 3000;
const users = {}; // Store connected users

app.use(cors());

io.on("connection", (socket) => {
```

```
    console.log(`User connected: ${socket.id}`);

    // Handle user joining with a username
    socket.on("setUsername", (username) => {
        users[socket.id] = username;
        io.emit("userList", Object.values(users));
        io.emit("notification", `${username} joined
the chat`);
    });

    // Handle incoming messages
    socket.on("message", (data) => {
        io.emit("message", { user: users[socket.id]
|| "Anonymous", text: data });
    });

    // Handle user disconnection
    socket.on("disconnect", () => {
        const username = users[socket.id];
        delete users[socket.id];
        io.emit("userList", Object.values(users));
        io.emit("notification", `${username} left
the chat`);
        console.log(`User disconnected:
${socket.id}`);
    });
});

server.listen(PORT, () => {
    console.log(`Chat server running on
http://localhost:${PORT}`);
});
```

How It Works

✓ **Handles user connections and stores usernames**

✓ **Broadcasts messages to all connected users**

✓ **Sends notifications when users join or leave**

✓ **Maintains a list of active users**

Now, let's build the **frontend** to connect and interact with this server.

Building the Frontend

For this, we will use **HTML, JavaScript, and Socket.io** to create a simple chat interface.

Step 1: Create `index.html`

```
<!DOCTYPE html>
<html lang="en">
<head>
    <meta charset="UTF-8">
    <title>Live Chat</title>
    <script
src="https://cdn.socket.io/4.0.1/socket.io.min.js">
</script>
    <style>
        body { font-family: Arial, sans-serif; }
        #chat-container { width: 50%; margin: auto;
}
        #messages { list-style: none; padding: 0; }
        #messages li { padding: 8px; border-bottom:
1px solid #ddd; }
        #user-list { margin-top: 20px; }
        #notification { color: green; font-style:
italic; }
    </style>
</head>
<body>
    <div id="chat-container">
        <h2>Live Chat</h2>
        <p id="notification"></p>
        <input id="username" type="text"
placeholder="Enter your name">
        <button onclick="setUsername()">Set
Name</button>
        <br><br>
        <input id="message" type="text"
placeholder="Type a message">
        <button
onclick="sendMessage()">Send</button>
        <ul id="messages"></ul>
        <h3>Active Users</h3>
        <ul id="user-list"></ul>
```

```
    </div>

    <script>
        const socket = io("http://localhost:3000");

        socket.on("connect", () => {
            console.log("Connected to chat
server");
        });

        function setUsername() {
            const username =
document.getElementById("username").value;
            socket.emit("setUsername", username);
        }

        function sendMessage() {
            const message =
document.getElementById("message").value;
            socket.emit("message", message);

document.getElementById("message").value = "";
        }

        socket.on("message", (data) => {
            const li =
document.createElement("li");
            li.textContent = `${data.user}:
${data.text}`;

document.getElementById("messages").appendChild(li)
;
        });

        socket.on("notification", (message) => {
document.getElementById("notification").textContent
= message;
            setTimeout(() => {
document.getElementById("notification").textContent
= "";
```

```
        }, 5000);
    });

        socket.on("userList", (users) => {
            const userList =
document.getElementById("user-list");
            userList.innerHTML = "";
            users.forEach(user => {
                const li =
document.createElement("li");
                li.textContent = user;
                userList.appendChild(li);
            });
        });
    </script>
</body>
</html>
```

How It Works

✓ **Users can set their usernames**.

✓ **Messages are sent and displayed instantly**.

✓ **Users see notifications when someone joins or leaves**.

✓ **A list of active users is displayed in real time**.

Running the Live Chat Application

Step 1: Start the Backend

```
node server.js
```

Step 2: Open `index.html` in Multiple Browser Tabs

Enter a username and send messages.

Messages will appear instantly across all tabs.

When a user joins or leaves, notifications will be displayed.

Enhancements and Future Improvements

1. Store Chat History in a Database

Modify `server.js` to save messages in **MongoDB**:

```
npm install mongoose
const mongoose = require("mongoose");

mongoose.connect("mongodb://localhost/chatDB", {
    useNewUrlParser: true,
    useUnifiedTopology: true
});

const MessageSchema = new mongoose.Schema({ user:
String, text: String, timestamp: Date });
const Message = mongoose.model("Message",
MessageSchema);

socket.on("message", async (data) => {
    const message = new Message({ user:
users[socket.id], text: data, timestamp: new Date()
});
    await message.save();
    io.emit("message", message);
});
```

Now, messages **persist in MongoDB**, allowing users to see previous chat history.

2. Implement Private Messaging

Modify `server.js` to **allow private messages**:

```
socket.on("privateMessage", ({ recipientId, message
}) => {
    io.to(recipientId).emit("privateMessage", {
sender: users[socket.id], text: message });
});
```

This allows users to **send direct messages to specific people**.

Add Emojis and File Sharing

Use **emoji libraries and file upload features** to enhance user experience.

```
socket.on("imageUpload", (data) => {
    io.emit("image", data);
```

```
});
```

By extending this project, you can create **advanced chat applications** for **customer support, gaming, and social networking**.

Live Notifications and Real-Time Data Streaming

In modern applications, **real-time updates** are crucial for enhancing user experience. Whether it's a **notification system**, a **live data dashboard**, or a **collaborative workspace**, users expect instant updates without refreshing the page.

Traditional request-response models **fall short** in handling live updates efficiently. This is where **WebSockets and real-time data streaming** come into play, enabling **instant communication between the server and the client**.

What Are Live Notifications?

Live notifications **instantly inform users of important events** in an application. Some common examples include:

Messaging apps → "You received a new message from Alice."

E-commerce platforms → "Your order has been shipped!"

Social media updates → "John liked your post."

These notifications **enhance engagement and usability** by keeping users informed **without requiring them to refresh the page**.

What Is Real-Time Data Streaming?

Real-time data streaming enables **continuous updates** of information, making it ideal for:

Stock market dashboards → Updating stock prices every second.

Live sports scores → Displaying real-time match updates.

IoT applications → Streaming sensor data from connected devices.

With **WebSockets**, updates are **pushed from the server to the client instantly**, ensuring **low-latency communication**.

Setting Up a Real-Time Notification System with Socket.io

Step 1: Install Dependencies

First, create a new project and install the required packages:

```
mkdir real-time-notifications
cd real-time-notifications
npm init -y
npm install express socket.io cors
```

express → Manages API routes and server setup.

socket.io → Enables real-time WebSocket communication.

cors → Allows frontend applications to access the server.

Step 2: Create a WebSocket Server for Notifications

Modify `server.js`:

```
const express = require("express");
const http = require("http");
const socketIo = require("socket.io");
const cors = require("cors");

const app = express();
const server = http.createServer(app);
const io = socketIo(server, {
    cors: {
        origin: "*",
        methods: ["GET", "POST"]
    }
});

const PORT = process.env.PORT || 3000;

app.use(cors());
```

```javascript
// Handle WebSocket connections
io.on("connection", (socket) => {
    console.log(`User connected: ${socket.id}`);

    // Send notifications to users
    setInterval(() => {
        io.emit("notification", {
            message: "You have a new update!",
            timestamp: new
Date().toLocaleTimeString()
        });
    }, 10000);

    socket.on("disconnect", () => {
        console.log(`User disconnected:
${socket.id}`);
    });
});

server.listen(PORT, () => {
    console.log(`Notification server running on
http://localhost:${PORT}`);
});
```

How It Works

✓ Users connect to the server via WebSockets.

✓ Every 10 seconds, a notification is sent to all connected users.

✓ Handles user disconnections gracefully.

Step 3: Connect a Frontend to Receive Notifications

Create an `index.html` file:

```html
<!DOCTYPE html>
<html lang="en">
<head>
    <meta charset="UTF-8">
    <title>Live Notifications</title>
    <script
src="https://cdn.socket.io/4.0.1/socket.io.min.js">
</script>
```

```html
    <style>
        body { font-family: Arial, sans-serif; }
        #notifications { list-style: none; padding:
0; }
        #notifications li { padding: 8px; border-
bottom: 1px solid #ddd; }
    </style>
</head>
<body>
    <h1>Live Notifications</h1>
    <ul id="notifications"></ul>

    <script>
        const socket = io("http://localhost:3000");

        socket.on("connect", () => {
            console.log("Connected to notification
server");
        });

        socket.on("notification", (data) => {
            const li =
document.createElement("li");
            li.textContent = `${data.message} -
${data.timestamp}`;

document.getElementById("notifications").appendChil
d(li);
        });
    </script>
</body>
</html>
```

✓ Users receive live notifications.

✓ New notifications appear instantly in the list.

Now, open multiple browser tabs to see notifications **broadcasted in real-time**.

Streaming Real-Time Data for Dashboards

Now, let's create a **real-time data streaming system** that continuously updates a **stock price dashboard**.

Step 1: Modify Server to Send Live Data Updates

Modify `server.js`:

```
io.on("connection", (socket) => {
    console.log(`User connected: ${socket.id}`);

    // Simulate live stock market data streaming
    setInterval(() => {
        io.emit("stockUpdate", {
            stock: "AAPL",
            price: (Math.random() *
1000).toFixed(2),
            timestamp: new
Date().toLocaleTimeString()
        });
    }, 3000);

    socket.on("disconnect", () => {
        console.log(`User disconnected:
${socket.id}`);
    });
});
```

Every 3 seconds, new stock data is generated and broadcasted.

Step 2: Create a Frontend for the Stock Dashboard

Modify `index.html`:

```
<h1>Live Stock Prices</h1>
<ul id="stocks"></ul>

<script>
    const socket = io("http://localhost:3000");

    socket.on("stockUpdate", (data) => {
        const li = document.createElement("li");
        li.textContent = `Stock: ${data.stock},
Price: $${data.price} (${data.timestamp})`;
```

```
document.getElementById("stocks").appendChild(li);
    });
</script>
```

✓ **Stock prices update in real-time without refreshing the page**.

✓ **Simulates a real-world financial dashboard**.

Optimizing Real-Time Data Handling for Scalability

1. Prevent Overloading with Too Many Events

Instead of sending updates to **all users every second**, use **rooms** to send data **only to subscribed clients**.

```
socket.on("subscribeToStock", (stockSymbol) => {
    socket.join(stockSymbol);
});

setInterval(() => {
    const stockData = {
        stock: "AAPL",
        price: (Math.random() * 1000).toFixed(2),
        timestamp: new Date().toLocaleTimeString()
    };
    io.to("AAPL").emit("stockUpdate", stockData);
}, 3000);
```

✓ **Users subscribe only to relevant stock updates**.

✓ **Reduces unnecessary data transmission**.

2. Implement Message Queue for Large-Scale Applications

For applications with **millions of active users**, use **Redis Pub/Sub or Kafka** to distribute messages efficiently.

Example with **Redis Pub/Sub**:

```
const redis = require("redis");
const pub = redis.createClient();
const sub = redis.createClient();

sub.subscribe("notifications");
```

```
sub.on("message", (channel, message) => {
    io.emit("notification", JSON.parse(message));
});

// Publish a new notification
setInterval(() => {
    pub.publish("notifications", JSON.stringify({
message: "New system update!" }));
}, 10000);
```

Scales WebSocket connections across multiple servers.

With **live notifications and real-time data streaming**, you can build **interactive applications** for **finance, gaming, customer support, and more**. WebSockets provide the foundation for **low-latency, high-performance real-time communication**, making applications more **engaging and responsive**.

Chapter 12: File Uploads and Processing

Many modern applications require file uploads, whether it's **profile pictures, document uploads, or media sharing**. Handling file uploads efficiently ensures **smooth performance, secure storage, and fast processing**.

Handling File Uploads with Multer

Uploading files is a **fundamental feature** in many modern web applications. Whether it's **profile pictures, documents, videos, or product images**, efficiently handling file uploads is essential for a smooth user experience.

When building a file upload system, you need to consider:

Where to store the files → Locally, in a database, or on cloud storage?

How to validate files → Ensuring correct file type, size limits, and security.

How to manage uploaded files → Storing metadata, processing images, or handling large file uploads efficiently.

To handle file uploads in **Node.js and Express**, we use **Multer**, a powerful middleware designed for processing **multipart/form-data** requests.

Installing and Setting Up Multer

Step 1: Install Required Packages

Before using Multer, install the necessary dependencies:

```
npm install express multer cors
```

express → The web framework for handling API routes.

multer → Middleware for handling file uploads.

cors → Enables the frontend to access the API without cross-origin issues.

Step 2: Create an Express Server with Multer

Modify `server.js` to include basic file upload functionality:

```javascript
const express = require("express");
const multer = require("multer");
const cors = require("cors");
const path = require("path");

const app = express();
app.use(cors());
app.use(express.json());

// Configure storage settings
const storage = multer.diskStorage({
    destination: "./uploads/",
    filename: (req, file, cb) => {
        cb(null, file.fieldname + "-" + Date.now()
+ path.extname(file.originalname));
    }
});

const upload = multer({ storage });

// Serve uploaded files statically
app.use("/uploads", express.static("uploads"));

// File upload endpoint
app.post("/upload", upload.single("file"), (req,
res) => {
    res.json({ message: "File uploaded
successfully!", filePath:
`/uploads/${req.file.filename}` });
});

app.listen(3000, () => {
    console.log("Server running on
http://localhost:3000");
});
```

How This Works:

✓ Multer stores files in the `uploads/` directory.

✓ The uploaded file's name includes a timestamp to prevent duplicates.

✓ Users can retrieve the uploaded file via `/uploads/{filename}`.

Step 3: Upload a File from the Frontend

To test file uploads, create a simple HTML form:

```html
<!DOCTYPE html>
<html lang="en">
<head>
    <meta charset="UTF-8">
    <title>File Upload</title>
</head>
<body>
    <h2>Upload a File</h2>
    <input type="file" id="fileInput">
    <button onclick="uploadFile()">Upload</button>
    <p id="status"></p>

    <script>
        function uploadFile() {
            const file =
document.getElementById("fileInput").files[0];
            const formData = new FormData();
            formData.append("file", file);

            fetch("http://localhost:3000/upload", {
                method: "POST",
                body: formData
            })
            .then(res => res.json())
            .then(data =>
document.getElementById("status").textContent =
data.message)
            .catch(error => console.error("Error:",
error));
        }
    </script>
</body>
</html>
```

Users can select a file and click "Upload".
The file is uploaded to the server and stored in the `/uploads/` folder.

Validating File Uploads

Restricting File Size and Type

To **prevent large or malicious files**, add validation rules in `server.js`:

```
const upload = multer({
    storage,
    limits: { fileSize: 5 * 1024 * 1024 }, // Limit
file size to 5MB
    fileFilter: (req, file, cb) => {
        const allowedTypes =
/jpeg|jpg|png|gif|pdf/;
        const extname =
allowedTypes.test(path.extname(file.originalname).t
oLowerCase());
        const mimetype =
allowedTypes.test(file.mimetype);

        if (mimetype && extname) {
            return cb(null, true);
        } else {
            return cb(new Error("Only images and
PDFs are allowed"));
        }
    }
});

app.post("/upload", upload.single("file"), (req,
res) => {
    res.json({ message: "File uploaded
successfully!", filePath:
`/uploads/${req.file.filename}` });
});
```

✓ **Limits uploads to 5MB**

✓ **Only allows images (JPG, PNG, GIF) and PDFs**

✓ **Rejects other file types with an error message**

Handling Multiple File Uploads

To allow users to upload multiple files at once, modify the upload route:

```
app.post("/upload-multiple", upload.array("files",
5), (req, res) => {
```

269

```
    const filePaths = req.files.map(file =>
`/uploads/${file.filename}`);
    res.json({ message: "Files uploaded
successfully!", filePaths });
});
```

✓ **Users can upload up to 5 files in a single request**

✓ **Returns an array of file paths for uploaded files**

To test this, modify the frontend script:

```
function uploadMultipleFiles() {
    const files =
document.getElementById("fileInput").files;
    const formData = new FormData();
    for (let i = 0; i < files.length; i++) {
        formData.append("files", files[i]);
    }

    fetch("http://localhost:3000/upload-multiple",
{
        method: "POST",
        body: formData
    })
    .then(res => res.json())
    .then(data => console.log("Uploaded Files:",
data.filePaths))
    .catch(error => console.error("Error:",
error));
}
```

Supports batch file uploads without multiple requests

Serving Uploaded Files Securely

By default, uploaded files are accessible via `/uploads/{filename}`. If security is a concern, restrict access to only **authenticated users**.

Modify `server.js` to **serve files only to authorized users**:

```
const authenticateUser = (req, res, next) => {
    const apiKey = req.header("x-api-key");
    if (apiKey === "secureapikey123") {
```

```
        return next();
    } else {
        return res.status(403).json({ message:
"Unauthorized access" });
    }
};


app.use("/uploads", authenticateUser,
express.static("uploads"));
```

Users must provide a valid API key to access uploaded files

To access a file securely:

```
curl -H "x-api-key: secureapikey123"
http://localhost:3000/uploads/file.jpg
```

Deleting Uploaded Files

To allow users to **delete their uploaded files**, add a DELETE route:

```
const fs = require("fs");

app.delete("/delete/:filename", (req, res) => {
    const filePath =
`uploads/${req.params.filename}`;

    fs.unlink(filePath, (err) => {
        if (err) {
            return res.status(400).json({ message:
"File not found" });
        }
        res.json({ message: "File deleted
successfully!" });
    });
});
```
To delete a file from the frontend:

```
fetch("http://localhost:3000/delete/file.jpg", {
method: "DELETE" })
    .then(res => res.json())
    .then(data => console.log(data.message))
    .catch(error => console.error("Error:",
error));
```

Users can delete files they no longer need

By following these best practices, your application will **handle file uploads securely and efficiently**, ensuring **fast performance, reduced storage costs, and better user experience**.

Storing Files in Cloud Services

Uploading files to a **cloud storage service** is essential for scalability, security, and accessibility. Unlike storing files locally, **cloud storage solutions** allow applications to:
Serve files globally with minimal latency.
Reduce server load and storage limitations.
Ensure data redundancy and security.

Uploading Files to AWS S3

Amazon S3 (Simple Storage Service) is a **highly scalable and durable** object storage service that supports:
✓ **Unlimited storage** → No limits on file size or number of files.
✓ **Automatic redundancy** → Data is stored across multiple locations.
✓ **Public and private access controls** → Securely control who can view/download files.

Step 1: Install Required Packages

```
npm install express multer aws-sdk multer-s3 dotenv
```
express → Web framework for handling API routes.

multer → Middleware for handling file uploads.

aws-sdk → AWS SDK for interacting with S3.

multer-s3 → Multer extension for direct S3 uploads.

dotenv → Load environment variables securely.

Step 2: Set Up AWS Credentials

Create a `.env` file to store AWS credentials:

```
AWS_ACCESS_KEY_ID=your-access-key
AWS_SECRET_ACCESS_KEY=your-secret-key
AWS_REGION=us-east-1
AWS_BUCKET_NAME=your-bucket-name
```

Step 3: Configure AWS S3 and Multer

Modify `server.js` to configure Multer for S3 uploads:

```
require("dotenv").config();
const express = require("express");
const multer = require("multer");
const AWS = require("aws-sdk");
const multerS3 = require("multer-s3");
const cors = require("cors");

const app = express();
app.use(cors());
app.use(express.json());

const s3 = new AWS.S3({
    accessKeyId: process.env.AWS_ACCESS_KEY_ID,
    secretAccessKey:
process.env.AWS_SECRET_ACCESS_KEY,
    region: process.env.AWS_REGION
});

const upload = multer({
    storage: multerS3({
        s3,
        bucket: process.env.AWS_BUCKET_NAME,
        acl: "public-read",
        metadata: (req, file, cb) => {
            cb(null, { fieldName: file.fieldname
});
        },
        key: (req, file, cb) => {
            cb(null, `${Date.now()}-
${file.originalname}`);
        }
    })
});
```

```
// Upload file to S3
app.post("/upload-s3", upload.single("file"), (req,
res) => {
    res.json({
        message: "File uploaded successfully!",
        fileUrl: req.file.location
    });
});

const PORT = process.env.PORT || 3000;
app.listen(PORT, () => console.log(`Server running
on http://localhost:${PORT}`));
```

Uploads files directly to S3 instead of storing them on the local server.
Generates a public URL for accessing the uploaded file.
Ensures secure file access control using ACL (Access Control List).

Step 4: Upload a File from the Frontend

Modify the frontend to send a file to the S3 upload endpoint:

```html
<input type="file" id="fileInput">
<button onclick="uploadToS3()">Upload to
S3</button>
<p id="status"></p>

<script>
    function uploadToS3() {
        const file =
document.getElementById("fileInput").files[0];
        const formData = new FormData();
        formData.append("file", file);

        fetch("http://localhost:3000/upload-s3", {
            method: "POST",
            body: formData
        })
        .then(res => res.json())
        .then(data => {

document.getElementById("status").textContent =
`Uploaded: ${data.fileUrl}`;
        })
```

```
        .catch(error => console.error("Error:",
error));
    }
</script>
```

Users can upload files and get a direct S3 URL for sharing or embedding.

Uploading Files to Cloudinary

Cloudinary is an **image and video management platform** that provides:

✓ **Automatic image optimization** for web performance.

✓ **On-the-fly transformations** (resizing, cropping, watermarking).

✓ **CDN delivery** for fast global access.

Step 1: Install Cloudinary SDK and Multer

```
npm install cloudinary multer multer-storage-
cloudinary dotenv
```

Step 2: Configure Cloudinary Credentials

Create a .env file with Cloudinary credentials:

```
CLOUDINARY_CLOUD_NAME=your-cloud-name
CLOUDINARY_API_KEY=your-api-key
CLOUDINARY_API_SECRET=your-api-secret
```

Step 3: Configure Multer for Cloudinary Uploads

Modify server.js to support Cloudinary uploads:

```
require("dotenv").config();
const express = require("express");
const multer = require("multer");
const { v2: cloudinary } = require("cloudinary");
const { CloudinaryStorage } = require("multer-
storage-cloudinary");
const cors = require("cors");

const app = express();
app.use(cors());
app.use(express.json());
```

```javascript
// Configure Cloudinary
cloudinary.config({
    cloud_name: process.env.CLOUDINARY_CLOUD_NAME,
    api_key: process.env.CLOUDINARY_API_KEY,
    api_secret: process.env.CLOUDINARY_API_SECRET
});

const storage = new CloudinaryStorage({
    cloudinary,
    params: {
        folder: "uploads",
        allowedFormats: ["jpg", "png", "gif",
"pdf"]
    }
});

const upload = multer({ storage });

// Upload file to Cloudinary
app.post("/upload-cloudinary",
upload.single("file"), (req, res) => {
    res.json({
        message: "File uploaded successfully!",
        fileUrl: req.file.path
    });
});

const PORT = process.env.PORT || 3000;
app.listen(PORT, () => console.log(`Server running
on http://localhost:${PORT}`));
```

✓ Stores files in Cloudinary instead of a local server.

✓ Supports multiple formats (JPEG, PNG, GIF, PDF, etc.).

✓ Returns a publicly accessible Cloudinary URL for the file.

Step 4: Upload a File from the Frontend

Modify the frontend script:

```html
<input type="file" id="fileInput">
<button onclick="uploadToCloudinary()">Upload to
Cloudinary</button>
```

```html
<p id="status"></p>

<script>
    function uploadToCloudinary() {
        const file =
document.getElementById("fileInput").files[0];
        const formData = new FormData();
        formData.append("file", file);

        fetch("http://localhost:3000/upload-
cloudinary", {
            method: "POST",
            body: formData
        })
        .then(res => res.json())
        .then(data => {

document.getElementById("status").textContent =
`Uploaded: ${data.fileUrl}`;
        })
        .catch(error => console.error("Error:",
error));
    }
</script>
```

Users can upload images directly to Cloudinary and receive a **URL for embedding**.

Best Practices for Cloud Storage

1. Restrict File Types to Prevent Security Risks

Modify `multer` settings to allow only specific file types:

```
fileFilter: (req, file, cb) => {
    const allowedTypes = /jpeg|jpg|png|pdf/;
    const extname =
allowedTypes.test(path.extname(file.originalname).t
oLowerCase());
    const mimetype =
allowedTypes.test(file.mimetype);

    if (mimetype && extname) {
```

```
        return cb(null, true);
    } else {
        return cb(new Error("Only images and PDFs
are allowed"));
    }
}
```

Prevents malicious file uploads.

2. Automatically Delete Old Files to Reduce Storage Costs

For **AWS S3**, set lifecycle policies to delete files after **X days**. For **Cloudinary**, use **expiration rules** to automatically remove old files.

Reduces cloud storage costs over time.

By integrating **cloud storage solutions**, you make file management **scalable, secure, and cost-effective**, ensuring **fast access and optimized performance** for your users.

Image Processing with Sharp

Handling images efficiently is crucial for **web applications, e-commerce platforms, social media apps, and content management systems**. Images often need to be **resized, compressed, optimized, and sometimes converted** before being stored or displayed.

Sharp is a **high-performance image processing library** for Node.js that allows:

✓ **Fast image resizing and compression** without losing quality.

✓ **Conversion between formats (JPEG, PNG, WebP, etc.)**.

✓ **Cropping, rotation, and watermarking**.

✓ **Processing images in memory for faster performance**.

Installing and Setting Up Sharp

Step 1: Install Sharp

Run the following command to install Sharp:

```
npm install sharp
```
Sharp has **zero dependencies** and is **faster than ImageMagick or GraphicsMagick**, making it an excellent choice for **server-side image processing**.

Step 2: Create an Express Server for Image Processing

Modify `server.js` to set up a basic image upload system:

```
const express = require("express");
const multer = require("multer");
const sharp = require("sharp");
const fs = require("fs");
const path = require("path");

const app = express();
const upload = multer({ dest: "uploads/" });

app.use(express.json());
app.use("/uploads", express.static("uploads"));

const PORT = process.env.PORT || 3000;

app.listen(PORT, () => {
    console.log(`Server running on
http://localhost:${PORT}`);
});
```

Multer stores uploaded images temporarily in uploads/ **before processing.**
Sharp will process images before saving them permanently.

Resizing and Compressing Images for Web Optimization

Many websites load **high-resolution images unnecessarily**, slowing down performance. **Resizing and compressing images** helps optimize load times while maintaining quality.

Step 1: Create an API Route for Resizing Images

Modify `server.js` to resize uploaded images before saving them:

```
app.post("/resize", upload.single("image"), async
(req, res) => {
    try {
        const inputPath = req.file.path;
        const outputPath = `uploads/resized-
${Date.now()}.jpg`;

        await sharp(inputPath)
            .resize(300, 300) // Resize to 300x300
pixels
            .jpeg({ quality: 80 }) // Compress with
80% quality
            .toFile(outputPath);

        fs.unlinkSync(inputPath); // Delete
original file to save space

        res.json({ message: "Image resized
successfully!", filePath: outputPath });
    } catch (error) {
        res.status(500).json({ message: "Error
processing image", error });
    }
});
```

✓ Resizes images to 300x300 pixels.

✓ Reduces image size while maintaining good quality.

✓ Deletes the original file to prevent unnecessary storage usage.

Step 2: Upload and Resize an Image from the Frontend

Modify `index.html` to send an image to the `/resize` endpoint:

```
<input type="file" id="fileInput">
<button onclick="uploadAndResize()">Upload &
Resize</button>
<p id="status"></p>

<script>
    function uploadAndResize() {
        const file =
document.getElementById("fileInput").files[0];
```

```javascript
      const formData = new FormData();
      formData.append("image", file);

      fetch("http://localhost:3000/resize", {
          method: "POST",
          body: formData
      })
      .then(res => res.json())
      .then(data => {

document.getElementById("status").textContent =
`Resized Image: ${data.filePath}`;
      })
      .catch(error => console.error("Error:",
error));
    }
</script>
```

Users can upload images, and they are resized automatically.
The resized image can be served via /uploads/{filename}.

Converting Images to Different Formats

Sharp allows **conversion between image formats** (e.g., PNG to JPEG, JPEG to WebP) to optimize storage and loading speeds.

Modify API Route to Convert Images to WebP

```javascript
app.post("/convert", upload.single("image"), async
(req, res) => {
    try {
        const inputPath = req.file.path;
        const outputPath = `uploads/converted-
${Date.now()}.webp`;

        await sharp(inputPath)
            .toFormat("webp")
            .toFile(outputPath);

        fs.unlinkSync(inputPath);

        res.json({ message: "Image converted to
WebP!", filePath: outputPath });
```

```
    } catch (error) {
        res.status(500).json({ message: "Error
processing image", error });
    }
});
```

Converts images to WebP format for better compression. Deletes the original file to save space.

Cropping, Rotating, and Adding Watermarks

1. Cropping an Image

Modify `server.js` to **crop images** before saving:

```
app.post("/crop", upload.single("image"), async
(req, res) => {
    try {
        const inputPath = req.file.path;
        const outputPath = `uploads/cropped-
${Date.now()}.jpg`;

        await sharp(inputPath)
            .extract({ left: 100, top: 100, width:
200, height: 200 }) // Crop a 200x200 section
            .toFile(outputPath);

        fs.unlinkSync(inputPath);

        res.json({ message: "Image cropped
successfully!", filePath: outputPath });
    } catch (error) {
        res.status(500).json({ message: "Error
cropping image", error });
    }
});
```

Extracts a 200x200 pixel section from the original image.

2. Rotating an Image

```
app.post("/rotate", upload.single("image"), async
(req, res) => {
```

```
    try {
        const inputPath = req.file.path;
        const outputPath = `uploads/rotated-
${Date.now()}.jpg`;

        await sharp(inputPath)
            .rotate(90) // Rotate by 90 degrees
            .toFile(outputPath);

        fs.unlinkSync(inputPath);

        res.json({ message: "Image rotated
successfully!", filePath: outputPath });
    } catch (error) {
        res.status(500).json({ message: "Error
rotating image", error });
    }
});
```

Rotates the image by 90 degrees.

3. Adding a Watermark

```
app.post("/watermark", upload.single("image"),
async (req, res) => {
    try {
        const inputPath = req.file.path;
        const outputPath = `uploads/watermarked-
${Date.now()}.jpg`;

        await sharp(inputPath)
            .composite([{ input: "watermark.png",
gravity: "southeast" }]) // Adds watermark in
bottom right
            .toFile(outputPath);

        fs.unlinkSync(inputPath);

        res.json({ message: "Watermark added
successfully!", filePath: outputPath });
    } catch (error) {
        res.status(500).json({ message: "Error
adding watermark", error });
```

```
        }
    });
```

Overlays a watermark image at the bottom-right corner.

Handling Large Image Uploads Efficiently

Large images can **slow down your application and consume excessive storage**. Here's how to optimize performance:

1. Limit File Size in Multer

```
const upload = multer({
    limits: { fileSize: 5 * 1024 * 1024 } // Limit
file size to 5MB
});
```

Prevents users from uploading excessively large files.

2. Stream Image Processing Instead of Storing in Memory

```
app.post("/stream-process", upload.single("image"),
(req, res) => {
    res.set("Content-Type", "image/jpeg");

    sharp(req.file.path)
        .resize(400, 400)
        .jpeg({ quality: 80 })
        .pipe(res); // Stream directly to the
response
});
```

Processes images in real-time without saving them to disk.

By integrating **Sharp**, you make image handling **faster, more efficient, and optimized for web performance**, ensuring a **seamless user experience**.

Handling Large File Uploads Efficiently

Large file uploads present **unique challenges** in web applications. When users upload **videos, high-resolution images, or large datasets**, the server must handle these files efficiently to **prevent crashes, optimize performance, and ensure a smooth user experience**.

Uploading large files inefficiently can cause:

Memory overflows → Server crashes due to excessive RAM usage.

Slow performance → Large files can clog the network and database.

Incomplete uploads → Users may face timeouts or dropped connections.

By default, when a file is uploaded using traditional methods, it is **fully loaded into RAM** before being processed. This is inefficient for **large files** as it can **consume too much memory and crash the server**.

Streaming allows us to **process files in chunks**, meaning that only a small portion is in memory at any given time.

Step 1: Install Required Packages

```
npm install express multer fs
```
express → Handles API requests.

multer → Middleware for handling file uploads.

fs → Used for file system operations (streaming files to disk).

Step 2: Create a Streaming File Upload Server

Modify `server.js` to **stream file uploads directly to disk instead of loading them into memory**:

```
const express = require("express");
const multer = require("multer");
const fs = require("fs");

const app = express();
const PORT = 3000;

// Configure Multer to store files in chunks
const storage = multer.diskStorage({
    destination: "uploads/",
    filename: (req, file, cb) => {
        cb(null, file.originalname);
```

```
    }
});

const upload = multer({ storage });

// Streaming large file upload
app.post("/upload", upload.single("file"), (req,
res) => {
    res.json({ message: "File uploaded
successfully!" });
});

app.listen(PORT, () => {
    console.log(`Server running on
http://localhost:${PORT}`);
});
```

How It Works

✓ **Files are written directly to disk instead of being held in memory.**

✓ **Prevents memory overflows on large file uploads.**

✓ **Uploads large files efficiently without slowing down the server.**

Step 3: Upload a Large File from the Frontend

Modify `index.html` to handle large file uploads efficiently:

```
<input type="file" id="fileInput">
<button onclick="uploadFile()">Upload Large
File</button>
<p id="status"></p>

<script>
    function uploadFile() {
        const file =
document.getElementById("fileInput").files[0];
        const formData = new FormData();
        formData.append("file", file);

        fetch("http://localhost:3000/upload", {
            method: "POST",
            body: formData
```

```
        })
        .then(res => res.json())
        .then(data => {

document.getElementById("status").textContent =
data.message;
        })
        .catch(error => console.error("Error:",
error));
    }
</script>
```

✓ **Allows users to upload large files without slowing down the page**.

✓ **The file is streamed and stored on the server efficiently**.

Implementing Chunked/Resumable File Uploads

When uploading **very large files**, network failures can **cause the upload to fail**. Instead of restarting from scratch, chunked uploads:

Split files into smaller parts (chunks).

Send each chunk separately to the server.

Reassemble the file once all chunks have been uploaded.

Step 1: Modify Backend to Handle Chunked Uploads

Modify `server.js` to allow **partial uploads**:

```
const path = require("path");

app.post("/upload-chunk", (req, res) => {
    const { chunkNumber, totalChunks, filename } =
req.headers;
    const filePath = path.join("uploads",
filename);

    const fileStream =
fs.createWriteStream(filePath, { flags: "a" }); //
Append mode

    req.on("data", (chunk) => {
```

```
        fileStream.write(chunk);
    });

    req.on("end", () => {
        fileStream.end();
        res.json({ message: `Chunk ${chunkNumber}
of ${totalChunks} received` });
    });
});
```

✓ **Uploads files in small chunks.**

✓ **Prevents failures due to network disconnections.**

✓ **Resumes an interrupted upload without restarting.**

Step 2: Modify Frontend to Upload Files in Chunks

Modify index.html to send chunks instead of full files:

```
<input type="file" id="fileInput">
<button onclick="uploadLargeFile()">Upload Large
File in Chunks</button>
<p id="status"></p>

<script>
    async function uploadLargeFile() {
        const file =
document.getElementById("fileInput").files[0];
        const chunkSize = 1 * 1024 * 1024; // 1MB
chunks
        const totalChunks = Math.ceil(file.size /
chunkSize);

        for (let i = 0; i < totalChunks; i++) {
            const start = i * chunkSize;
            const end = Math.min(start + chunkSize,
file.size);
            const chunk = file.slice(start, end);

            const formData = new FormData();
            formData.append("file", chunk);
```

```javascript
                await
fetch("http://localhost:3000/upload-chunk", {
                method: "POST",
                headers: {
                        "chunkNumber": i + 1,
                        "totalChunks": totalChunks,
                        "filename": file.name
                },
                body: chunk
            });


document.getElementById("status").textContent =
`Uploaded ${i + 1} of ${totalChunks} chunks`;
        }


document.getElementById("status").textContent =
"File upload complete!";
    }
</script>
```

✓ **Uploads large files in chunks, preventing failures due to network issues**.

✓ **Improves upload reliability and performance**.

Storing Large Files in Cloud Storage (AWS S3)

Storing files in AWS S3 instead of the local server:

✓ **Reduces storage costs** → Only pay for what you use.

✓ **Handles large files efficiently** → No server limitations.

✓ **Provides global access** → Files are available anywhere via URLs.

Step 1: Modify Backend to Upload Large Files to S3

Modify `server.js` to **upload large files directly to AWS S3**:

```javascript
const AWS = require("aws-sdk");

const s3 = new AWS.S3({
    accessKeyId: process.env.AWS_ACCESS_KEY_ID,
```

289

```
    secretAccessKey:
process.env.AWS_SECRET_ACCESS_KEY,
    region: process.env.AWS_REGION
});

app.post("/upload-s3", upload.single("file"), async
(req, res) => {
    const fileStream =
fs.createReadStream(req.file.path);

    const params = {
        Bucket: process.env.AWS_BUCKET_NAME,
        Key: req.file.originalname,
        Body: fileStream,
        ACL: "public-read"
    };

    s3.upload(params, (error, data) => {
        fs.unlinkSync(req.file.path); // Delete
local file
        if (error) return res.status(500).json({
error: "S3 upload failed" });
        res.json({ message: "File uploaded to S3!",
fileUrl: data.Location });
    });
});
```

✓ **Uploads files directly to S3, reducing server storage load**.

✓ **Deletes local files after successful upload to save space**.

By applying these techniques, your application will **handle large file uploads seamlessly, prevent crashes, and optimize storage costs** while delivering a smooth user experience.

Chapter 13: Microservices and API Gateways

As applications grow, maintaining a **monolithic architecture** becomes increasingly difficult. Scaling, deploying, and managing services in a single codebase can lead to **performance bottlenecks, slower deployments, and complex maintenance**.

This is where **microservices** come into play. Microservices allow developers to **break down a large application into smaller, independent services**, making applications more **scalable, maintainable, and fault-tolerant**.

Introduction to Microservices in Node.js

Microservices are an **architectural style** where an application is broken into **smaller, loosely coupled services**, each responsible for a specific function. These services communicate with each other **via APIs** and can be developed, deployed, and scaled **independently**.

Each microservice:

✓ **Has its own codebase** and can be managed separately.

✓ **Communicates with other services** through HTTP APIs, WebSockets, gRPC, or message queues.

✓ **Can be written in different programming languages** based on requirements.

✓ **Can be deployed independently**, reducing downtime and enabling rapid development cycles.

How Microservices Solve Common Problems

Challenge in Monolithic Apps	Solution with Microservices
Difficult to scale	Each service can scale independently
Large codebase is hard to maintain	Smaller, more manageable codebases

Challenge in Monolithic Apps	Solution with Microservices
Deployments require full system restart	Deploy individual services without downtime
One failure can crash the entire application	Failures are isolated to specific services
Difficult to introduce new technologies	Different services can use different technologies

When to Use Microservices?

Microservices are not always the best choice. They add complexity, and for small projects, a monolithic approach might be simpler. However, microservices **excel in large-scale applications** where:

The system has **multiple independent business functions** (e.g., user management, payments, analytics).

Teams are working on **different parts of the application simultaneously**.

Services need to be **scaled independently** (e.g., high-traffic services vs. low-traffic services).

There's a need for **different technology stacks for different functionalities** (e.g., Node.js for APIs, Python for machine learning).

A good example is **Netflix**, which transitioned from a monolithic architecture to microservices to handle **millions of requests per second efficiently**.

How Microservices Communicate

Since microservices are **independent units**, they must communicate with each other to exchange data. The most common communication methods include:

1. HTTP/REST APIs

Each service exposes an **HTTP API** that other services can call.

Example: A User Service and Order Service in an E-Commerce App

`GET /users/{id}` → Fetch user details.

```
GET /orders/{user_id}
```
→ Fetch orders for a user.

Requesting user details from the frontend:

```
fetch("http://localhost:4001/users/1")
    .then(res => res.json())
    .then(data => console.log("User:", data));
```

Requesting orders for a user:

```
fetch("http://localhost:4002/orders?user_id=1")
    .then(res => res.json())
    .then(data => console.log("Orders:", data));
```

✓ **Simple to implement**

✓ **Works well for most applications**

✗ **Can lead to performance issues if services depend heavily on each other**

2. Messaging Queues (RabbitMQ, Kafka, NATS)

For **asynchronous communication**, services send messages via **message brokers** instead of calling APIs directly.

Example: A Payment Service Notifying an Order Service When Payment Is Completed

The **Payment Service** sends a message:

```
const amqp = require("amqplib");

async function sendMessage() {
    const connection = await
amqp.connect("amqp://localhost");
    const channel = await
connection.createChannel();
    const queue = "order_updates";

    await channel.assertQueue(queue);
    channel.sendToQueue(queue,
Buffer.from(JSON.stringify({ orderId: 123, status:
"PAID" })));
```

```
    console.log("Sent payment update for order
123");
}

sendMessage();
```

The **Order Service** listens for updates:

```
async function receiveMessages() {
    const connection = await
amqp.connect("amqp://localhost");
    const channel = await
connection.createChannel();
    const queue = "order_updates";

    await channel.assertQueue(queue);
    console.log("Waiting for messages...");

    channel.consume(queue, (msg) => {
        const data =
JSON.parse(msg.content.toString());
        console.log(`Received update: Order
${data.orderId} is now ${data.status}`);
    }, { noAck: true });
}

receiveMessages();
```

✓ **Decouples services, making them more resilient**

✓ **Handles spikes in traffic efficiently**

✗ **Adds complexity and requires managing a message broker**

3. gRPC (Faster Communication Between Services)

gRPC is a **high-performance RPC framework** that allows services to communicate **faster** than REST by using **binary protocols** instead of text-based JSON.

✓ **Faster than REST (uses Protocol Buffers instead of JSON)**

✓ **Supports streaming, making it great for real-time applications**

✗ **Requires both services to use gRPC-compatible languages**

Setting Up a Basic Microservices Example with Node.js

Let's build two microservices:

User Service → Manages user data.

Product Service → Manages products.

API Gateway → Manages requests to microservices.

Step 1: Create the User Service

```
mkdir user-service
cd user-service
npm init -y
npm install express cors
```

user-service/server.js

```
const express = require("express");
const app = express();
const PORT = 4001;

app.use(express.json());
app.use(require("cors")());

const users = [
    { id: 1, name: "Alice" },
    { id: 2, name: "Bob" }
];

app.get("/users", (req, res) => {
    res.json(users);
});

app.listen(PORT, () => console.log(`User Service
running on port ${PORT}`));
```

Step 2: Create the Product Service

```
mkdir ../product-service
cd ../product-service
npm init -y
npm install express cors
```

product-service/server.js

```javascript
const express = require("express");
const app = express();
const PORT = 4002;

app.use(express.json());
app.use(require("cors")());

const products = [
    { id: 1, name: "Laptop", price: 1200 },
    { id: 2, name: "Phone", price: 800 }
];

app.get("/products", (req, res) => {
    res.json(products);
});

app.listen(PORT, () => console.log(`Product Service
running on port ${PORT}`));
```

Step 3: Create an API Gateway

```
mkdir ../api-gateway
cd ../api-gateway
npm init -y
npm install express axios cors
```

api-gateway/server.js

```javascript
const express = require("express");
const axios = require("axios");
const app = express();
const PORT = 4000;

app.use(express.json());
app.use(require("cors")());

// Proxy request to User Service
app.get("/users", async (req, res) => {
    const response = await
axios.get("http://localhost:4001/users");
    res.json(response.data);
```

```
});

// Proxy request to Product Service
app.get("/products", async (req, res) => {
    const response = await
axios.get("http://localhost:4002/products");
    res.json(response.data);
});

app.listen(PORT, () => console.log(`API Gateway
running on port ${PORT}`));
```

Step 4: Start All Services

```
node user-service/server.js
node product-service/server.js
node api-gateway/server.js
```

Now, instead of calling multiple APIs, the frontend only needs to interact with **http://localhost:4000/users** and **http://localhost:4000/products**.

✓ **Microservices run independently**.

✓ **API Gateway manages service communication**.

With microservices, applications become **modular, scalable, and easier to maintain**, allowing for **faster deployments and improved reliability**.

Building Scalable Microservices with Express.js

Microservices have transformed how modern applications are built, enabling **scalability, flexibility, and maintainability**. Instead of a **monolithic** architecture where everything is tightly coupled, microservices allow applications to be **broken into independent services**, each handling a specific function.

When building microservices, **Express.js** is an excellent choice due to its **lightweight nature, simplicity, and robust ecosystem**. It allows developers to create APIs quickly while maintaining flexibility for **service-to-service communication, database interactions, and scaling strategies**.

When building microservices, a **well-defined structure** ensures:

Easy maintainability – Services are independent but well-organized.

Scalability – Each service can scale independently.

Efficient debugging – Logs and errors are isolated to specific services.

Recommended Folder Structure for a Microservice

```
user-service/
|— controllers/
|     |— userController.js
|— routes/
|     |— userRoutes.js
|— models/
|     |— userModel.js
|— services/
|     |— userService.js
|— config/
|     |— database.js
|— app.js
|— server.js
|— package.json
```

✓ **Separation of concerns** → Controllers, services, and models are decoupled.
✓ **Easier debugging** → Each service has its own logs, errors, and business logic.

Setting Up a Scalable Microservice with Express.js

Step 1: Create a User Microservice

```
mkdir user-service
cd user-service
npm init -y
npm install express mongoose cors dotenv
```

Step 2: Configure Express and MongoDB

config/database.js

```
const mongoose = require("mongoose");

const connectDB = async () => {
    try {
        await
mongoose.connect(process.env.MONGO_URI, {
            useNewUrlParser: true,
            useUnifiedTopology: true
        });
        console.log("MongoDB Connected");
    } catch (error) {
        console.error("MongoDB Connection Failed",
error);
        process.exit(1);
    }
};

module.exports = connectDB;
```

✓ **Handles database connection separately** for easy reusability.
✓ **Ensures the database connection is established before running queries**.

Step 3: Define the User Model

models/userModel.js

```
const mongoose = require("mongoose");

const UserSchema = new mongoose.Schema({
```

299

```
    name: { type: String, required: true },
    email: { type: String, unique: true, required:
true }
}, { timestamps: true });

module.exports = mongoose.model("User",
UserSchema);
```

✓ Creates a schema for user data.

✓ Ensures `name` and `email` are required fields.

✓ Automatically adds timestamps for created/updated fields.

Step 4: Implement the User Service

services/userService.js

```
const User = require("../models/userModel");

const createUser = async (userData) => {
    return await User.create(userData);
};

const getUsers = async () => {
    return await User.find();
};

module.exports = { createUser, getUsers };
```

✓ Encapsulates database logic into a separate service layer.

✓ Prepares microservices for scalability by keeping controllers lightweight.

Step 5: Define API Endpoints

controllers/userController.js

```
const { createUser, getUsers } =
require("../services/userService");

const addUser = async (req, res) => {
    try {
        const user = await createUser(req.body);
```

```
        res.status(201).json(user);
    } catch (error) {
        res.status(400).json({ error: error.message
});
    }
};

const listUsers = async (req, res) => {
    try {
        const users = await getUsers();
        res.json(users);
    } catch (error) {
        res.status(500).json({ error: error.message
});
    }
};

module.exports = { addUser, listUsers };
```

✓ **Keeps business logic in services** to keep controllers clean.

✓ **Ensures error handling is centralized and standardized**.

Step 6: Create Routes

routes/userRoutes.js

```
const express = require("express");
const { addUser, listUsers } =
require("../controllers/userController");

const router = express.Router();

router.post("/users", addUser);
router.get("/users", listUsers);

module.exports = router;
```

Defines clean RESTful endpoints for the user service.

Step 7: Initialize Express and Start the Microservice

server.js

```
require("dotenv").config();
const express = require("express");
const connectDB = require("./config/database");
const userRoutes = require("./routes/userRoutes");

const app = express();
app.use(express.json());
app.use(require("cors")());

connectDB(); // Connect to MongoDB

app.use("/api", userRoutes);

const PORT = process.env.PORT || 4001;
app.listen(PORT, () => console.log(`User Service
running on port ${PORT}`));
```

✓ **Loads environment variables** using dotenv.

✓ **Connects to MongoDB before starting the server**.

✓ **Registers routes under /api for clarity**.

Handling Communication Between Microservices

Using an API Gateway

Instead of having the frontend **call multiple microservices separately**, an API Gateway acts as a **single entry point**.

Step 1: Set Up an API Gateway

```
mkdir ../api-gateway
cd ../api-gateway
npm init -y
npm install express axios cors
```

Step 2: Configure API Gateway Routes

api-gateway/server.js

```
const express = require("express");
const axios = require("axios");
const app = express();
const PORT = 4000;
```

302

```
app.use(express.json());
app.use(require("cors")());

app.get("/users", async (req, res) => {
    const response = await
axios.get("http://localhost:4001/api/users");
    res.json(response.data);
});

app.listen(PORT, () => console.log(`API Gateway
running on port ${PORT}`));
```

✓ **Frontends now only communicate with the API Gateway**.

✓ **The gateway handles routing requests to the correct microservices**.

Scaling Microservices Efficiently

1. Deploy Each Microservice in a Separate Container (Docker)

Each service can be containerized using **Docker** to allow easy deployment and scaling.

Dockerfile (For Each Microservice)

```
FROM node:14
WORKDIR /app
COPY package*.json ./
RUN npm install
COPY . .
CMD ["node", "server.js"]
EXPOSE 4001
```

To build and run the container:

```
docker build -t user-service .
docker run -p 4001:4001 user-service
```

Ensures microservices run independently inside containers.

2. Deploy with Kubernetes for Scalability

Kubernetes can manage multiple instances of microservices dynamically.

303

```
apiVersion: apps/v1
kind: Deployment
metadata:
  name: user-service
spec:
  replicas: 2
  selector:
    matchLabels:
      app: user-service
  template:
    metadata:
      labels:
        app: user-service
    spec:
      containers:
        - name: user-service
          image: user-service:latest
          ports:
            - containerPort: 4001
```

Automatically scales microservices based on demand.

By following these **best practices**, you ensure your application is **modular, resilient, and scalable**, ready for **high-performance production deployments**.

API Gateway and Service Communication Strategies

Microservices architecture allows applications to be **modular, scalable, and independently deployable**. However, with multiple services handling different functionalities, managing **service-to-service communication** efficiently is crucial.

One of the best solutions for handling **microservices communication** is an **API Gateway**. Instead of exposing multiple microservices directly to clients, an API Gateway acts as a **single entry point** that:

✓ **Routes requests** to the correct microservice.

✓ **Manages authentication and security centrally**.

✓ **Handles load balancing and rate limiting**.

✓ **Reduces client-side complexity by aggregating responses from multiple services**.

In a **monolithic** system, the frontend communicates with a **single backend**. In a **microservices** architecture, however, different services handle separate functionalities:

User Service → Manages user data.

Order Service → Handles customer orders.

Product Service → Manages product inventory.

Without an API Gateway, the **frontend must call each service separately**, increasing complexity:

```
fetch("http://localhost:4001/users")
fetch("http://localhost:4002/orders")
fetch("http://localhost:4003/products")
```

With an API Gateway, all requests go through a **single endpoint**:

```
fetch("http://localhost:4000/api/users")
fetch("http://localhost:4000/api/orders")
fetch("http://localhost:4000/api/products")
```

✓ **Simplifies API requests**.

✓ **Provides centralized security, authentication, and caching**.

✓ **Improves performance through request aggregation**.

Building an API Gateway with Express.js

Step 1: Create the API Gateway Service

```
mkdir api-gateway
cd api-gateway
npm init -y
npm install express axios cors
```

Step 2: Implement API Routing

Modify `server.js` to route API requests to microservices:

```javascript
const express = require("express");
const axios = require("axios");
const cors = require("cors");

const app = express();
app.use(cors());
app.use(express.json());

const services = {
    users: "http://localhost:4001",
    orders: "http://localhost:4002",
    products: "http://localhost:4003"
};

// Route requests to microservices
app.use("/api/:service/:endpoint?", async (req,
res) => {
    const { service, endpoint } = req.params;
    const serviceUrl = services[service];

    if (!serviceUrl) {
        return res.status(404).json({ error:
"Service not found" });
    }

    try {
        const response = await axios({
            method: req.method,
            url: `${serviceUrl}/${endpoint || ""}`,
            data: req.body
        });
        res.json(response.data);
    } catch (error) {
        res.status(500).json({ error: "Service
communication error", details: error.message });
    }
});

const PORT = 4000;
app.listen(PORT, () => console.log(`API Gateway
running on http://localhost:${PORT}`));
```

✓ **Dynamically routes requests to different services**

✓ **Acts as a single API entry point**

Now, calling http://localhost:4000/api/users fetches user data from http://localhost:4001/users.

Service Communication Strategies

Microservices need to communicate efficiently. There are three main strategies:

1. Synchronous Communication (REST/HTTP)

Example:

API Gateway calls `http://localhost:4001/users`

Waits for a response before proceeding

Code Example:

```
const getUsers = async () => {
    const response = await
axios.get("http://localhost:4001/users");
    console.log(response.data);
};
getUsers();
```

✓ **Simple to implement**

✓ **Works well for most APIs**

✗ **Can lead to bottlenecks if services depend too much on each other**

2. Asynchronous Communication (Message Queues - RabbitMQ, Kafka)

For **decoupled services**, use **message queues** where services send and receive messages without waiting for an immediate response.

Example:

The **Order Service** processes a new order.

Instead of calling the **Inventory Service** directly, it **sends a message** to a queue.

The **Inventory Service** listens and processes the message asynchronously.

Step 1: Install RabbitMQ Client

```
npm install amqplib
```

Step 2: Send Message to RabbitMQ (Publisher - Order Service)

```
const amqp = require("amqplib");

async function sendMessage(order) {
    const connection = await
amqp.connect("amqp://localhost");
    const channel = await
connection.createChannel();
    const queue = "order_queue";

    await channel.assertQueue(queue);
    channel.sendToQueue(queue,
Buffer.from(JSON.stringify(order)));

    console.log("Order placed:", order);
}

sendMessage({ orderId: 123, product: "Laptop",
quantity: 1 });
```

Step 3: Process Messages (Consumer - Inventory Service)

```
async function receiveMessages() {
    const connection = await
amqp.connect("amqp://localhost");
    const channel = await
connection.createChannel();
    const queue = "order_queue";

    await channel.assertQueue(queue);
    console.log("Waiting for messages...");

    channel.consume(queue, (msg) => {
```

```
        const order =
JSON.parse(msg.content.toString());
        console.log(`Processing order:
${order.orderId}`);
    }, { noAck: true });
}

receiveMessages();
```

✓ **Decouples services** for better fault tolerance.

✓ **Handles spikes in traffic efficiently**.

✗ **Adds complexity and requires managing a message broker**.

3. Event-Driven Communication (WebSockets, gRPC)

For **real-time communication**, use **WebSockets or gRPC**.

Example: A chat application where **messages are instantly delivered** to connected users.

Step 1: Install Socket.io

```
npm install socket.io
```

Step 2: Implement WebSocket Communication in API Gateway

```
const io = require("socket.io")(server, {
    cors: { origin: "*" }
});

io.on("connection", (socket) => {
    console.log("User connected:", socket.id);

    socket.on("message", (data) => {
        io.emit("message", data);
    });

    socket.on("disconnect", () => {
        console.log("User disconnected:",
socket.id);
    });
});
```

✓ Enables real-time updates without repeated requests.

✓ Ideal for chat applications and live dashboards.

Optimizing API Gateway Performance

1. Implement Caching for Faster Responses

```
npm install node-cache
const NodeCache = require("node-cache");
const cache = new NodeCache({ stdTTL: 60 });

app.get("/api/:service/:endpoint?", async (req,
res) => {
    const cacheKey = `${req.params.service}-
${req.params.endpoint}`;

    if (cache.has(cacheKey)) {
        return res.json(cache.get(cacheKey));
    }

    try {
        const response = await
axios.get(`${services[req.params.service]}/${req.pa
rams.endpoint}`);
        cache.set(cacheKey, response.data);
        res.json(response.data);
    } catch (error) {
        res.status(500).json({ error: "Service
communication error", details: error.message });
    }
});
```

Reduces API load by caching frequently accessed responses.

With **API Gateways and efficient service communication**, microservices become **faster, more scalable, and easier to maintain**, ensuring **high availability and optimal performance**.

Deploying Microservices on the Cloud

Building microservices locally is one thing; **deploying them to a cloud platform** for scalability, high availability, and security is another. Cloud deployment allows microservices to **run efficiently in production**, handling thousands or even millions of requests seamlessly.

A well-deployed microservices system should:

✓ **Scale automatically** based on traffic.

✓ **Ensure high availability** with redundancy.

✓ **Maintain security** with proper access controls.

✓ **Optimize costs** by only using necessary resources.

When deploying microservices, your choice of cloud provider depends on:

Ease of deployment → How quickly can you deploy and scale services?

Cost-effectiveness → Pay-as-you-go pricing vs. fixed server costs.

Managed services → Does the provider offer built-in Kubernetes, databases, and monitoring?

Security & Compliance → Does it meet security requirements like GDPR, HIPAA?

Popular Cloud Providers for Microservices

Cloud Provider	Features
AWS (Amazon Web Services)	Scalable infrastructure, AWS Lambda, ECS, EKS, S3, RDS
Google Cloud Platform (GCP)	Google Kubernetes Engine (GKE), Cloud Run, Firebase
Microsoft Azure	Azure Kubernetes Service (AKS), Functions, SQL Database
DigitalOcean	Affordable managed Kubernetes, Droplets, App Platform

For this guide, we will use **AWS**, but the same principles apply to **GCP, Azure, or DigitalOcean**.

Deploying Microservices Using Docker

Why Use Docker?

Docker allows us to:

✓ **Package each microservice into a lightweight container**.

✓ **Ensure consistency across development and production environments**.

✓ **Run services anywhere (AWS, GCP, Azure, or even local machines)**.

Step 1: Create a Dockerfile for a Microservice

Let's assume we have a **User Service** running on Express.js.

user-service/Dockerfile

```
# Use official Node.js image
FROM node:14

# Set working directory
WORKDIR /app

# Copy package.json and install dependencies
COPY package*.json ./
RUN npm install

# Copy the rest of the application files
COPY . .

# Expose the application port
EXPOSE 4001

# Start the application
CMD ["node", "server.js"]
```

This Dockerfile creates a containerized microservice that runs on port **4001**.

Step 2: Build and Run the Docker Container Locally

```
docker build -t user-service .
docker run -p 4001:4001 user-service
```

The microservice is now running inside a Docker container.

Step 3: Push the Docker Image to Docker Hub (or AWS ECR/GCP Artifact Registry)

```
docker tag user-service your-dockerhub-
username/user-service
docker push your-dockerhub-username/user-service
```

The microservice is now available for deployment on any cloud provider.

Deploying Microservices to Kubernetes (AWS EKS / GCP GKE / Azure AKS)

Kubernetes provides:

✓ **Auto-scaling** → Services scale up/down based on demand.

✓ **Self-healing** → If a service crashes, Kubernetes restarts it automatically.

✓ **Load balancing** → Routes traffic across multiple instances of a service.

Step 1: Create Kubernetes Deployment Files

user-service-deployment.yaml

```
apiVersion: apps/v1
kind: Deployment
metadata:
  name: user-service
spec:
  replicas: 3
  selector:
    matchLabels:
      app: user-service
  template:
    metadata:
      labels:
        app: user-service
    spec:
      containers:
        - name: user-service
          image: your-dockerhub-username/user-
service:latest
          ports:
            - containerPort: 4001
---
```

```
apiVersion: v1
kind: Service
metadata:
  name: user-service
spec:
  selector:
    app: user-service
  ports:
    - protocol: TCP
      port: 80
      targetPort: 4001
  type: LoadBalancer
```

✓ Defines a Kubernetes deployment with 3 replicas (instances) of the service.

✓ Automatically scales the service.

✓ Exposes the service via a LoadBalancer.

Step 2: Deploy the Service to Kubernetes

```
kubectl apply -f user-service-deployment.yaml
```

Now, Kubernetes will automatically manage and scale the microservice.

Deploying to AWS ECS (Alternative to Kubernetes)

For smaller projects, **AWS ECS (Elastic Container Service)** is a simpler alternative to Kubernetes.

Step 1: Create an ECS Cluster

```
aws ecs create-cluster --cluster-name
microservices-cluster
```

Step 2: Register a Task Definition for the User Service

ecs-task-definition.json

```
{
  "family": "user-service",
  "containerDefinitions": [
    {
      "name": "user-service",
```

314

```
      "image": "your-dockerhub-username/user-
service",
      "memory": 512,
      "cpu": 256,
      "essential": true,
      "portMappings": [{ "containerPort": 4001,
"hostPort": 4001 }]
    }
  ]
}
```

Step 3: Deploy the Service to ECS

```
aws ecs create-service --cluster microservices-
cluster --service-name user-service --task-
definition user-service
```

AWS ECS manages and deploys the microservice without requiring Kubernetes.

Setting Up CI/CD for Automated Deployment

A CI/CD pipeline automates:

✓ **Building and testing** new code changes.

✓ **Pushing updates to Docker Hub or AWS ECR**.

✓ **Deploying the latest version automatically to Kubernetes or ECS**.

Step 1: Define a GitHub Actions Pipeline

.github/workflows/deploy.yml

```
name: Deploy Microservice

on:
  push:
    branches:
      - main

jobs:
  build-and-deploy:
    runs-on: ubuntu-latest
```

```
    steps:
       - name: Checkout code
         uses: actions/checkout@v2

       - name: Log in to Docker Hub
         run: echo "${{ secrets.DOCKER_PASSWORD }}"
| docker login -u "${{ secrets.DOCKER_USERNAME }}"
--password-stdin

       - name: Build Docker Image
         run: docker build -t your-dockerhub-
username/user-service .

       - name: Push Docker Image
         run: docker push your-dockerhub-
username/user-service

       - name: Deploy to Kubernetes
         run: kubectl apply -f user-service-
deployment.yaml
```

Every time new code is pushed, the pipeline builds, tests, and deploys the microservice automatically.

By following these **best practices**, you can ensure your microservices are **scalable, resilient, and easy to maintain in production**, making them ready to handle real-world application demands.

Chapter 14: Serverless and Cloud Deployment

Deploying applications to the cloud has evolved significantly. Traditional server-based architectures required **managing infrastructure, scaling resources, and handling maintenance tasks manually**. However, with the rise of **serverless computing**, cloud providers now **manage servers dynamically**, allowing developers to focus solely on building applications.

Introduction to Serverless Computing

Serverless computing is a **cloud execution model** where cloud providers manage the infrastructure required to run applications. Developers simply deploy **functions or applications**, and the provider **automatically provisions and scales resources as needed**.

Even though the term **"serverless"** implies no servers, in reality, there are still servers running in the background. The difference is that **you don't have to manage them**—they are dynamically allocated and abstracted by the cloud provider.

How Serverless Works

A function or application is triggered – This could be an API request, a file upload, a database update, or an event like a user logging in.

The cloud provider allocates resources – Instead of a permanently running server, the provider creates an execution environment **on demand**.

The function executes and returns a response – Once execution is complete, the environment is **automatically shut down**, reducing costs.

For example, when a user uploads an image to a cloud storage service, a **serverless function** can be triggered to **resize the image, store metadata in a database, and send a notification**, all without manually provisioning any servers.

Benefits of Serverless Computing

No Server Management – The cloud provider handles scaling, maintenance, and updates.

Pay-as-You-Go Pricing – You only pay for the execution time and resources used.

Automatic Scaling – Resources scale up or down dynamically based on demand.

High Availability – Cloud providers distribute workloads across multiple locations.

Faster Development – Focus on writing code instead of managing infrastructure.

When Should You Use Serverless Computing?

Serverless is best suited for applications that:

Have unpredictable workloads – If your app experiences traffic spikes (e.g., a viral social media post), serverless scales automatically.

Require event-driven processing – Functions trigger based on events like HTTP requests, database changes, or file uploads.

Need cost optimization – If your app has periods of low activity, you don't pay for idle server time.

Perform background tasks – Ideal for scheduled jobs, image processing, or notifications.

Handle short-lived tasks – Each execution is stateless and typically runs for seconds or minutes.

However, serverless is **not ideal for applications that require long-running processes** (e.g., real-time multiplayer games or video streaming) because execution times are typically **limited to a few minutes** per request.

Real-World Examples of Serverless Computing

1. Image Processing in an E-Commerce Platform

Scenario: A user uploads a high-resolution product image.
Solution: A serverless function is triggered:

Resizes the image into multiple sizes (thumbnail, medium, high resolution).

Stores resized images in a cloud storage bucket.

Updates the database with image metadata.
Outcome: The entire process runs **automatically and scales based on demand**, ensuring quick processing even during high traffic.

2. Chatbot for Customer Support

Scenario: A customer interacts with a chatbot on a website.
Solution: Serverless functions handle:

Processing user messages.

Querying an FAQ database for responses.

Returning relevant answers.
Outcome: The chatbot **scales dynamically** based on the number of concurrent users.

3. Real-Time Notifications for a Ride-Sharing App

Scenario: A driver updates their location in a ride-sharing app.
Solution: A serverless function:

Updates the rider's UI with the driver's new location.

Sends push notifications when the driver arrives.
Outcome: The application **only uses compute power when updates are required**, reducing costs.

Deploying a Serverless Function with AWS Lambda

AWS Lambda is a **popular serverless computing service** that allows you to run code **without provisioning or managing servers**. It automatically scales, bills only for execution time, and integrates with various AWS services.

Step 1: Install AWS CLI and Set Up an IAM Role

Install AWS CLI

```
pip install awscli
aws configure
```

Create an IAM Role for Lambda Execution

```
aws iam create-role --role-name lambda-basic --
assume-role-policy-document file://trust-
policy.json
```

trust-policy.json:

```json
{
  "Version": "2012-10-17",
  "Statement": [
    {
      "Effect": "Allow",
      "Principal": {
        "Service": "lambda.amazonaws.com"
      },
      "Action": "sts:AssumeRole"
    }
  ]
}
```

Step 2: Write a Lambda Function

Create a new folder and add an **index.js** file:

```js
exports.handler = async (event) => {
    return {
        statusCode: 200,
        body: JSON.stringify({ message: "Hello from
AWS Lambda!" })
    };
};
```

Step 3: Deploy the Function

Zip the function:

```
zip function.zip index.js
```

Deploy it to AWS Lambda:

```
aws lambda create-function --function-name
myLambdaFunction \
--zip-file fileb://function.zip --handler
index.handler \
--runtime nodejs14.x --role
arn:aws:iam::YOUR_ACCOUNT_ID:role/lambda-basic
```

The function is now deployed and can be triggered via AWS API Gateway.

Deploying Serverless Functions on Vercel

Vercel provides **fast, serverless deployments** for Node.js applications.

Step 1: Install Vercel CLI

```
npm install -g vercel
```

Step 2: Create a Serverless Function

Create an `api/hello.js` file:

```
module.exports = (req, res) => {
    res.json({ message: "Hello from Vercel
Serverless!" });
};
```

Step 3: Deploy the Function

```
vercel
```

The function is deployed and available online instantly

Comparing Serverless Providers

Feature	AWS Lambda	Vercel	Google Cloud Functions	Azure Functions
Best for	Scalable backend logic	Frontend APIs	& Event-driven apps	Enterprise apps
Cold start time	Fast	Fast	Fast	Fast
Auto-scaling	Yes	Yes	Yes	Yes
Free tier available	Yes	Yes	Yes	Yes

✓ **Choose AWS Lambda for backend processing.**

✓ **Choose Vercel for frontend-friendly deployments.**

✓ **Choose Google Cloud Functions for AI/ML integrations.**

With **serverless computing**, applications become **more agile, cost-efficient, and scalable**, making it an essential tool for modern cloud-based development.

Deploying Node.js Apps on AWS, Vercel, and Heroku

Deploying a **Node.js application** to the cloud is a critical step in making it accessible to users. Whether you're building an API, a web application, or a microservice, **choosing the right cloud provider and deployment strategy** determines how well your app performs in production.

Deploying a Node.js App on AWS

AWS (Amazon Web Services) is a **highly scalable and reliable cloud platform** used by companies worldwide. It offers multiple ways to deploy Node.js applications, including:

EC2 (Elastic Compute Cloud) → Gives you full control over a virtual server.

Elastic Beanstalk → A fully managed platform for deploying applications easily.

Lambda (Serverless) → Executes code on-demand without managing servers.

For this guide, we'll **deploy a Node.js app on EC2 and Elastic Beanstalk**.

Deploying a Node.js App on AWS EC2

EC2 instances are virtual servers that provide **full control over the operating system, network settings, and software configurations**.

Step 1: Launch an EC2 Instance

Log in to **AWS Console** → Go to **EC2** → Click **Launch Instance**.
Choose **Ubuntu 20.04** as the operating system.
Select **t2.micro** (Free Tier).
Configure security groups → **Allow inbound HTTP (port 80) and SSH (port 22)**.
Click **Launch** and **connect via SSH** using the provided key pair.

Step 2: Install Node.js and Set Up the App

Once connected to the EC2 instance, update the system and install Node.js:

```
sudo apt update -y
sudo apt install nodejs npm -y
```

Clone a Node.js application from GitHub:

```
git clone https://github.com/your-repository/node-app.git
cd node-app
npm install
```

Step 3: Run the Application

Start the application:

```
node index.js
```

To keep the app running in the background, use **PM2**:

```
npm install -g pm2
pm2 start index.js
pm2 save
pm2 startup
```

The Node.js application is now running on AWS EC2.

Deploying a Node.js App on AWS Elastic Beanstalk

Elastic Beanstalk is **AWS's Platform-as-a-Service (PaaS)**, which automatically manages the deployment process, scaling, and load balancing.

Step 1: Install the AWS CLI and Elastic Beanstalk CLI

```
pip install awscli
pip install awsebcli --upgrade
```

Step 2: Initialize the Beanstalk Environment

Navigate to your Node.js app directory and initialize Beanstalk:

```
eb init
```

Follow the prompts to:

Select AWS **region**.

Choose **Node.js** as the platform.

Step 3: Deploy the Application

```
eb create my-node-app
```

✓ **AWS Beanstalk automatically provisions resources and deploys the application.**

✓ **You get a URL to access your live application.**

Deploying a Node.js App on Vercel

Vercel is a **serverless deployment platform** optimized for frontend and API deployments. It offers:

Zero configuration deployments.

Automatic scalability.

Fast global CDN for low-latency requests.

Step 1: Install Vercel CLI

```
npm install -g vercel
```

Step 2: Deploy a Node.js API

Create an `api/index.js` file:

```
module.exports = (req, res) => {
    res.json({ message: "Hello from Vercel
Serverless!" });
};
```

Step 3: Deploy to Vercel

Run the following command:

```
vercel
```

**Vercel detects the project and deploys it automatically.
You get a production-ready URL instantly.**

Deploying a Node.js App on Heroku

Heroku is a **developer-friendly PaaS** that simplifies deployments by
abstracting infrastructure management.

Step 1: Install Heroku CLI

```
npm install -g heroku
```

Step 2: Deploy a Node.js App to Heroku

Create a Simple Express App

```
mkdir heroku-app
cd heroku-app
npm init -y
npm install express
```

Create index.js:

```
const express = require("express");
const app = express();
const PORT = process.env.PORT || 3000;

app.get("/", (req, res) => {
    res.send("Hello from Heroku!");
});

app.listen(PORT, () => console.log(`Server running
on port ${PORT}`));
```

Create a Procfile (Required by Heroku)

```
echo "web: node index.js" > Procfile
```
Deploy the Application

```
heroku login
heroku create my-heroku-app
git init
```

```
git add .
git commit -m "Deploy to Heroku"
git push heroku master
```

The app is now deployed and accessible via a Heroku-provided URL.

Comparing Deployment Options

Feature	AWS EC2	AWS Beanstalk	Vercel	Heroku
Best For	Full server control	Auto-managed scaling	APIs & frontend apps	Simple backend hosting
Scaling	Manual	Automatic	Automatic	Limited free tier
Complexity	High	Medium	Low	Low
Cost	Pay-per-use	Pay-per-use	Free for small apps	Free with limitations

Use AWS EC2 for full control over infrastructure.
Use AWS Beanstalk for managed deployments with auto-scaling.
Use Vercel for fast, serverless deployments.
Use Heroku for easy backend hosting with minimal configuration.

Automating Deployments with CI/CD Pipelines

Instead of manually deploying updates, use **Continuous Integration and Continuous Deployment (CI/CD)** to **automate the process**.

Step 1: Set Up a GitHub Actions Workflow

Create `.github/workflows/deploy.yml`:

```
name: Deploy to Heroku

on:
  push:
    branches:
```

```
      - main

jobs:
  deploy:
    runs-on: ubuntu-latest
    steps:
      - name: Checkout code
        uses: actions/checkout@v2

      - name: Setup Node.js
        uses: actions/setup-node@v2
        with:
          node-version: 14

      - name: Install Dependencies
        run: npm install

      - name: Deploy to Heroku
        run: |
          echo "${{ secrets.HEROKU_API_KEY }}" |
heroku auth:token
          heroku git:remote -a my-heroku-app
          git push heroku main
```

✓ **Automatically deploys when new code is pushed to GitHub**.
✓ **Ensures consistent and error-free deployments**.

By understanding **the strengths of each platform**, you can **choose the right deployment strategy** based on your application's needs, whether it's **serverless, auto-scaling, or traditional hosting**.

CI/CD Pipelines for Node.js Applications

In modern software development, **continuous integration (CI) and continuous deployment (CD)** are critical practices that enable teams to **automate testing, build processes, and deployments**. Without CI/CD, updates to an application require **manual testing and deployment**, which can be time-consuming, error-prone, and inefficient.

Continuous Integration (CI) – The practice of frequently integrating code changes into a shared repository, followed by automated testing. **Continuous Deployment (CD)** – The automated process of deploying successfully tested code to production.

Example Workflow:
A developer pushes new code to a Git repository (GitHub, GitLab, Bitbucket).
The CI system automatically:

Installs dependencies

Runs tests

Builds the application
If all tests pass, the CD system **deploys** the application automatically.

Setting Up a CI/CD Pipeline for a Node.js App

Step 1: Create a Simple Node.js App

If you don't have a Node.js application yet, create one:

```
mkdir node-ci-cd
cd node-ci-cd
npm init -y
npm install express jest supertest
```

Create `index.js`:

```
const express = require("express");
const app = express();
const PORT = process.env.PORT || 3000;

app.get("/", (req, res) => {
    res.send("Hello from CI/CD pipeline!");
});

app.listen(PORT, () => console.log(`Server running
on port ${PORT}`));

module.exports = app;
```

Create `tests/index.test.js`:

```js
const request = require("supertest");
const app = require("../index");

test("GET / should return status 200", async () =>
{
    const response = await request(app).get("/");
    expect(response.status).toBe(200);
    expect(response.text).toBe("Hello from CI/CD
pipeline!");
});
```

We now have a simple Express app with a test suite.

Automating CI/CD with GitHub Actions

GitHub Actions allows you to **run tests, build, and deploy automatically** when code is pushed to the repository.

Step 1: Create a GitHub Repository

```
git init
git add .
git commit -m "Initial commit"
git branch -M main
git remote add origin https://github.com/your-username/node-ci-cd.git
git push -u origin main
```

Step 2: Define a CI/CD Workflow

Create the folder `.github/workflows/` and add a file named `ci-cd.yml`:

```yaml
name: CI/CD Pipeline for Node.js

on:
  push:
    branches:
        - main
  pull_request:
    branches:
        - main
```

329

```
jobs:
  build:
    runs-on: ubuntu-latest

    steps:
      - name: Checkout code
        uses: actions/checkout@v2

      - name: Setup Node.js
        uses: actions/setup-node@v2
        with:
          node-version: 16

      - name: Install dependencies
        run: npm install

      - name: Run tests
        run: npm test

      - name: Build application
        run: npm run build || echo "No build step
defined"

  deploy:
    needs: build
    runs-on: ubuntu-latest
    if: github.ref == 'refs/heads/main'

    steps:
      - name: Deploy to Heroku
        run: |
          echo "${{ secrets.HEROKU_API_KEY }}" |
heroku auth:token
          heroku git:remote -a your-heroku-app-name
          git push heroku main
```

This GitHub Actions workflow runs tests and automatically deploys to Heroku.

Step 3: Add Secrets for Secure Deployment

Go to your GitHub repository → **Settings** → **Secrets** → **Actions**.
Click **New Repository Secret** and add:

`HEROKU_API_KEY` → Get this from Heroku by running:

```
heroku auth:token
```

Push your code to GitHub:

```
git add .
git commit -m "Setup GitHub Actions"
git push origin main
```

Now, every time code is pushed to `main`, the app is tested and deployed automatically!

Deploying a Node.js App Using GitHub Actions

Deploying to AWS (EC2 or Elastic Beanstalk)

Modify `ci-cd.yml` to deploy to AWS:

```
deploy:
  needs: build
  runs-on: ubuntu-latest

  steps:
    - name: Configure AWS credentials
      uses: aws-actions/configure-aws-
credentials@v1
      with:
        aws-access-key-id: ${{
secrets.AWS_ACCESS_KEY_ID }}
        aws-secret-access-key: ${{
secrets.AWS_SECRET_ACCESS_KEY }}
        aws-region: us-east-1

    - name: Deploy to Elastic Beanstalk
      run: eb deploy my-app-env
```

Ensures fully automated AWS deployment on each push.

Deploying to Vercel

Modify `ci-cd.yml` to deploy to Vercel:

```
deploy:
```

```
    needs: build
    runs-on: ubuntu-latest

    steps:
      - name: Deploy to Vercel
        run: vercel --prod --token ${{
secrets.VERCEL_TOKEN }}
```

Ensures Node.js apps are deployed instantly to Vercel.

Optimizing CI/CD for Performance

1. Caching Dependencies for Faster Builds

Modify `ci-cd.yml` to cache `node_modules`:

```
- name: Cache dependencies
  uses: actions/cache@v2
  with:
    path: ~/.npm
    key: ${{ runner.os }}-node-${{
hashFiles('**/package-lock.json') }}
    restore-keys: |
      ${{ runner.os }}-node-
```

Reduces install time by caching dependencies.

2. Running Tests in Parallel

Modify `ci-cd.yml` to speed up test execution:

```
- name: Run tests in parallel
  run: npm test -- --maxWorkers=2
```

Speeds up testing by running on multiple CPU cores.

3. Deploying to Multiple Environments (Staging & Production)

Modify `ci-cd.yml` to deploy to **staging first, then production**:

```
deploy:
  needs: build
  runs-on: ubuntu-latest
```

```
steps:
  - name: Deploy to Staging
    run: vercel --prod --token ${{
secrets.VERCEL_TOKEN }} --env staging

  - name: Deploy to Production
    if: github.ref == 'refs/heads/main'
    run: vercel --prod --token ${{
secrets.VERCEL_TOKEN }} --env production
```

Ensures safe deployment to staging before production.

By implementing **CI/CD**, you ensure that your application is **always production-ready**, with every code change tested, built, and deployed automatically. 🚀

Chapter 15: Optimizing Node.js Applications

Optimizing a Node.js application ensures **faster response times, better scalability, and efficient resource utilization**. As applications grow, handling **high traffic, reducing latency, and preventing bottlenecks** becomes crucial.

Identifying Performance Bottlenecks

Performance issues in a **Node.js application** can lead to **slow response times, high CPU usage, memory leaks, and poor user experience**. When an application slows down, the key to fixing it is **accurate identification of bottlenecks** before optimization.

If you try to optimize without identifying the root cause, you may **waste time on the wrong areas** or introduce unnecessary complexity. A systematic approach to profiling and debugging helps pinpoint the exact issues affecting performance.

A **performance bottleneck** occurs when **one part of the application is significantly slowing down the entire system**.

Common Bottlenecks in Node.js Applications

Blocking Operations – Synchronous code that prevents other operations from running.
Slow Database Queries – Inefficient queries causing delays.
Memory Leaks – Unreleased objects consuming system memory over time.
High CPU Usage – Intensive computations running on the main thread.
Unoptimized Middleware – Middleware that increases response times.
Network Latency – Delays caused by slow external API calls.

Each of these issues **affects request handling speed, server load, and overall user experience**.

Measuring Response Times with Basic Logging

Before using complex tools, start by **measuring how long key parts of your application take to execute**.

Using console.time() to Measure Execution Time

Node.js has a built-in `console.time()` function to measure how long operations take:

```
console.time("DB Query");
const result = await database.find(); // Simulate
database call
console.timeEnd("DB Query");
```

This logs:

```
DB Query: 240ms
```

✓ **Quick way to find slow sections in your code.**

✓ **Pinpoints specific functions causing delays.**

Profiling Application Performance with Node.js Built-in Tools

Using `perf_hooks` to Track Execution Performance

The `perf_hooks` module provides detailed performance measurements.

Example: Measuring Function Execution Time

```
const { performance, PerformanceObserver } =
require("perf_hooks");

const obs = new PerformanceObserver((items) => {
    console.log(items.getEntries()[0]);
});
obs.observe({ entryTypes: ["measure"] });

performance.mark("start");
setTimeout(() => {
    performance.mark("end");
    performance.measure("Slow Function", "start",
"end");
}, 500);
```

Shows detailed execution time in milliseconds.

Detecting High CPU Usage and Slow Functions

Using Node.js CPU Profiling with Chrome DevTools

Start the Node.js application with profiling enabled:

```
node --prof index.js
```
After running for a while, stop the application and generate a report:

```
node --prof-process isolate-*.log > cpu-profile.txt
```
Analyze `cpu-profile.txt` for slow-running functions.

✓ **Identifies high CPU usage areas in your code.**

✓ **Finds functions that should be optimized.**

Identifying and Fixing Memory Leaks

Memory leaks happen when an application **keeps holding onto memory that is no longer needed**, leading to **high memory usage and potential crashes**.

Detecting Memory Leaks with process.memoryUsage()

```
setInterval(() => {
    console.log(process.memoryUsage());
}, 5000);
```

Monitors memory usage over time to detect unexpected growth.

Common Causes of Memory Leaks in Node.js

Global Variables – Unused variables held in memory. **Event Listeners Not Removed** – Accumulating unused listeners. **Uncleared Timers** – `setTimeout()` or `setInterval()` running indefinitely.

Fix: Remove Unused Event Listeners

```
const EventEmitter = require("events");
const emitter = new EventEmitter();

const handler = () => console.log("Event
triggered");

emitter.on("testEvent", handler);
```

```
emitter.off("testEvent", handler); // Proper
cleanup
```

Ensures event listeners don't accumulate in memory.

Optimizing Database Queries to Reduce Response Times

Slow database queries often **block requests and increase latency**.

1. Index Frequently Queried Fields

Instead of:

```
const users = await User.find({ email:
"user@example.com" });
```

Add an **index** to speed up lookups:

```
User.createIndexes({ email: 1 });
```

Drastically improves query speed for large datasets.

2. Use Pagination to Avoid Large Data Fetches

Instead of returning **thousands of records** at once:

```
const users = await User.find().limit(10).skip(20);
```

Prevents excessive data transfer, improving performance.

Fixing Blocking Code in the Event Loop

Node.js runs **on a single thread**, meaning if one function blocks execution, **everything else slows down**.

Using Asynchronous Code Instead of Blocking Calls

Blocking function:

```
const fs = require("fs");

const data = fs.readFileSync("large-file.txt"); //
Blocks event loop
console.log("File read complete");
Non-blocking function:
fs.readFile("large-file.txt", (err, data) => {
```

337

```
    console.log("File read complete");
});
```

Prevents other requests from being delayed.

Monitoring Performance in Production

Tools like PM2, New Relic, and Datadog help monitor performance and detect real-time bottlenecks.

Using PM2 to Monitor Node.js Applications

Install PM2:

```
npm install -g pm2
```
Start the application with monitoring:

```
pm2 start index.js --name="node-app"
```
Check real-time statistics:

```
pm2 monit
```

Shows CPU, memory usage, and request latency in real time.

Example: Optimizing a Slow API Endpoint

Original Code (Slow API with Blocking Query and No Caching):

```
app.get("/users", async (req, res) => {
    const users = await database.find(); //
Expensive DB query
    res.json(users);
});
```
Optimized Code (Uses Caching and Pagination):

```
const redis = require("redis");
const client = redis.createClient();

// Middleware to check cache
const cache = (req, res, next) => {
    client.get("users", (err, data) => {
        if (data) {
            res.json(JSON.parse(data));
        } else {
```

338

```
            next();
        }
    });
};

// Optimized API
app.get("/users", cache, async (req, res) => {
    const users = await database.find().limit(10);
    client.setex("users", 3600,
JSON.stringify(users)); // Cache for 1 hour
    res.json(users);
});
```

✓ **Improves response time with caching**.

✓ **Prevents unnecessary database queries**.

By identifying and fixing **performance bottlenecks**, your Node.js application will **run faster, handle more traffic, and provide a better user experience**.

Load Balancing and Clustering in Node.js

Node.js is known for its **event-driven, non-blocking architecture**, making it an excellent choice for handling concurrent requests efficiently. However, by default, **Node.js runs on a single thread**, which means it can only process one request at a time per instance.

As traffic increases, this **single-threaded model can become a bottleneck**, leading to slow response times and unresponsive applications. To solve this, we need to **scale our application horizontally** using **load balancing and clustering**.

A single Node.js instance running on **one CPU core** has **limited processing power**. If multiple requests arrive simultaneously, some will have to **wait until the event loop processes the earlier ones**, leading to:

Increased response times for users.

Higher CPU utilization on the single-threaded process.

339

Reduced reliability because if the single instance crashes, the entire application goes down.

Load Balancing → Distributes incoming traffic across multiple servers or instances.

Clustering → Runs multiple instances of Node.js **on different CPU cores** within the same machine.

Combining both techniques allows for **horizontal scaling**, ensuring your application can **handle high traffic efficiently**.

How Clustering Works

The **Cluster module** allows Node.js to **fork multiple worker processes** from a **single master process**, with each worker **running on a separate CPU core**.

If one worker crashes, another takes over.
Each worker shares the same port, distributing traffic automatically.

Step 1: Create a Basic Clustered Server

Modify `server.js` to utilize multiple CPU cores:

```
const cluster = require("cluster");
const os = require("os");
const express = require("express");

if (cluster.isMaster) {
    console.log(`Master process ${process.pid} is
running`);

    // Fork workers (one for each CPU core)
    for (let i = 0; i < os.cpus().length; i++) {
        cluster.fork();
    }

    cluster.on("exit", (worker) => {
        console.log(`Worker ${worker.process.pid}
died`);
        cluster.fork(); // Restart worker if one
crashes
    });
} else {
```

```
    const app = express();

    app.get("/", (req, res) => {
        res.send(`Handled by worker
${process.pid}`);
    });

    app.listen(3000, () => console.log(`Worker
${process.pid} started`));
}
```

How This Works

✓ **The master process forks multiple worker processes**, each running on a separate CPU core.

✓ **Incoming requests are distributed among the workers**, improving performance.

✓ **If a worker crashes, the master process automatically restarts it**, ensuring availability.

Implementing Load Balancing with Nginx

While clustering **distributes traffic within a single server**, **load balancing distributes traffic across multiple servers**, ensuring:

✓ **High availability** – If one server fails, traffic is rerouted.

✓ **Improved performance** – Incoming requests are spread across multiple servers.

✓ **Scalability** – Add more servers as needed.

Step 1: Install and Configure Nginx

Install Nginx (Linux/Ubuntu):

```
sudo apt update
sudo apt install nginx
```
Modify Nginx Configuration

Edit the configuration file:

```
sudo nano /etc/nginx/sites-available/default
```

341

Add the following **reverse proxy and load balancer** configuration:

```
server {
    listen 80;

    location / {
        proxy_pass http://node_servers;
    }
}

upstream node_servers {
    server 127.0.0.1:3001;
    server 127.0.0.1:3002;
    server 127.0.0.1:3003;
    server 127.0.0.1:3004;
}
```

Restart Nginx to Apply Changes

```
sudo systemctl restart nginx
```

How This Works

✓ **Nginx listens on port 80 and forwards requests to available Node.js servers**.

✓ **The load balancer distributes requests among multiple instances**, preventing overload on a single server.

Running Multiple Node.js Instances with PM2

While clustering allows using multiple CPU cores, **PM2** (Process Manager 2) helps **manage multiple Node.js instances efficiently**.

Step 1: Install PM2

```
npm install -g pm2
```

Step 2: Start Multiple Instances of Node.js Application

```
pm2 start server.js -i max
```

✓ `-i max` runs **one instance per CPU core**.

✓ PM2 **automatically restarts instances** if one crashes.

342

Step 3: Monitor Performance

```
pm2 monit
```

Shows real-time CPU and memory usage per process.

Scaling Node.js in the Cloud

For large-scale applications, deploying on **AWS, Google Cloud, or Azure** ensures:

✓ **Automatic scaling** – Services like AWS Elastic Load Balancer distribute traffic dynamically.

✓ **Global availability** – Deploy across multiple regions for faster response times.

✓ **Managed load balancing** – Cloud providers optimize resource allocation.

Deploying Node.js Behind AWS Elastic Load Balancer (ELB)

Launch multiple EC2 instances running Node.js.
Configure an AWS Application Load Balancer (ALB).
Add EC2 instances as target groups.
Use Auto Scaling Groups to automatically adjust instance count based on traffic.

AWS automatically distributes requests across multiple instances, ensuring optimal performance.

Example: A Fully Scalable Node.js Architecture

Scenario: A Node.js application handles **100,000+ concurrent users**.

Step 1: Use **Node.js Clustering** to utilize all CPU cores.
Step 2: Deploy multiple instances on **AWS EC2**.
Step 3: Set up **Nginx as a Load Balancer** for traffic distribution.
Step 4: Use **Redis caching** to speed up API responses.
Step 5: Monitor and scale using **AWS Auto Scaling** and **PM2**.

Testing Load Balancing and Performance

1. Using Apache Benchmark (ab) for Load Testing

Run this command to **simulate 1000 requests with 100 concurrent users**:

```
ab -n 1000 -c 100 http://localhost/
```

Measures request handling capacity and response times.

2. Using Artillery for Stress Testing

Install **Artillery**, a powerful load-testing tool:

```
npm install -g artillery
```
Run a **stress test** simulating 500 users per second for 30 seconds:

```
artillery quick --count 500 -n 30 http://localhost/
```

Generates detailed reports on system performance.

By applying these techniques, **your Node.js application will be highly scalable, fault-tolerant, and capable of handling massive traffic loads**, ensuring smooth user experience even during peak demand. 🚀

Caching Strategies with Redis

Efficient caching is one of the most effective ways to **improve the performance, scalability, and reliability** of a Node.js application. By caching frequently accessed data, we can **reduce database load, lower response times, and handle more concurrent users** with fewer resources.

Why Caching Matters in Node.js Applications

Every time a user makes a request, the server typically **fetches data from a database or an external API**, processes it, and sends it back to the client. If the same request is made repeatedly, this leads to:

Increased database queries – The database is asked for the same data multiple times.

Slow response times – Waiting for the database to return results.

Higher infrastructure costs – More CPU and memory usage due to redundant processing.

Instead of **re-fetching the same data over and over**, we can store it in a **high-speed cache** like Redis, allowing **instant access without hitting the database**.

Understanding Redis as a Caching Solution

Redis (Remote Dictionary Server) is an **in-memory data store** that is extremely fast because it **keeps data in RAM** instead of reading from disk-based storage. It supports **key-value storage**, allowing us to cache:

✓ **Database query results** – Speed up API responses.

✓ **Sessions and authentication tokens** – Reduce database lookups for logged-in users.

✓ **Computed results** – Store expensive calculations to avoid recalculating frequently.

How Redis Works for Caching

Step 1: The application first checks Redis to see if the requested data is cached.

Step 2: If the data is **found in Redis**, it is returned instantly (**cache hit**).

Step 3: If the data is **not in Redis**, it is fetched from the database, stored in Redis, and then returned (**cache miss**).

Setting Up Redis in a Node.js Application

Step 1: Install Redis

For Linux/Ubuntu:

```
sudo apt update
sudo apt install redis-server
```

Start Redis:

```
sudo systemctl enable redis
sudo systemctl start redis
```

To verify Redis is running:

```
redis-cli ping
```

If Redis responds with "PONG", it is working correctly.

Step 2: Install Redis Client for Node.js

```
npm install redis
```

Step 3: Connect to Redis in a Node.js Application

Modify `server.js` to integrate Redis:

```
const express = require("express");
const redis = require("redis");

const app = express();
const client = redis.createClient(); // Connect to
Redis

client.on("error", (err) => console.error("Redis
error:", err));

// Example route without caching
app.get("/no-cache", async (req, res) => {
    const data = await slowDatabaseQuery();
    res.json(data);
});

// Example route with caching
app.get("/cache", async (req, res) => {
    client.get("cachedData", async (err,
cachedResult) => {
        if (cachedResult) {
            return
res.json(JSON.parse(cachedResult)); // Return
cached data
        }

        const data = await slowDatabaseQuery(); //
Fetch fresh data
        client.setex("cachedData", 3600,
JSON.stringify(data)); // Store data in Redis for 1
hour

        res.json(data);
    });
});
```

```
async function slowDatabaseQuery() {
    return new Promise((resolve) => {
        setTimeout(() => resolve({ message:
"Fetched from database" }), 2000);
    });
}

app.listen(3000, () => console.log("Server running
on port 3000"));
```

✓ Caches API responses, reducing load on the database.

✓ If Redis contains the data, it returns instantly.

✓ If not, data is fetched from the database, stored in Redis, and then returned.

Implementing Expiry and Cache Invalidation

Storing data **indefinitely** in the cache can cause **stale data issues**. Redis allows setting **expiry times** for cached items, ensuring data is refreshed periodically.

Using TTL (Time-to-Live) for Expiry

```
client.setex("user_123", 600,
JSON.stringify(userData)); // Expires in 600
seconds (10 minutes)
```

Ensures cached data is updated periodically.

Manual Cache Invalidation (Deleting Stale Cache)

When updating the database, the cache must be cleared to prevent outdated data from being served:

```
client.del("user_123"); // Removes cached data for
this user
```

Prevents serving old data after an update.

Caching Strategies for Different Use Cases

1. Full Page Caching (Improving API Response Times)

For **frequently accessed API endpoints**, caching **entire API responses** speeds up delivery.

```
app.get("/products", async (req, res) => {
    client.get("all_products", async (err,
cachedProducts) => {
        if (cachedProducts) {
            return
res.json(JSON.parse(cachedProducts)); // Return
cached data
        }

        const products = await database.find(); //
Fetch products from DB
        client.setex("all_products", 1800,
JSON.stringify(products)); // Cache for 30 minutes

        res.json(products);
    });
});
```

Reduces database load for high-traffic endpoints.

2. User Session Caching (Faster Authentication and Authorization)

Instead of storing sessions in a database, **store them in Redis** for quick lookups.

```
app.post("/login", async (req, res) => {
    const user = await
database.findUser(req.body.email);

    if (!user || user.password !==
req.body.password) {
        return res.status(401).json({ error:
"Invalid credentials" });
    }

    const sessionToken = generateToken();
    client.setex(`session_${sessionToken}`, 3600,
JSON.stringify(user)); // Cache session for 1 hour
```

```
    res.json({ sessionToken });
});
```

Speeds up authentication without querying the database every time.

3. Rate Limiting (Preventing API Abuse)

Redis can be used to limit how many times a user can **access an API in a given time** to prevent **DDoS attacks or spam requests**.

```
const rateLimit = (req, res, next) => {
    const ip = req.ip;

    client.get(ip, (err, record) => {
        if (record && record >= 10) {
            return res.status(429).json({ error:
"Too many requests" });
        }

        client.incr(ip);
        client.expire(ip, 60); // Reset count every
60 seconds

        next();
    });
};

app.use(rateLimit);
```

Restricts users to 10 requests per minute to prevent abuse.

Monitoring Redis Cache Performance

1. Checking Cache Hit Ratio

To see how often requests are served from the cache instead of the database:

```
redis-cli info stats | grep keyspace_hits
```

Higher hit ratio means better cache utilization.

2. Monitoring Memory Usage

```
redis-cli info memory
```

Ensures Redis is not consuming excessive memory.

Deploying Redis in Production

For high-traffic applications, **use Redis Cluster** to distribute cache across multiple nodes.

Setting Up Redis Cluster on AWS (Elasticache)

Go to AWS Elasticache Console.
Create a Redis Cluster with at least **3 nodes**.
Connect to Redis Cluster from Node.js:

```
const Redis = require("ioredis");
const client = new Redis.Cluster([
    { host: "redis-cluster-endpoint", port: 6379 }
]);
```

Ensures high availability and fault tolerance.

By implementing **Redis caching strategies**, your Node.js application will be **significantly faster, more scalable, and resilient under heavy traffic**, providing a **smooth experience for users** while reducing infrastructure costs.

Chapter 16: Testing and Debugging

Ensuring that a Node.js application runs reliably and without errors is crucial, especially as applications grow in complexity. Bugs, performance issues, and regressions can sneak into the codebase, making thorough **testing and debugging** essential parts of the development process.

Why Testing and Debugging Matter

Prevents Bugs – Catching issues early avoids major production failures.
Ensures Stability – Automated tests prevent breaking changes.
Speeds Up Development – Debugging tools help quickly identify issues.
Improves Code Maintainability – Tests document expected behavior.

Writing Unit Tests with Jest

Unit testing is a **crucial practice** in modern software development that ensures each function in an application behaves as expected. Without proper tests, applications can **break unexpectedly**, leading to **downtime, security vulnerabilities, and frustrated users**.

Jest is a **fast, powerful, and easy-to-use** testing framework that allows developers to write **unit tests**, ensuring individual components function correctly.

A **unit test** focuses on testing a **single function or module** in isolation, meaning external dependencies (like databases or APIs) are **mocked or replaced with test doubles**.

When unit tests are properly written:
✓ **Bugs are detected early** – Issues are caught before deployment.
✓ **Code is more reliable** – Prevents unexpected regressions.
✓ **Refactoring is safer** – Code can be changed without breaking functionality.
✓ **Speeds up development** – Developers get instant feedback on code behavior.

Setting Up Jest in a Node.js Project

Step 1: Install Jest

```
npm install --save-dev jest
```

Step 2: Configure Jest in package.json

Modify the `package.json` file to include a test script:

```
"scripts": {
    "test": "jest"
}
```

Now, Jest will automatically run all test files with the `.test.js` or `.spec.js` extension.

Writing Basic Unit Tests with Jest

Step 1: Create a Simple Function

Create `math.js` in your project:

```
function add(a, b) {
    return a + b;
}

function multiply(a, b) {
    return a * b;
}

module.exports = { add, multiply };
```

Step 2: Write Unit Tests for the Functions

Create a test file `math.test.js`:

```
const { add, multiply } = require("./math");

test("adds 2 + 3 to equal 5", () => {
    expect(add(2, 3)).toBe(5);
});

test("multiplies 4 * 5 to equal 20", () => {
    expect(multiply(4, 5)).toBe(20);
});
```

Step 3: Run the Tests

Execute the following command:

```
npm test
```

Jest will output:

```
PASS    ./math.test.js

✓ adds 2 + 3 to equal 5

✓ multiplies 4 * 5 to equal 20
```

Confirms expected behavior for both functions.
If any test fails, Jest provides detailed error messages for debugging.

Using Matchers in Jest for Assertions

Jest provides a variety of **matchers** to validate different types of outputs.

Testing Object Equality

```
test("object assignment", () => {
    const data = { name: "Alice" };
    data.age = 30;
    expect(data).toEqual({ name: "Alice", age: 30
});
});
```

Ensures objects have the expected properties and values.

Checking for Null or Undefined Values

```
test("null check", () => {
    const value = null;
    expect(value).toBeNull();
    expect(value).not.toBeUndefined();
});
```

Validates null and undefined cases correctly.

Testing Arrays and Strings

```
test("Array contains specific item", () => {
```

353

```
    const shoppingList = ["milk", "eggs", "bread"];
    expect(shoppingList).toContain("milk");
});
```
Confirms the presence of an item in an array.

Mocking External Dependencies in Unit Tests

Unit tests should **not depend on external APIs or databases** because:

Network requests slow down tests.

Data can change unpredictably.

Tests should be isolated and deterministic.

Mocking an API Call with Jest

Modify userService.js:

```
const axios = require("axios");

async function getUserData(userId) {
    const response = await
axios.get(`https://api.example.com/users/${userId}`
);
    return response.data;
}

module.exports = { getUserData };
```

Mocking the API in Tests

Create userService.test.js:

```
const { getUserData } = require("./userService");
const axios = require("axios");

jest.mock("axios"); // Mock axios

test("fetches user data successfully", async () =>
{
    axios.get.mockResolvedValue({ data: { id: 1,
name: "Alice" } });
```

```
    const user = await getUserData(1);
    expect(user.name).toBe("Alice");
});
```

Prevents actual network requests while testing API behavior.

Testing Asynchronous Code

Jest supports testing **async/await** functions and promises.

Testing a Delayed Function

Modify `asyncFunctions.js`:

```
function delayedFunction() {
    return new Promise((resolve) => {
        setTimeout(() => resolve("Completed"),
1000);
    });
}

module.exports = { delayedFunction };
```

Write a Test for the Asynchronous Function

```
const { delayedFunction } =
require("./asyncFunctions");

test("resolves after 1 second", async () => {
    await
expect(delayedFunction()).resolves.toBe("Completed"
);
});
```

Ensures the function correctly handles asynchronous behavior.

Running Tests in Watch Mode

During development, use Jest's watch mode to **rerun tests automatically when files change**:

```
npm test -- --watch
```

Instant feedback while coding.

Measuring Test Coverage

To measure **how much of the code is tested**, use Jest's built-in coverage tool:

```
npm test -- --coverage
```

Example output:

```
--------------------|---------|----------|--------
-|---------
File                | % Stmts | % Branch | % Funcs
| % Lines
--------------------|---------|----------|--------
-|---------
math.js             | 100%    | 100%     | 100%    |
100%
--------------------|---------|----------|--------
-|---------

Test coverage: 100%
```

Identifies untested parts of the codebase.

Organizing Tests for Large Applications

For large projects, group tests into **separate directories**:

```
/tests
    ├── unit
    │    ├── math.test.js
    │    ├── userService.test.js
    ├── integration
    │    ├── api.test.js
```

Keeps unit and integration tests structured for better maintainability.

Automating Tests with Continuous Integration (CI/CD)

To automatically run tests **on every GitHub commit**, use **GitHub Actions**.

Step 1: Create `.github/workflows/test.yml`

```yaml
name: Node.js CI

on: [push, pull_request]

jobs:
  test:
    runs-on: ubuntu-latest
    steps:
      - name: Checkout code
        uses: actions/checkout@v2

      - name: Setup Node.js
        uses: actions/setup-node@v2
        with:
          node-version: 16

      - name: Install dependencies
        run: npm install

      - name: Run tests
        run: npm test
```

Runs tests automatically when code is pushed to GitHub.

By implementing **unit testing with Jest**, you ensure **code reliability, prevent regressions, and improve software quality**, making development faster and more efficient. 🚀

Integration Testing with Mocha and Chai

Ensuring that different components of an application **work together correctly** is just as important as verifying individual functions. This is where **integration testing** comes in.

While **unit tests focus on isolated functions**, integration tests **verify interactions between modules, APIs, databases, and external services**. Without integration testing, you may have **working individual components that fail when combined** due to unexpected behaviors or dependencies.

357

Integration testing **verifies that multiple components work together as expected**. For example, if an API interacts with a database, integration tests ensure that:

The API correctly handles requests and responses.

Database queries return expected results.

Error handling works correctly when data is missing or invalid.

While **unit tests** check individual functions, **integration tests** ensure that **multiple pieces work together smoothly**.

Setting Up Mocha and Chai for Integration Testing

Step 1: Install Required Packages

```
npm install --save-dev mocha chai supertest
```
Mocha – A test framework that runs JavaScript tests.

Chai – Provides powerful assertions (`expect`, `should`, `assert`).

Supertest – Simplifies testing HTTP endpoints.

Step 2: Configure Mocha in package.json

Modify `package.json` to include a test script:

```
"scripts": {
  "test": "mocha --exit"
}
```

Now, running `npm test` will execute all test files.

Writing an Express API for Testing

Let's create a **simple Express API** that we will test.

Step 1: Create an Express Server

Modify `server.js`:

```
const express = require("express");
const app = express();
```

358

```
app.use(express.json());

const users = [{ id: 1, name: "Alice" }];

app.get("/users", (req, res) => {
    res.json(users);
});

app.post("/users", (req, res) => {
    const newUser = { id: users.length + 1, name:
req.body.name };
    users.push(newUser);
    res.status(201).json(newUser);
});

module.exports = app;
```

This API has two endpoints:

GET /users → Returns a list of users.

POST /users → Adds a new user.

Writing Integration Tests with Mocha and Chai

Now, let's write tests to **verify that the API endpoints work correctly**.

Step 1: Create a Test File

Create test/server.test.js:

```
const request = require("supertest");
const app = require("../server");
const { expect } = require("chai");

describe("User API", () => {

    it("should return an array of users", async ()
=> {
        const res = await
request(app).get("/users");
        expect(res.status).to.equal(200);
        expect(res.body).to.be.an("array");
        expect(res.body[0].name).to.equal("Alice");
    });
```

```
it("should create a new user", async () => {
    const newUser = { name: "Bob" };

    const res = await request(app)
        .post("/users")
        .send(newUser);

    expect(res.status).to.equal(201);
    expect(res.body).to.have.property("id");
    expect(res.body.name).to.equal("Bob");
});

});
```

✓ The first test verifies that the GET /users endpoint returns a valid response.

✓ The second test ensures that POST /users correctly adds a user.

Step 2: Run the Tests

Execute:

```
npm test
```

✓ Mocha runs all integration tests and verifies API behavior.

✓ If a test fails, Mocha provides detailed error messages for debugging.

Testing API Error Handling

What happens if a user **sends an invalid request**? The API should return **a proper error response** instead of crashing.

Modify server.js to include error handling:

```
app.post("/users", (req, res) => {
    if (!req.body.name) {
        return res.status(400).json({ error: "Name
is required" });
    }

    const newUser = { id: users.length + 1, name:
req.body.name };
```

```
    users.push(newUser);
    res.status(201).json(newUser);
});
```

Writing a Test for Error Cases

Modify `test/server.test.js` to add an invalid request test:

```
it("should return 400 if name is missing", async ()
=> {
    const res = await
request(app).post("/users").send({});
    expect(res.status).to.equal(400);
    expect(res.body).to.have.property("error",
"Name is required");
});
```

Now, the API is validated for both success and failure scenarios.

Testing Database Integration

A real-world application interacts with a **database** instead of using an in-memory array. Let's modify the API to use MongoDB and test it.

Step 1: Install Mongoose for MongoDB

```
npm install mongoose
```

Modify `server.js` to connect to MongoDB:

```
const mongoose = require("mongoose");

mongoose.connect("mongodb://localhost:27017/testdb"
, {
    useNewUrlParser: true,
    useUnifiedTopology: true,
});

const UserSchema = new mongoose.Schema({
    name: String
});

const User = mongoose.model("User", UserSchema);
```

```
app.get("/users", async (req, res) => {
    const users = await User.find();
    res.json(users);
});

app.post("/users", async (req, res) => {
    if (!req.body.name) {
        return res.status(400).json({ error: "Name
is required" });
    }

    const newUser = new User({ name: req.body.name
});
    await newUser.save();
    res.status(201).json(newUser);
});
```

Step 2: Modify the Test to Use a Test Database

Modify `test/server.test.js`:

```
const mongoose = require("mongoose");

before(async () => {
    await
mongoose.connect("mongodb://localhost:27017/testdb"
, {
        useNewUrlParser: true,
        useUnifiedTopology: true
    });
});

after(async () => {
    await mongoose.connection.dropDatabase();
    await mongoose.connection.close();
});
```

Ensures tests run on a separate database to avoid affecting production data.

The database is cleared after tests to prevent contamination.

Running Tests in a CI/CD Pipeline

To **automate testing** in a **GitHub Actions workflow**, add:

Step 1: Create `.github/workflows/test.yml`

```
name: Run API Integration Tests

on: [push, pull_request]

jobs:
  test:
    runs-on: ubuntu-latest
    services:
      mongodb:
        image: mongo:latest
        ports:
          - 27017:27017

    steps:
      - name: Checkout Code
        uses: actions/checkout@v2

      - name: Install Node.js
        uses: actions/setup-node@v2
        with:
          node-version: 16

      - name: Install Dependencies
        run: npm install

      - name: Run Tests
        run: npm test
```

Runs API integration tests automatically on every code push.

By implementing **integration tests with Mocha and Chai**, you **prevent API failures, detect regressions, and ensure database interactions work correctly**, leading to a **more stable and reliable** Node.js application. 🚀

Debugging Node.js Applications with Chrome DevTools

Debugging is an essential skill for every Node.js developer. Even with **automated tests and code reviews**, some bugs only surface **when the application runs in a real environment**.

A poorly debugged application can lead to:
Slow performance – Inefficient code or memory leaks.
Crashes and downtime – Unhandled errors causing service failures.
Security risks – Unvalidated inputs leading to vulnerabilities.

Instead of using **console.log() everywhere**, Chrome DevTools provides a **powerful debugging environment** to:
✓ **Set breakpoints** – Pause code execution at specific lines.
✓ **Inspect variables** – View real-time values of objects and arrays.
✓ **Analyze memory usage** – Detect and fix memory leaks.
✓ **Profile CPU performance** – Identify slow functions.

Setting Up Chrome DevTools for Node.js

Step 1: Start Node.js with the `--inspect` Flag

To enable debugging, start your Node.js application with:

```
node --inspect server.js
```

This enables a WebSocket connection for Chrome DevTools.

Step 2: Open Chrome DevTools for Node.js

Open **Google Chrome**.
Navigate to `chrome://inspect`.
Click **"Open Dedicated DevTools for Node"**.
Click **"Inspect"** next to your running Node.js process.

You now have full access to Chrome's debugging tools for Node.js.

Using Breakpoints to Pause and Inspect Code Execution

Instead of using **console.log() to debug**, **set breakpoints** to pause execution and inspect variables.

Step 1: Add a Debugger Statement

Modify `server.js`:

```
const express = require("express");
const app = express();

app.get("/", (req, res) => {
    let message = "Hello, world!";
    debugger; // Execution will pause here
    res.send(message);
});

app.listen(3000, () => console.log("Server running
on port 3000"));
```

Step 2: Trigger the Breakpoint

Start the application with:

```
node --inspect server.js
```

Open `http://localhost:3000/` in your browser.
Chrome DevTools pauses execution at `debugger;`.
Inspect **variable values, call stack, and scope** in DevTools.

You can step through the code line by line to understand how it executes.

Inspecting Variables and Watch Expressions

When paused at a breakpoint, **check the state of variables**:

Scope Panel – Displays local and global variables.
Watch Panel – Add specific variables to monitor their values.

Example: Watching a Variable in DevTools

Modify `server.js`:

```
app.get("/calculate", (req, res) => {
    let num1 = 10;
    let num2 = 20;
    let sum = num1 + num2;

    debugger; // Pause execution here
```

365

```
    res.json({ sum });
});
```

Steps to Debug in DevTools

Start the app with `node --inspect server.js`.
Visit `http://localhost:3000/calculate`.
In Chrome DevTools:

Add **num1, num2, sum** to the **Watch Panel**.

See how their values change step by step.

Allows real-time monitoring of variable changes.

Viewing the Call Stack and Understanding Execution Flow

The **Call Stack panel** in Chrome DevTools **shows the sequence of function calls** leading to a breakpoint.

Example: Tracing Function Calls

Modify `server.js`:

```
function multiply(a, b) {
    return a * b;
}

function calculateTotal(price, quantity) {
    return multiply(price, quantity);
}

app.get("/total", (req, res) => {
    let total = calculateTotal(100, 2);
    debugger; // Pause execution here
    res.json({ total });
});
```

Steps to Analyze the Call Stack

Start the app and visit `http://localhost:3000/total`.
In Chrome DevTools:

View the **Call Stack panel** to trace execution back to `multiply()`.

366

Step through functions to see how values are passed.

Helps identify incorrect function calls or unexpected arguments.

Detecting and Fixing Memory Leaks

Memory leaks occur when **objects are not properly released**, causing **increasing memory usage** over time.

Step 1: Monitor Memory Usage in DevTools

Start the app with:

```
node --inspect server.js
```

Open **Chrome DevTools** and go to the **Memory Tab**.
Click **Heap Snapshot** → Take a snapshot.
Interact with the application, then take another snapshot.
Compare snapshots to see **if objects persist in memory** unnecessarily.

Detects memory leaks by showing growing object counts.

Step 2: Fixing Memory Leaks in Node.js

Example: Improper Event Listener Handling

Problem: Event listeners that are never removed cause memory leaks.

```
const EventEmitter = require("events");
const emitter = new EventEmitter();

function onDataReceived(data) {
    console.log("Data received:", data);
}

emitter.on("data", onDataReceived); // Listener
added
```

If `onDataReceived` **is never removed**, it stays in memory indefinitely.

Solution: Always clean up event listeners:

```
emitter.off("data", onDataReceived); // Proper cleanup
```

✓ **Prevents memory leaks by removing unused listeners.**

Profiling CPU Performance to Find Slow Functions

Slow applications may have **CPU-intensive operations** blocking execution.

Step 1: Start CPU Profiling in DevTools

Start the application with:

```
node --inspect server.js
```

Open Chrome DevTools → Go to the **Profiler Tab**.
Click **Start Profiling and Run Your Code**.
Perform actions in the app, then **stop profiling**.
Analyze the results:

Identify **functions consuming the most CPU**.

Optimize or refactor inefficient code.

Helps pinpoint slow functions and optimize performance.

Step 2: Optimizing a CPU-Heavy Function

Problem: A synchronous function blocking execution.

```
app.get("/heavy", (req, res) => {
    let sum = 0;
    for (let i = 0; i < 1e9; i++) { // Heavy
computation
        sum += i;
    }
    res.json({ sum });
});
```

Solution: Move computation to a separate worker thread.

```
const { Worker } = require("worker_threads");

app.get("/heavy", (req, res) => {
    const worker = new Worker("./worker.js");
    worker.on("message", (sum) => res.json({ sum
})));
});
```

worker.js:

```
const { parentPort } = require("worker_threads");

let sum = 0;
for (let i = 0; i < 1e9; i++) {
    sum += i;
}

parentPort.postMessage(sum);
```

Prevents blocking the main thread, improving responsiveness.

By mastering **debugging with Chrome DevTools**, you ensure your **Node.js applications are stable, efficient, and error-free**, leading to **better performance and improved user experience**.

Chapter 17: Security Best Practices in Node.js

Security is a **critical aspect of any Node.js application**. A single vulnerability can lead to **data breaches, financial losses, or unauthorized access to sensitive information**. As a developer, it's your responsibility to **proactively secure your application** against attacks.

Preventing Common Security Vulnerabilities

Security should never be an afterthought in software development. Applications that fail to **properly validate and sanitize user input** are vulnerable to **attacks that compromise user data, expose system vulnerabilities, and cause financial or reputational damage**.

Cross-Site Scripting (XSS) – Injecting Malicious Scripts

XSS occurs when **an attacker injects JavaScript code** into a web page, and the browser executes it **as if it were safe content**. This allows attackers to:

Steal user cookies and authentication tokens.

Redirect users to malicious sites.

Modify content on a webpage without authorization.

How XSS Attacks Work

Example: An Insecure Search Route in an Express App

```
app.get("/search", (req, res) => {
    const query = req.query.q;
    res.send(`<h1>Search Results for:
${query}</h1>`); // Vulnerable
});
```
An attacker can send a request like this:

```
http://localhost:3000/search?q=<script>alert('Hacke
d!')</script>
```

The page renders:

```
<h1>Search Results for:
<script>alert('Hacked!')</script></h1>
```

The script executes, triggering an alert box. In a real-world scenario, this script could **steal session cookies** or **redirect users to a phishing site**.

How to Prevent XSS

1. Sanitize User Input

Install **sanitize-html**, a library that removes potentially harmful scripts:

```
npm install sanitize-html
```
Modify the search route to **sanitize user input before rendering it**:

```
const sanitizeHtml = require("sanitize-html");

app.get("/search", (req, res) => {
    const query = sanitizeHtml(req.query.q);
    res.send(`<h1>Search Results for:
${query}</h1>`);
});
```

This ensures that scripts cannot be injected and executed.

2. Use HTTP Security Headers

Install **helmet**, a middleware that sets security headers to prevent XSS:

```
npm install helmet
```
Enable **Content Security Policy (CSP)** to block unauthorized scripts:

```
const helmet = require("helmet");
app.use(helmet());
```

Prevents browsers from executing inline scripts or loading untrusted content.

Cross-Site Request Forgery (CSRF) – Unauthorized Actions on Behalf of Users

CSRF exploits **a logged-in user's active session** to perform actions they **did not intend to execute**.

For example, a logged-in user visits a **malicious website** that secretly makes a request to:

```
POST http://bank.com/transfer
{ recipient: "attacker", amount: "5000" }
```

If the user is **already logged in**, the bank **processes the request**, and **money is stolen**.

How to Prevent CSRF

1. Use CSRF Tokens

Install **csurf**, a middleware that generates a unique token for each form submission:

```
npm install csurf cookie-parser
```

Modify the Express app to **include CSRF protection**:

```
const csrf = require("csurf");
const cookieParser = require("cookie-parser");

app.use(cookieParser());
app.use(csrf({ cookie: true }));

app.get("/form", (req, res) => {
    res.send(`
        <form action="/transfer" method="POST">
            <input type="hidden" name="_csrf"
value="${req.csrfToken()}">
            <button type="submit">Transfer
Money</button>
        </form>
    `);
});
```

Now, **requests must include the CSRF token, preventing unauthorized actions.**

2. Require SameSite Cookies

Setting **SameSite=Strict** in cookies ensures that cookies **are only sent in requests originating from the same website**:

```
app.use(require("cookie-session")({
    name: "session",
    secret: "your-secret-key",
    cookie: { sameSite: "strict", secure: true }
}));
```

 Prevents cookies from being sent along with cross-site requests.

SQL Injection (SQLi) – Manipulating Database Queries

SQL Injection happens when **user input is directly inserted into a SQL query** without validation. Attackers **alter the SQL query** to gain **unauthorized access to databases**, retrieve sensitive data, or even **delete entire tables**.

How SQL Injection Works

Example: Vulnerable SQL Query in Node.js

```
app.get("/user", async (req, res) => {
    const userId = req.query.id;
    const user = await db.query(`SELECT * FROM
users WHERE id = '${userId}'`);
    res.json(user);
});
```

An attacker enters:

```
1'; DROP TABLE users; --
```

This modifies the query to:

```
SELECT * FROM users WHERE id = '1'; DROP TABLE
users; --'
```

The entire users table is deleted.

How to Prevent SQL Injection

1. Use Parameterized Queries

Modify the query to **use placeholders (?) instead of inserting user input directly**:

```
app.get("/user", async (req, res) => {
    const userId = req.query.id;
    const user = await db.query("SELECT * FROM users WHERE id = ?", [userId]);
    res.json(user);
});
```

User input is treated as a value, not SQL code, preventing injections.

2. Use an ORM like Sequelize

ORMs (Object-Relational Mappers) **automatically sanitize queries**:

```
const user = await User.findOne({ where: { id: req.query.id } });
```

Prevents SQL injection while simplifying database queries.

3. Escape User Input in Raw SQL Queries

If raw SQL must be used, sanitize inputs using libraries like `mysql2`:

```
npm install mysql2
const mysql = require("mysql2");

const connection = mysql.createConnection({ /* database config */ });

app.get("/user", async (req, res) => {
    const userId = req.query.id;
    const query = "SELECT * FROM users WHERE id = ?";
    connection.query(query, [userId], (err, results) => {
        res.json(results);
    });
});
```

Ensures input is safely escaped before execution.

By following these **best practices**, you ensure that your **Node.js application is secure against common web vulnerabilities**, protecting user data and system integrity.

Data Encryption and Securing User Information

Securing user data is **non-negotiable** in modern applications. Sensitive information, such as **passwords, financial records, and personal data**, must be **protected against unauthorized access, leaks, and cyberattacks**.

Encryption plays a **critical role** in data security, ensuring that even if data is intercepted or compromised, it remains **unreadable without proper authorization**.

Why Data Encryption is Essential

Protects sensitive user information from hackers. **Prevents data leaks** in case of database breaches. **Ensures compliance** with regulations like **GDPR, HIPAA, and PCI DSS**. **Secures authentication systems** by storing passwords safely.

Hashing Passwords Before Storing Them

Storing passwords **as plain text** is one of the **worst security mistakes** a developer can make. If an attacker **gains access to the database**, they can:

Use stolen passwords to log into user accounts.

Exploit users who reuse passwords across multiple sites.

Sell sensitive user data on the dark web.

How to Securely Hash Passwords with Bcrypt

Step 1: Install Bcrypt

Bcrypt is an industry-standard library for **secure password hashing**.

```
npm install bcrypt
```

Step 2: Hash and Store Passwords

Modify authService.js:

```javascript
const bcrypt = require("bcrypt");

async function hashPassword(password) {
    const saltRounds = 10;
    return await bcrypt.hash(password, saltRounds);
}

// Example usage
(async () => {
    const hashedPassword = await
hashPassword("MySecurePassword");
    console.log("Hashed Password:",
hashedPassword);
})();
```

Even if the database is compromised, hashed passwords remain unreadable.

Step 3: Verify Passwords During Login

Modify authService.js to check the hashed password:

```javascript
async function checkPassword(inputPassword,
storedHash) {
    return await bcrypt.compare(inputPassword,
storedHash);
}

// Example usage
(async () => {
    const storedHash = await
hashPassword("MySecurePassword");
    const isMatch = await
checkPassword("MySecurePassword", storedHash);
    console.log("Password match:", isMatch);
})();
```

Users can authenticate securely without exposing passwords.

Encrypting Sensitive Data in the Database

Not all data should be stored **as plain text**, especially sensitive information like:

Credit card details

Personal Identification Numbers (PINs)

Social Security Numbers (SSNs)

Encryption ensures that **even if a database breach occurs, attackers cannot read the stolen data**.

How to Encrypt and Decrypt Data Using Crypto Module

Node.js provides the **crypto** module for **AES (Advanced Encryption Standard) encryption**.

Step 1: Encrypt Data Before Storing It

Modify `encryptionService.js`:

```
const crypto = require("crypto");

const algorithm = "aes-256-cbc";
const secretKey = crypto.randomBytes(32);
const iv = crypto.randomBytes(16); //
Initialization Vector

function encrypt(text) {
    const cipher = crypto.createCipheriv(algorithm,
secretKey, iv);
    let encrypted = cipher.update(text, "utf8",
"hex");
    encrypted += cipher.final("hex");
    return { encryptedData: encrypted, iv:
iv.toString("hex") };
}

// Example usage
const result = encrypt("SensitiveUserData");
console.log("Encrypted:", result);
```

Even if attackers access the database, they won't be able to read the data.

Step 2: Decrypt Data When Retrieving It

Modify `encryptionService.js` to add decryption:

```javascript
function decrypt(encryptedData, ivHex) {
    const decipher =
crypto.createDecipheriv(algorithm, secretKey,
Buffer.from(ivHex, "hex"));
    let decrypted = decipher.update(encryptedData,
"hex", "utf8");
    decrypted += decipher.final("utf8");
    return decrypted;
}

// Example usage
console.log("Decrypted:",
decrypt(result.encryptedData, result.iv));
```

Data is securely stored and can only be decrypted with the correct key.

Securing Data in Transit with HTTPS & TLS

When data is sent over **HTTP**, it is transmitted in **plain text**, making it easy for attackers to **intercept login credentials, session cookies, and personal data** using techniques like **Man-in-the-Middle (MITM) attacks**.

How to Enforce HTTPS in an Express.js App

Step 1: Obtain an SSL Certificate

For free SSL certificates, use **Let's Encrypt**:

```
sudo certbot --nginx
```

Step 2: Configure Express to Use HTTPS

Modify `server.js`:

```javascript
const fs = require("fs");
const https = require("https");
const express = require("express");

const app = express();

// Load SSL certificate
const options = {
```

```
    key: fs.readFileSync("private-key.pem"),
    cert: fs.readFileSync("certificate.pem")
};

// Redirect HTTP to HTTPS
app.use((req, res, next) => {
    if (!req.secure) {
        return res.redirect("https://" +
req.headers.host + req.url);
    }
    next();
});

https.createServer(options, app).listen(443, () =>
{
    console.log("Secure server running on port
443");
});
```

Encrypts data in transit, preventing interception.

Securing API Keys and Environment Variables

Storing API keys and credentials directly in the source code **exposes them to public repositories and attackers**.

How to Secure API Keys Using dotenv

Step 1: Install dotenv

```
npm install dotenv
```

Step 2: Store API Keys in a `.env` File

Create a `.env` file:

```
DATABASE_URL=mongodb://username:password@host:port/
dbname
JWT_SECRET=your-secret-key
```

Step 3: Load API Keys in Node.js

Modify `config.js`:

```
require("dotenv").config();

module.exports = {
    databaseUrl: process.env.DATABASE_URL,
    jwtSecret: process.env.JWT_SECRET
};
```

Secrets are now loaded from environment variables, preventing accidental leaks.

Implementing Secure Session Storage

Using cookies **without encryption** makes session data **vulnerable to theft**.

How to Secure Sessions with Signed Cookies

```
npm install express-session
```

Modify `server.js`:

```
const session = require("express-session");

app.use(session({
    secret: process.env.SESSION_SECRET,
    resave: false,
    saveUninitialized: true,
    cookie: { secure: true, httpOnly: true,
sameSite: "strict" }
}));
```

Prevents session hijacking and CSRF attacks.

By following these **data encryption and security best practices**, you ensure that **user data remains safe**, preventing unauthorized access and minimizing security risks.

Security Auditing Tools for Node.js

Security vulnerabilities can **go unnoticed** even in well-structured applications. Attackers are **constantly looking for weaknesses** to exploit, whether it's outdated dependencies, exposed secrets, or misconfigured security settings.

Instead of relying on **manual code reviews**, security auditing tools can **automatically scan your Node.js application** for vulnerabilities and misconfigurations.

Using `npm audit` to Detect Vulnerable Dependencies

Third-party libraries **introduce security risks** if they contain vulnerabilities. If your project depends on an insecure package, an attacker could: **Execute remote code** on your server. **Exploit known vulnerabilities** to gain access to sensitive data. **Compromise authentication mechanisms** using outdated cryptographic methods.

Running `npm audit` to Scan for Vulnerabilities

Execute the following command in your project:

```
npm audit
```

If vulnerabilities are found, you'll see an output like this:

```
found 5 vulnerabilities (2 low, 1 moderate, 2 high)
in 1000 scanned packages
```

Fixing Issues Automatically

To fix vulnerabilities automatically:

```
npm audit fix
```

For critical issues requiring **major version updates**, use:

```
npm audit fix --force
```

Warning: `--force` may introduce breaking changes, so review the updates carefully.

Ensures that all dependencies are up-to-date and secure.

Scanning for Security Risks with Snyk

Snyk is a powerful **security scanner** that goes beyond `npm audit` by: **Detecting vulnerabilities in private dependencies**.

Providing real-time alerts for newly discovered threats.
Suggesting fixes with minimal breaking changes.

Step 1: Install Snyk

```
npm install -g snyk
```

Step 2: Scan Your Project for Security Issues

```
snyk test
```

Sample output:

```
✗ High severity vulnerability found in express
- Upgrade to express@4.17.2 to fix
```

Step 3: Monitor for Future Vulnerabilities

Set up continuous monitoring:

```
snyk monitor
```

Automatically alerts you when vulnerabilities are found in dependencies.

Using OWASP ZAP for Penetration Testing

OWASP ZAP (Zed Attack Proxy) is a tool for **scanning web applications**
for vulnerabilities like:
 Cross-Site Scripting (XSS)
 SQL Injection (SQLi)
 Insecure authentication flows

Step 1: Install OWASP ZAP

On Linux/macOS:

```
sudo apt install zaproxy
```
On Windows, download it from the official site.

Step 2: Run OWASP ZAP and Scan Your App

Start OWASP ZAP
Enter your **application's URL** (e.g., `http://localhost:3000`).

Click **"Attack"** → ZAP will crawl the site, identifying vulnerabilities. Review the **scan results** and fix issues found.

Provides real-time security assessments with actionable insights.

Checking for Exposed Secrets with GitLeaks

Hardcoding secrets like **API keys, database credentials, and JWT secrets** in your code can lead to:
Unauthorized access to sensitive data.
Massive data breaches if credentials are leaked in a public repository.
Financial loss if an attacker abuses API keys (e.g., AWS or Stripe).

Using GitLeaks to Detect Exposed Secrets

Step 1: Install GitLeaks

```
brew install gitleaks
```

Step 2: Scan for Leaked Secrets

```
gitleaks detect
```

If GitLeaks detects sensitive information, remove it immediately.

Step 3: Secure Secrets with Environment Variables

Instead of storing secrets in code, use **environment variables**.

1. Install dotenv to Load Secrets from `.env`

```
npm install dotenv
```

2. Store Secrets in a `.env` File

```
DATABASE_URL=mongodb://username:password@host:port/
dbname
JWT_SECRET=super-secret-key
```

3. Load Secrets in Your Node.js Application

```
require("dotenv").config();

const dbUrl = process.env.DATABASE_URL;
const jwtSecret = process.env.JWT_SECRET;
```

Prevents secrets from being accidentally committed to Git repositories.

Automating Security Audits in a CI/CD Pipeline

Prevents vulnerabilities from being merged into production. Ensures all security checks run before deploying new code. Automates dependency scanning, penetration testing, and secret detection.

Using GitHub Actions for Automated Security Audits

Create a **GitHub Actions workflow** to **run security checks on every push**.

Step 1: Create `.github/workflows/security-audit.yml`

```yaml
name: Security Audit

on: [push, pull_request]

jobs:
  security-check:
    runs-on: ubuntu-latest

    steps:
      - name: Checkout Code
        uses: actions/checkout@v2

      - name: Install Dependencies
        run: npm install

      - name: Run npm Audit
        run: npm audit --json > npm-audit-report.json || true

      - name: Run Snyk Security Scan
        run: snyk test

      - name: Run GitLeaks
        run: gitleaks detect --source=.

      - name: Run OWASP ZAP (Web Security Scan)
        run: |
          zap-cli start
```

```
zap-cli open-url http://localhost:3000
zap-cli spider http://localhost:3000
zap-cli active-scan http://localhost:3000
zap-cli report -o zap-report.html -f html
zap-cli shutdown
```

Step 2: Add Snyk API Key as a Secret in GitHub

Go to your **GitHub repository**.
Click **Settings → Secrets and Variables → Actions**.
Add a new secret named **SNYK_TOKEN**.

Modify the workflow to use it:

```
- name: Authenticate with Snyk
  run: snyk auth ${{ secrets.SNYK_TOKEN }}
```

Automatically scans for vulnerabilities and secrets on every push.

By integrating **security auditing tools into your development workflow**, you create a **proactive defense against cyber threats**, ensuring your Node.js application remains **secure, resilient, and compliant** with industry best practices.

Conclusion

Node.js has transformed modern **full-stack development** by providing a **scalable, efficient, and fast** environment for building web applications. Over the course of this book, we have explored how Node.js enables **server-side JavaScript programming**, allowing developers to build applications that are both responsive and capable of handling a high volume of concurrent requests.

By leveraging its **asynchronous event-driven architecture**, Node.js allows applications to remain **lightweight and efficient**, making it an excellent choice for **real-time applications, RESTful APIs, microservices, and serverless architectures**. Its extensive package ecosystem, powered by **npm (Node Package Manager)**, provides developers with a vast collection of tools and libraries that simplify development while maintaining flexibility.

Through structured learning and hands-on exercises, we have covered essential topics including **server-side programming, database integration, authentication, security best practices, caching strategies, and performance optimization**. The goal has been to provide a **comprehensive understanding of how to build, secure, and scale Node.js applications effectively**.

The Future of Node.js in Full-Stack Development

As **web technologies evolve**, Node.js continues to play a significant role in full-stack development. The shift towards **real-time applications, microservices, and serverless computing** has increased its relevance in the industry. Companies building **scalable and high-performance applications** continue to adopt Node.js due to its **non-blocking architecture** and ability to handle **thousands of concurrent connections efficiently**.

The adoption of **JavaScript-based full-stack development** has also contributed to its growth. With frameworks like **Next.js, NestJS, and Fastify**, developers can build highly performant applications while maintaining a **consistent JavaScript codebase across both frontend and backend**.

Newer enhancements in **WebAssembly (WASM)** and **Deno (an alternative runtime to Node.js built by the original Node.js creator)** indicate that **server-side JavaScript will continue to expand** with improved security, performance, and developer-friendly features. While these newer technologies are growing, Node.js remains a **core technology** in backend development due to its **maturity, large ecosystem, and strong community support**.

Looking ahead, Node.js will likely continue to evolve in areas such as **multithreading improvements, better TypeScript support, enhanced security mechanisms, and deeper integration with cloud-native solutions**. Developers who stay updated with these advancements will be well-positioned to build the next generation of full-stack applications.

Next Steps and Further Learning Resources

To continue improving as a **full-stack Node.js developer**, ongoing learning and hands-on practice are essential. Building real-world projects is the most effective way to **strengthen your understanding** of concepts such as **API development, security best practices, database design, and application deployment**.

Expanding your knowledge in **related technologies** will also enhance your skillset. Learning **TypeScript** can improve the maintainability of your Node.js applications by adding static typing. Exploring **GraphQL** as an alternative to RESTful APIs can help build more flexible and efficient data-fetching systems. Understanding **containerization with Docker and orchestration with Kubernetes** will prepare you for **deploying and scaling applications in production environments**.

Engaging with the **developer community** is another excellent way to stay informed about the latest advancements. Platforms like **GitHub, Stack Overflow, and Dev.to** provide valuable discussions and open-source projects that can accelerate your learning. Following official documentation, attending Node.js conferences, and contributing to open-source projects will further enhance your expertise.

As new best practices and technologies emerge, continuous learning will ensure that you remain a **skilled and adaptable developer**.

Node.js has proven to be a **powerful and versatile tool** for backend development, offering the speed, scalability, and flexibility required for modern applications. By understanding **its core concepts, best practices, and**

real-world applications, developers can build **secure, efficient, and maintainable applications** that meet industry demands.

The knowledge gained from this book provides a **strong foundation** in Node.js development. Applying these concepts in real-world projects will reinforce your understanding and help you refine your skills. As you continue exploring advanced topics such as **microservices, serverless computing, real-time applications, and cloud deployments**, you will be well-equipped to build and maintain **robust full-stack applications**.

Technology is always evolving, and staying ahead requires **curiosity, problem-solving skills, and a commitment to lifelong learning**. By continuously improving and applying new concepts, you will not only **master Node.js** but also be prepared for the future of **full-stack development**.

www.ingramcontent.com/pod-product-compliance
Lightning Source LLC
LaVergne TN
LVHW081513050326
832903LV00025B/1469